Interactive Computer Graphics

Interactive Computer Graphics

Henry Lloyd

STATES
ACADEMIC PRESS
www.statesacademicpress.com

Published by States Academic Press,
109 South 5th Street,
Brooklyn, NY 11249, USA

ISBN: 978-1-63989-295-2

Cataloging-in-Publication Data

Interactive computer graphics / Henry Lloyd.
    p. cm.
Includes bibliographical references and index.
ISBN 978-1-63989-295-2
1. Computer graphics. 2. Interactive computer systems.
I. Lloyd, Henry.
T385 .I58 2022
006.686 9--dc23

For information on all States Academic Press publications
visit our website at www.statesacademicpress.com

Contents

Preface

Computer graphics is a sub-discipline of computer science which focuses on the techniques used for digital synthesis and manipulation of visual content. It is an interdisciplinary field which makes use of the principles of applied mathematics, image processing, computational geometry, computer vision and information visualisation. Interactive computer graphics is a sub-field of computer graphics which studies the methods employed for generating images and animations at interactive frame rates. It has various benefits over passive computer graphics such as higher image quality, lower design cost and more precise results. The basic components of an interactive computer graphics system are a frame buffer, a monitor and a display controller. Most of the topics introduced in this book cover new techniques and the applications of interactive computer graphics. Different approaches, evaluations and methodologies on this discipline have been included herein. Those in search of information to further their knowledge will be greatly assisted by this book.

A foreword of all Chapters of the book is provided below:

Chapter 1 - The use of computers for creating and manipulating pictures on a display device is known as computer graphics. They are broadly classified into two categories, namely, master graphics and vector graphics. This is an introductory chapter which will introduce briefly all significant aspects of computer graphics; **Chapter 2** - The physical components of a computer that can be touched are termed as hardware. The collection of instructions and procedures which are used to perform different tasks on a computer is known as computer software. This chapter has been carefully written to provide an easy understanding of the hardware and software aspects of computer graphics like open source vector graphics and open source games development software, etc.; **Chapter 3** - The study of 2-dimensional shapes is known as plane geometry. Few fundamental concepts of plane geometry are Euclidean geometry, 2D geometry, points and lines, ellipse, 2D viewing, etc. The diverse types of plane geometry in computer graphics have been thoroughly discussed in this chapter; **Chapter 4** - The graphics that use a representation of three dimensional geometric data stored in a computer in order to perform calculations is termed as 3D. The concepts explained in this chapter will help in gaining a better perspective about 3D computer graphics as well as 3D geometry modeling and 3D transformations; **Chapter 5** - There are many applications of computer graphics. Some of them are special effects, web design, computer generated imagery, scientific visualization, morphing, etc. These diverse applications of computer graphics have been thoroughly discussed in this chapter.

I would like to thank the entire editorial team who made sincere efforts for this book and my family who supported me in my efforts of working on this book. I take this opportunity to thank all those who have been a guiding force throughout my life.

Henry Lloyd

Introduction to Computer Graphics

The use of computers for creating and manipulating pictures on a display device is known as computer graphics. They are broadly classified into two categories, namely, master graphics and vector graphics. This is an introductory chapter which will introduce briefly all significant aspects of computer graphics.

Computer Graphics involves technology to access. The Process transforms and presents information in a visual form. The role of computer graphics insensible. In today life, computer graphics has now become a common element in user interfaces, T.V. commercial motion pictures. Computer Graphics is the creation of pictures with the help of a computer. The end product of the computer graphics is a picture it may be a business graph, drawing, and engineering.

In computer graphics, two or three-dimensional pictures can be created that are used for research. Many hardware devices algorithm has been developing for improving the speed of picture generation with the passes of time. It includes the creation storage of models and image of objects. These models for various fields like engineering, mathematical and so on.

Today computer graphics is entirely different from the earlier one. It is not possible. It is an interactive user can control the structure of an object of various input devices. It is the use of computers to create and manipulate pictures on a display device. It comprises of software techniques to create, store, modify, represents pictures.

Why are Computer Graphics Used?

Suppose a shoe manufacturing company want to show the sale of shoes for five years. For this vast amount of information is to store. So a lot of time and memory will be needed. This method will be tough to understand by a common man. In this situation graphics is a better alternative. Graphics tools are charts and graphs. Using graphs, data can be represented in pictorial form. A picture can be understood easily just with a single look.

Interactive computer graphics work using the concept of two-way communication between computer users. The computer will receive signals from the input device, and the picture is modified accordingly. Picture will be changed quickly when we apply command.

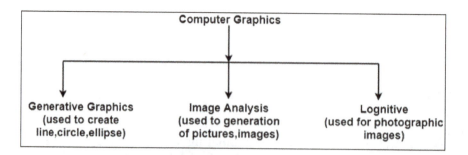

Types of Computer Graphics

The computer graphics contains two types. They are:

- Raster (Bitmap) graphics

- Vector graphics

Many individuals are likely to consider pictures on computers (or phones, tablets, or some other electronic gadget with a picture interface) without worrying about how the graphic is processed and displayed on the computer device. That's great when you're just a graphic user, but it is essential to note the image's specific design for all who would like to construct or modify computer graphics images.

Raster (Bitmap) Graphics

You are probably familiar with raster graphics if you have ever captured or downloaded a digital picture; even if you're not conscious, this is what digital pictures are. By considering the graphics field as a rectangle shape and separating the rectangle into some kind of two-dimensional array of small pixels, a raster represents an image.

For Example- An image generated by a high-resolution digital camera may also contain horizontal and vertical measurements of 4128 pixels and 3096 pixels, enabling the overall image to be 4128 x 3096 = 12,780,288 pixels. Each pixel describes standard pixel values for the picture at that level. (raster graphics typically require significant numbers of pixels, but devices are very adept at handling a large number of objects).

If you enlarge the above image, you can see each pixel of the image. You can now see the borders of the pixels here and measure them to ensure that the picture is actually 16×16 pixels (involving the white pixels at the vertices). The enlarged picture actually looks unconscionably messy, but as the picture will usually not be displayed at this zoom stage, it is decent enough to be used as an icon. In certain instances, there are several pixels in the bitmap image, like digital photos, that our eye cannot discern them at regular display sizes, so you see the picture as a constant collection of tones.

Here, we have an image to represent the bitmap graphics.

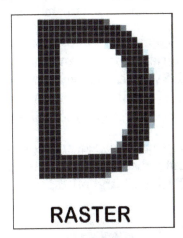

Without visible loss, bitmap graphics contains a "resolution" that reduces the amount to which you may amplify the picture. Graphics that have better image quality numbers have a higher resolution. Since raster image files are typically huge, being able to aggregate the pixel chart in a certain manner is beneficial, but there are several excellently-known approaches to do this. The drawback is that the worse picture appears to display, the more saturation you apply. JPEG (a standard developed by the Collaborative Photographic Specialists' Group) is one of the best known and is designed to facilitate you to add variable amounts of distortion to digital photos. For Example- Photoshop, Paint, etc.

Benefits of Raster Graphics

- It is simple to construct raster files through existing pixel information stored in a sequence in memory space.

- It is also possible to retrieve pixel information stored in a raster file while using a collection of coordinates that enables the information to be characterized in the grid form.

- If available, pixel values can be changed separately or as huge sets by changing a gradient.

- Raster graphics can transform well to external devices like CRTs and printers in spot-format.

Drawbacks of Raster Graphics

Vector Graphics

The optimal key to build a digital picture is to compile a list of commands that explain how to depict the picture and then save the list as an image file. The machine perceives each command and redraws the full image while the file is opened, normally as a bit-map for demonstration purposes. This mechanism is called rasterization.

This can seem to be an overly complicated approach for a graphical picture to be produced. There are several specifications for vector graphics, and some of those (– for example, AI, CDR) are patented. SVG (Scalable Vector Graphics) is one more open vector graphics standard that becomes incredibly famous. A Vector format file can be accessed by opening it with a text editor (like Notepad) software.

Nowadays, vector images are usually placed in graphical file formats like SVG, EPS, PDF, or AI, which are inherently distinct from the more traditional raster image formats such as JPEG, PNG, APNG, GIF, and MPEG4. For Example- Corel Draw, Adobe Illustrator, etc.

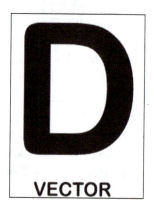

Standards of Vector Graphics

Scalable Vector Graphics (SVG) is the World Wide Web Consortium (W3C) specification for vector format. The norm is complicated and has been extremely slow to be developed due to commercial entities, at least in some parts. There is now some help for displaying SVG information for many internet browsers, but complete implementation of the standard is still relatively uncommon.

SVG seems to be a basic in recent decades that is entirely separate from the rendering system resolution, usually a printer or display monitor. In essence, Vector format documents are customizable text illustrating both straight and curved routes and other properties. For photos such as basic maps, line diagrams, coats of arms, and flags, which are usually not like pictures or other constant pictures, we prefer SVG. Rendering SVG contains bitmap format conversion at a resolution that is suitable for the current mission. SVG is also a medium for images that are animated.

For smartphones, there is also a variant of Scalable Vector Graphics. The basic format for smartphones is known as SVGT (SVG Tiny version) in general. These graphics can calculate connections and manipulate anti-aliasing as well. They can also be shown as wallpaper.

Standards of Vector Graphics

Usually, vector image editors allow conversion, rotation, mirroring, stretching, skewing, affine transformations, z-order shift broadly, what's in front of what and primitives to be combined into more complicated objects. The set activities on closed curves (union, difference, intersection, etc.) offer greater complex transformations. Vector images are perfect for basic or hybrid designs required being device-independent or do not require to attain a series of pictures. For instance, a vector-based graphics model is used in PostScript and PDF page description languages.

Conversion between Raster and Vector Graphics

Converting a vector graphic into a raster image is often required, and less. so, converting a raster image into a vector graphic. Any time when you try to display the content of a vector file, the transformation of vector images to raster happens all the time. The message includes the document's commands when you access a vector file and creates the outlines into the transient bitmap that it shows for you.

The Software application is required to transform raster to vector images. Typically, the method is called "Tracing." You had to have additional compensation tracing applications years ago, but most vector painting software now offers designed tracing capabilities. As the name indicates, by "sketching around the outlines of the raster, tracing technology operates so that patterns and outlines describing the picture are formed. The effect of the procedure is a collection of mathematical curves representing the vector image generated by the program.

Benefits of Vector Graphics

- Vector files are thin in size since they have less information than bitmap image files.

- Vector images are more versatile than bitmap graphics because the graphical fidelity can be increased up and down quickly without any loss.

- Vector image files have sharper lines compared to rectangular, pixel-based bitmap graphics, so they are stronger than raster images with straight lines and flowing curves.

Drawbacks of Vector Graphics

- When a vector image has minor defects, these are shown when the vector image is greatly expanded.

- A static color or gradient is usually loaded with vector images. Comprehensive picture (photo) attributes cannot be viewed as bitmap graphics.

Images

An image consists of a rectangular array of dots called pixels. The size of the image is specified in terms of width X height, in numbers of the pixels. The physical size of the image, in inches or centimeters, depends on the resolution of the device on which the image is displayed. The resolution is usually measured in DPI (Dots Per Inch). An image will appear smaller on a device with a higher resolution than on one with a lower resolution. For color images, one needs enough bits per pixel to represent all the colors in the image. The number of the bits per pixel is called the depth of the image.

Image Data Types

Images can be created by using different techniques of representation of data called data type like monochrome and colored images. Monochrome image is created by using single color whereas colored image is created by using multiple colors. Some important data types of images are following:

- 1-bit images: An image is a set of pixels. Note that a pixel is a picture element in digital image. In 1-bit images, each pixel is stored as a single bit (0 or 1). A bit has only two states either on or off, white or black, true or false. Therefore, such an image is also referred to as a binary image, since only two states are available. 1-bit image is also known as 1-bit monochrome images because it contains one color that is black for off state and white for on state.

  A 1-bit image with resolution 640*480 needs a storage space of 640*480 bits.

  640 x 480 bits. = (640 x 480) / 8 bytes = (640 x 480) / (8 x 1024) KB= 37.5KB.

  The clarity or quality of 1-bit image is very low.

- 8-bit Gray level images: Each pixel of 8-bit gray level image is represented by a single byte (8 bits). Therefore each pixel of such image can hold 2^8=256 values between 0 and 255. Therefore each pixel has a brightness value on a scale from black (0 for no brightness or intensity) to white (255 for full brightness or intensity). For example, a dark pixel might have a value of 15 and a bright one might be 240.

  A grayscale digital image is an image in which the value of each pixel is a single sample, which carries intensity information. Images are composed exclusively of gray shades, which vary from black being at the weakest intensity to white being at the strongest. Grayscale images carry many shades of gray from black to white. Grayscale images are also called monochromatic, denoting the presence of only one (mono) color (chrome). An image is represented by bitmap. A bitmap is a simple matrix of the tiny dots (pixels) that form an image and are displayed on a computer screen or printed.

A 8-bit image with resolution 640 x 480 needs a storage space of 640 x 480 bytes=(640 x 480)/1024 KB= 300KB. Therefore an 8-bit image needs 8 times more storage space than 1-bit image.

- 24-bit color images: In 24-bit color image, each pixel is represented by three bytes, usually representing RGB (Red, Green and Blue). Usually true color is defined to mean 256 shades of RGB (Red, Green and Blue) for a total of 16777216 color variations. It provides a method of representing and storing graphical image information an RGB color space such that a colors, shades and hues in large number of variations can be displayed in an image such as in high quality photo graphic images or complex graphics.

  Many 24-bit color images are stored as 32-bit images, and an extra byte for each pixel used to store an alpha value representing special effect information.

  A 24-bit color image with resolution 640 x 480 needs a storage space of 640 x 480 x 3 bytes = (640 x 480 x 3) / 1024=900KB without any compression. Also 32-bit color image with resolution 640 x 480 needs a storage space of 640 x 480 x 4 bytes= 1200KB without any compression.

Disadvantages:

  ○ Require large storage space.

  ○ Many monitors can display only 256 different colors at any one time. Therefore, in this case it is wasteful to store more than 256 different colors in an image.

- 8-bit color images: 8-bit color graphics is a method of storing image information in a computer's memory or in an image file, where one byte (8 bits) represents each pixel. The maximum number of colors that can be displayed at once is 256. 8-bit color graphics are of two forms. The first form is where the image stores not color but an 8-bit index into the color map for each pixel, instead of storing the full 24-bit color value. Therefore, 8-bit image formats consists of two parts: a color map describing what colors are present in the image and the array of index values for each pixel in the image. In most color maps each color is usually chosen from a palette of 16,777,216 colors (24 bits: 8 red, 8green, 8 blue).

  The other form is where the 8-bits use 3 bits for red, 3 bits for green and 2 bits for blue. This second form is often called 8-bit true color as it does not use a palette at all. When a 24-bit full color image is turned into an 8-bit image, some of the colors have to be eliminated, known as color quantization process. A 8-bit color image with resolution 640 x 480 needs a storage space of 640 x 480 bytes=(640 x 480) / 1024KB= 300KB without any compression.

Color Lookup Tables

A color loop-up table (LUT) is a mechanism used to transform a range of input colors into another range of colors. Color look-up table will convert the logical color numbers stored in each pixel of video memory into physical colors, represented as RGB triplets, which can be displayed on a computer monitor. Each pixel of image stores only index value or logical color number. For example if a pixel stores the value 30, the meaning is to go to row 30 in a color look-up table (LUT). The LUT is often called a Palette. Characteristic of LUT are following:

- The number of entries in the palette determines the maximum number of colors which can appear on screen simultaneously.

- The width of each entry in the palette determines the number of colors which the wider full palette can represent.

A common example would be a palette of 256 colors that is the number of entries is 256 and thus each entry is addressed by an 8-bit pixel value. Each color can be chosen from a full palette, with a total of 16.7 million colors that is the each entry is of 24 bits and 8 bits per channel which sets the total combinations of 256 levels for each of the red, green and blue components 256 x 256 x 256 =16,777,216 colors.

Image File Formats

- GIF: Graphics Interchange Formats- The GIF format was created by Compuserve. It supports 256 colors. GIF format is the most popular on the Internet because of its compact size. It is ideal for small icons used for navigational purpose and simple diagrams. GIF creates a table of up to 256 colors from a pool of 16 million. If the image has less than 256 colors, GIF can easily render the image without any loss of quality. When the image contains more colors, GIF uses algorithms to match the colors of the image with the palette of optimum set of 256 colors available. Better algorithms search the image to find and the optimum set of 256 colors.

  Thus GIF format is lossless only for the image with 256 colors or less. In case of a rich, true color image GIF may lose 99.998% of the colors. GIF files can be saved with a maximum of 256 colors. This makes it is a poor format for photographic images.

  GIFs can be animated, which is another reason they became so successful. Most animated banner ads are GIFs. GIFs allow single bit transparency that is when you are creating your image, you can specify which color is to be transparent. This provision allows the background colors of the web page to be shown through the image.

- JPEG- Joint Photographic Experts Group: The JPEG format was developed by the Joint Photographic Experts Group. JPEG files are bitmapped images. It store information as 24-bit color. This is the format of choice for nearly all photograph images on the internet. Digital cameras save images in a JPEG format by default. It has become the main graphics file format for the World Wide Web and any browser can support it without plug-ins. In order to make the file small, JPEG uses lossy compression. It works well on photographs, artwork and similar materials but not so well on lettering, simple cartoons or line drawings. JPEG images work much better than GIFs. Though JPEG can be interlaced, still this format lacks many of the other special abilities of GIFs, like animations and transparency, but they really are only for photos.

- PNG- Portable Network Graphics: PNG is the only lossless format that web browsers support. PNG supports 8 bit, 24 bits, 32 bits and 48 bits data types. One version of the format PNG-8 is similar to the GIF format. But PNG is the superior to the GIF. It produces smaller files and with more options for colors. It supports partial transparency also. PNG-24 is another flavor of PNG, with 24-bit color supports, allowing ranges of color akin to high color JPEG. PNG-24 is in no way a replacement format for JPEG because it is a lossless compression format. This means that file size can be rather big against a comparable JPEG. Also PNG supports for up to 48 bits of color information.

- TIFF- Tagged Image File Format: The TIFF format was developed by the Aldus Corporation in the 1980 and was later supported by Microsoft. TIFF file format is widely used bitmapped file format. It is supported by many image editing applications, software used by scanners and photo retouching programs.

- TIFF can store many different types of image ranging from 1 bit image, grayscale image, 8 bit color image, 24 bit RGB image etc. TIFF files originally use lossless compression. Today TIFF files also use lossy compression according to the requirement. Therefore, it is a very flexible format. This file format is suitable when the output is printed. Multi-page documents can be stored as a single TIFF file and that is way this file format is so popular. The TIFF format is now used and controlled by Adobe.

- BMP- Bitmap: The bitmap file format (BMP) is a very basic format supported by most Windows applications. BMP can store many different type of image: 1 bit image, grayscale image, 8 bit color image, 24 bit RGB image etc. BMP files are uncompressed. Therefore, these are not suitable for the internet. BMP files can be compressed using lossless data compression algorithms.

- EPS- Encapsulated Postscript: The EPS format is a vector based graphic. EPS is popular for saving image files because it can be imported into nearly any kind of application. This file format is suitable for printed documents. Main disadvantage of this format is that it requires more storage as compare to other formats.

- PDF - Portable Document Format: PDF format is vector graphics with embedded pixel graphics with many compression options. When your document is ready to be shared with others or for publication. This is only format that is platform independent. If you have Adobe Acrobat you can print from any document to a PDF file. From illustrator you can save as .PDF.

- EXIF- Exchange Image File: Exif is an image format for digital cameras. A variety of tage are available to facilitate higher quality printing, since information about the camera and picture - taking condition can be stored and used by printers for possible color correction algorithms.it also includes specification of file format for audio that accompanies digital images.

- WMF- Windows MetaFile: WMF is the vector file format for the MS-Windows operating environment. It consists of a collection of graphics device interface function calls to the MS-Windows graphice drawing library. Metafiles are both small and flexible, hese images can be displayed properly by their proprietary softwares only.

- PICT: PICT images are useful in Macintosh software development, but you should avoid them in desktop publishing. Avoid using PICT format in electronic publishing-PICT images are prone to corruption.

- Photoshop: This is the native Photoshop file format created by Adobe. You can import this format directly into most desktop publishing applications.

How to Calculate Pixels

Display resolution indicates how many pixels are contained in a screen. So, a 1080x1920 display is just a grid that's 1080 pixels tall and 1920 pixels wide. To calculate the number of pixels in a display, multiply the height of the grid by the width. In the case of a 1080x1920 display, there's a total of 2,073,600 pixels within the grid.

How Pixels Create Colors

Each individual point blends with those around it to create a smooth transition of color. Think of it like an absurdly detailed impressionist painting. The more colors each point can display, the more natural and crisp the image looks.

The number of bits used to represent a pixel determines how many colors it can display. So, an 8-bit pixel only allows for 256 colors, while a 24-bit pixel displays 16,777,216 colors.

How Pixels Determine Display Resolution

Resolution is measured in PPI (pixels per inch), so it's a measurement of the pixel density in a given image or display. Both the PPI and the size of the image can affect the resolution.

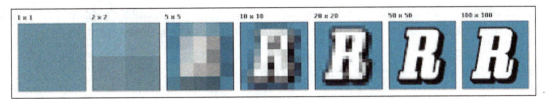

If the pixel density is too low, it can cause some real problems.

The Importance of Pixel Density

Pixel density helps determine the clarity of an image.

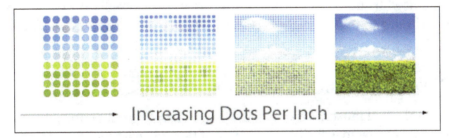

The pixel density of an image must complement the size of that image. If, for example, you're displaying a large image, you'll need a higher PPI to avoid pixalation.

The Importance of Pixel Depth

Pixel depth describes the amount of data that can be stored in each individual square. The number of bits that represent a pixel determine how many colors it can display.

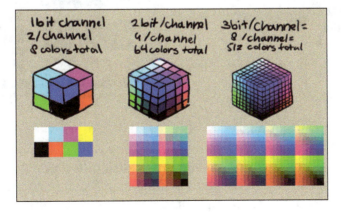

The more colors a pixel can display, the better the tone of the photo and the more lifelike it will look. A quality image is not just determined by the number of pixels in the image, but also the depth of those pixels.

How to Utilize Pixels in Modern Design

Understanding pixels and how to use them is a must for today's designers. It's the building blocks for everything we see digitally. Here are a few times you'll use them:

When You're Designing for Specific Devices

You need to understand both screen specs and CSS pixels to create brilliant, device-specific designs. This enables you to make smart decisions for the project. The resolution and PPI of a device are almost always provided by the manufacturer. You can also find direct device comparisons on third-party websites.

However, in design, CSS pixels are just as important. They're abstract (but still related) units used by designers that don't directly correspond with regular pixels. In modern devices with high-density screens, there are often two device pixels per CSS pixel.

When You're Creating a Responsive Website

In today's world, you must have a responsive website. Very few people, if any, will stick around on your outdated website -- especially if they're on a mobile device. Responsive websites are all about looking great at different sizes and resolutions.

Each screen size will present your website in a slightly different way. You'll notice content is getting scaled down and broken up differently. Small images may get pixelated as a result. Make sure to run tests at all common sizes and resolutions to make sure the site is actually as usable—across every device.

When you're Trying to Improve Image Quality

Increasing an image's resolution or shrinking the size can help increase PPI for a grainy image. Displaying fewer pixels—and more data for each pixel—can help enhance the color, tone, and weight of an image. Size, pixel density, pixel depth, and color are all settings that can drastically change the quality of a photo.

Resolution

Resolution measures the number of pixels in a digital image or display. It is defined as width by height, or W x H, where W is the number of horizontal pixels and H is the number of vertical pixels. For example, the resolution of an HDTV is 1920 x 1080.

Image Resolution

A digital photo that is 3,088 pixels wide by 2,320 pixels tall has a resolution of 3088 × 2320. Multiplying these numbers together produces 7,164,160 total pixels. Since the photo contains just over seven million pixels, it is considered a "7 megapixel" image. Digital camera resolution is often measured in megapixels, which is simply another way to express the image resolution.

"Resolution" is often used synonymously with "size" when describing the dimensions of a digital image. However, the term "size" can be a bit ambiguous, since it may refer to the file size of the image or its dimensions. Therefore, it is best to use "resolution" when describing the dimensions of a digital image.

Display Resolution

Every monitor and screen has a specific resolution. An HD display has a resolution of 1920 x 1080 pixels. A 4K display has twice the resolution of HD, or 3840 x 2160 pixels. It is called "4K" since the screen is nearly 4,000 pixels across horizontally. The total number of pixels in a 4K display is 8,294,400, or just over eight megapixels.

Monitor resolution defines how many pixels a screen can display, but it does not describe how fine the image is. For example, a 27" iMac 5K display has a resolution of 5120 x 2880 while an older 27" Apple Thunderbolt Display has exactly half the resolution of 2560 x 1440. Since the 27" iMac is the same physical size as the Thunderbolt Display but has twice the resolution, it has twice the pixel density, measured in pixels per inch, or PPI.

Raster Image versus Vector Image

Here are the three most important differences between raster and vector.

Pixels versus Math

Since raster images are comprised of colored pixels arranged to form an image, they cannot be scaled without sacrificing quality. If you enlarge a raster, it will pixelate, or become blurry. The lower its resolution (pixels-per-inch), the smaller the image must be to maintain quality.

In contrast, the mathematical equations that form the foundations for vectors recalculate when they're resized; thus, you can infinitely scale a vector graphic and maintain crisp, sharp edges. The difference is easy to see when you zoom on in a raster versus a vector; you can see individual pixels in the raster file, but the vector is still smooth. With vectors, resolution is not a concern.

Raster images are capable of displaying a myriad of colors in a single image and allow for color editing beyond that of a vector image. They can display finer nuances in light and shading at the right resolution. Vector images are scalable, so that the same image can be designed once and resized infinitely for any size application - from business card to billboard.

True-to-life graphics

Though it's possible to make a vector resemble a photograph, the minute nuances of blended colors, shading, shadows, and gradient make it impossible to get a true-to-life representation of a photograph with vectors. Even if it were possible, the process would be excruciatingly tedious, as every color change would require a new shape to be created.

Rasterized effects can be added to vectors, but it's not the same as a true vector and things like scalability and resolution become factors to consider. Rasterized images, on the other hand, are perfectly capable of rendering true-to-life graphics: visually-perfect color blends, shades, gradients, and shadows. Of course, unlike vectors, they're still limited by dimensional size and resolution.

File Type and Size

The most common raster file types include JPG, GIF, PNG, TIF, BMP, and PSD. The most common vector file types are AI, CDR, and SVG. Both rasters and vectors can be rendered in EPS and PDF format, where the software that created the file dictates whether it's a raster or vector file. Common vector creation and editing programs include Adobe Illustrator, CorelDraw, and InkScape. The most popular raster editors are Photoshop (which has limited vector capabilities) and GIMP.

Because rasterized images must contain all the information necessary to render the image (pixels, colors, arrangement of pixels, etc.), they can have large file sizes – and the higher resolution and dimensional size, the larger the file.

Compression can help minimize those file sizes, but compared to vectors, rasters take up a lot of space. Why? Since vectors rely on calculations to be performed by the programs that load them, the only information they need to contain are their mathematical formulas. This table compares some of the differences, advantage (pros), and disadvantages (cons) between raster and vector images.

Raster	Vector
Comprised of pixels, arranged to form an image	Comprised of paths, dictated by mathematical formulas
Constrained by resolution and dimensions	Infinitely scalable
Capable of rich, complex color blends	Difficult to blend colors without rasterizing
Large file sizes (but can be compressed)	Small file sizes
File types include .jpg, .gif, .png, .tif, .bmp, .psd; plus .eps and .pdf when created by raster programs	File types include .ai, .cdr, .svg; plus .eps and .pdf when created by vector programs
Raster software includes Photoshop and GIMP	Vector software includes Illustrator, CorelDraw, and InkScape
Perfect for "painting"	Perfect for "drawing"
Capable of detailed editing	Less detailed, but offers precise paths

When should you Use Raster or Vector?

Raster images are best for photos, while vectors are best for logos, illustrations, engravings, etchings, product artwork, signage, and embroidery. Some liken raster images to paintings and vectors to drawing; if your project requires complex color blends, such as in painting, raster is the preferred format; if your project requires scalable shapes and solid colors, such as in drawing, vector is the best choice.

Many projects combine raster and vector images together: a brochure, for example, might include a corporate logo (vector) and a photo of happy customers (raster) – often coupled in layout software such as InDesign or QuarkXpress (though Illustrator and Photoshop can also be used to pair raster and vector images).

Other examples include printing postcards that feature an illustrated background (vector) with a foreground photo (raster), online catalog printing that features scalable product information tables vector) alongside product images (raster), and business greeting card printing that combines corporate logos (vectors) with photos (rasters).

Ultimately, it boils down to what you're creating and its intended use. If you need a brand logo that will be used time and again in multiple media – print, digital, television, product etching, signage, etc. – you should create a vector that can be scaled as-needed then output in whichever format you need at any given time. If you want to edit a photo or make a sweet digital painting, you should create a raster that's capable of rendering complex color blends and mimicking the natural qualities of light.

Display Devices

Display devices are also known as output devices. Most commonly used output device in a graphics system is a video monitor.

Cathode-ray-tubes

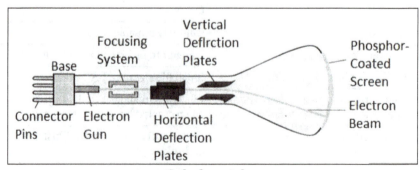

Cathode ray tube.

- It is an evacuated glass tube.

- An electron gun at the rear of the tube produce a beam of electrons which is directed towards the screen of the tube by a high voltage typically 15000 to 20000 volts.

- Inner side screen is coated with phosphor substance which gives light when it is stroked bye electrons.

- Control grid controls velocity of electrons before they hit the phosphor.

- The control grid voltage determines how many electrons are actually in the electron beam. The negativethe control voltage is the fewer the electrons that pass through the grid.

- Thus control grid controls Intensity of the spot where beam strikes the screen.

- The focusing system concentrates the electron beam so it converges to small point when hits thephosphor coating.

- Deflection system directs beam which decides the point where beam strikes the screen.

- Deflection system of the CRT consists of two pairs of parallel plates which are vertical and horizontaldeflection plates.

- Voltage applied to vertical and horizontal deflection plates is control vertical and horizontal deflectionrespectively.

- There are two techniques used for producing images on the CRT screen:

  ○ Vector scan/Random scan display.

  ○ Raster scan display.

Vector scan/Random Scan Display

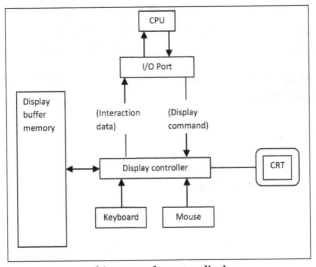

Architecture of a vector display.

- Vector scan display directly traces out only the desired lines on CRT.

- If we want line between point p1 & p2 then we directly drive the beam deflection circuitry which focus beam directly from point p1 to p2.

- If we do not want to display line from p1 to p2 and just move then we can blank the beam as we move it.

- To move the beam across the CRT, the information about both magnitude and direction is required. This information is generated with the help of vector graphics generator.

- Figure shows architecture of vector display. It consists of display controller, CPU, display buffer memory and CRT.

- Display controller is connected as an I/O peripheral to the CPU.

- Display buffer stores computer produced display list or display program.

- The Program contains point & line plotting commands with end point co-ordinates as well as character plotting commands.

- Display controller interprets command and sends digital and point co-ordinates to a vector generator.

- Vector generator then converts the digital co-ordinate value to analog voltages for beam deflection circuits that displace an electron beam which points on the CRT's screen.

- In this technique beam is deflected from end point to end point hence this techniques is also called random scan.

- We know as beam strikes phosphors coated screen it emits light but that light decays after few milliseconds and therefore it is necessary to repeat through the display list to refresh the screen at least 30 times per second to avoid flicker.

- As display buffer is used to store display list and used to refreshing, it is also called refresh buffer.

Raster Scan Display

- Figure shows the architecture of Raster display. It consists of display controller, CPU, video controller, refresh buffer, keyboard, mouse and CRT.

- The display image is stored in the form of 1's and 0's in the refresh buffer.

- The video controller reads this refresh buffer and produces the actual image on screen.

- It will scan one line at a time from top to bottom & then back to the top.

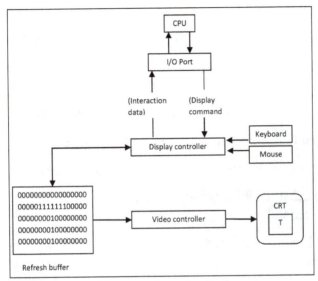

Architecture of a raster display.

- In this method the horizontal and vertical deflection signals are generated to move the beam all over the screen in a pattern shown in figure.

- Here beam is swept back & forth from left to the right.

- When beam is moved from left to right it is ON. When beam is moved from right to left it is OFF and process of moving beam from right to left after completion of row is known as Horizontal Retrace.

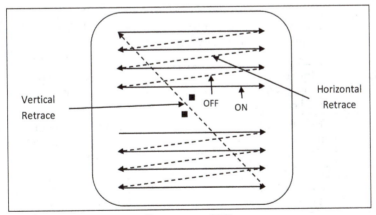

Raster scan CRT.

- When beam is reach at the bottom of the screen. It is made OFF and rapidly retraced back to the top left to start again and process of moving back to top is known as Vertical Retrace.

- The screen image is maintained by repeatedly scanning the same image. This process is known as Refreshing of Screen.

- In raster scan displays a special area of memory is dedicated to graphics only. This memory is called Frame Buffer.

- Frame buffer holds set of intensity values for all the screen points.

- That intensity is retrieved from frame buffer and display on screen one row at a time.

- Each screen point referred as pixel or Pel (Picture Element).

- Each pixel can be specified by its row and column numbers.

- It can be simply black and white system or color system.

- In simple black and white system each pixel is either ON or OFF, so only one bit per pixel is needed.

- Additional bits are required when color and intensity variations can be displayed up to 24-bits per pixel are included in high quality display systems.

- On a black and white system with one bit per pixel the frame buffer is commonly called a Bitmap. And for systems with multiple bits per pixel, the frame buffer is often referred as a Pixmap.

Table: Difference between random scan and raster scan.

Base of Difference	Raster Scan System	Random Scan System
Electron Beam	The electron beam is swept across the screen, one row at a time, from top to bottom.	The electron beam is directed only to the parts of screen where a picture is to be drawn.
Resolution	Its resolution is poor because raster system in contrast produces zigzag lines that are plotted as discrete point sets.	Its resolution is good because this system produces smooth lines drawings because CRT beam directly follows the line path.
Picture Definition	Picture definition is stored as a set of intensity values for all screen points, called pixels in a refresh buffer area.	Picture definition is stored as a set of line drawing instructions in a display file.
Realistic Display	The capability of this system to store intensity values for pixel makes it well suited for the realistic display of scenes contain shadow and color pattern.	These systems are designed for line-drawing and can't display realistic shaded scenes.
Draw an Image	Screen points/pixels are used to draw an image.	Mathematical functions are used to draw an image.

Color CRT monitors

- A CRT monitors displays color pictures by using a combination of phosphors that emit different colored light.

- It produces range of colors by combining the light emitted by different phosphors.

- There are two basic techniques for color display:
  - Beam-penetration technique.
  - Shadow-mask technique.

Beam-penetration Technique

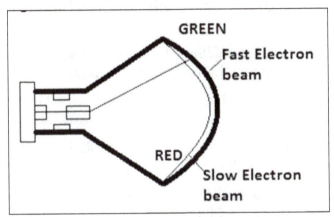

Beam-penetration CRT

- This technique is used with random scan monitors.

- In this technique inside of CRT coated with two phosphor layers usually red and green. The outer layer of red and inner layer of green phosphor.

- The color depends on how far the electron beam penetrates into the phosphor layer.

- A beam of fast electron penetrates more and excites inner green layer while slow electron excites outer red layer.

- At intermediate beam speed we can produce combination of red and green lights which emit additional two colors orange and yellow.

- The beam acceleration voltage controls the speed of the electrons and hence color of pixel.

- It is a low cost technique to produce color in random scan monitors.

- It can display only four colors.

- Quality of picture is not good compared to other techniques.

Shadow-mask technique

- It produces wide range of colors as compared to beam-penetration technique.

- This technique is generally used in raster scan displays. Including color TV.

- In this technique CRT has three phosphor color dots at each pixel position. One dot for red, one for green and one for blue light. This is commonly known as Dot Triangle.

- Here in CRT there are three electron guns present, one for each color dot. And a shadow mask grid just behind the phosphor coated screen.

- The shadow mask grid consists of series of holes aligned with the phosphor dot pattern.

- Three electron beams are deflected and focused as a group onto the shadow mask and when they pass through a hole they excite a dot triangle.

- In dot triangle three phosphor dots are arranged so that each electron beam can activate only its corresponding color dot when it passes through the shadow mask.

- A dot triangle when activated appears as a small dot on the screen which has color of combination of three small dots in the dot triangle.

- By changing the intensity of the three electron beams we can obtain different colors in the shadow mask CRT.

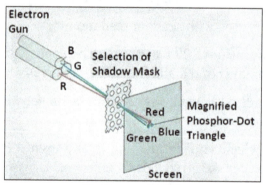

Shadow-mask CRT.

Direct-view Storage Tubes (DVST)

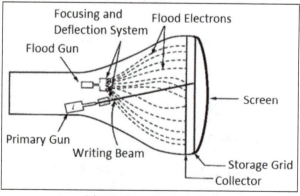

Direct-view storage tube.

- In raster scan display we do refreshing of the screen to maintain a screen image.

- DVST gives alternative method for maintaining the screen image.

- DVST uses the storage grid which stores the picture information as a charge distribution just behind the phosphor coated screen.

- DVST consists two electron guns a primary gun and a flood gun.

- A primary gun stores the picture pattern and the flood gun maintains the picture display.

- A primary gun emits high speed electrons which strike on the storage grid to draw the picture pattern.

- As electron beam strikes on the storage grid with high speed, it knocks out electrons from the storage grid keeping the net positive charge.

- The knocked out electrons are attracted towards the collector.

- The net positive charge on the storage grid is nothing but the picture pattern.

- The continuous low speed electrons from flood gun pass through the control grid and are attracted to the positive charged area of the storage grid.

- The low speed electrons then penetrate the storage grid and strike the phosphor coating without affecting the positive charge pattern on the storage grid.

- During this process the collector just behind the storage grid smooth out the flow of flood electrons.

Advantage of DVST

- Refreshing of CRT is not required.

- Very complex pictures can be displayed at very high resolution without flicker.

- Flat screen.

Disadvantage of DVST

- They do not display color and are available with single level of line intensity.

- For erasing it is necessary to removal of charge on the storage grid so erasing and redrawing process take several second.

- Erasing selective part of the screen cannot be possible.

- Cannot used for dynamic graphics application as on erasing it produce unpleasant flash over entire screen.

- It has poor contrast as a result of the comparatively low accelerating potential applied to the flood electrons.

- The performance of DVST is somewhat inferior to the refresh CRT.

Flat Panel Display

- The term flat panel display refers to a class of video device that have reduced volume, weight & power requirement compared to a CRT.

- As flat panel display is thinner than CRTs, we can hang them on walls or wear on our wrists.

- Since we can even write on some flat panel displays they will soon be available as pocket notepads.

- We can separate flat panel display in two categories:

  ○ Emissive displays: the emissive display or emitters are devices that convert electrical energy into light. For Ex. Plasma panel, thin film electroluminescent displays and light emitting diodes.

  ○ Non emissive displays: non emissive display or non-emitters use optical effects to convert sunlight or light from some other source into graphics patterns. For Ex. LCD (Liquid Crystal Display).

Plasma Panels Displays

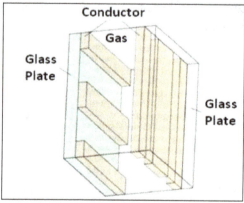

Basic design of a plasma-panel display device.

- This is also called gas discharge displays.

- It is constructed by filling the region between two glass plates with a mixture of gases that usually includes neon.

- A series of vertical conducting ribbons is placed on one glass panel and a set of horizontal ribbon is built into the other glass panel.

- Firing voltage is applied to a pair of horizontal and vertical conductors cause the gas at the intersection of the two conductors to break down into glowing plasma of electrons and ions.

- Picture definition is stored in a refresh buffer and the firing voltages are applied to refresh the pixel positions, 60 times per second.

- Alternating current methods are used to provide faster application of firing voltages and thus brighter displays.

- Separation between pixels is provided by the electric field of conductor.

- One disadvantage of plasma panels is they were strictly monochromatic device that means shows only one color other than black like black and white.

Thin Film Electroluminescent Displays

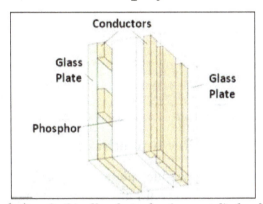

Basic design of a thin-film electro luminescent display device.

- It is similar to plasma panel display but region between the glass plates is filled with phosphors such as zinksulphide doped with magnesium instead of gas.

- When sufficient voltage is applied the phosphors becomes a conductor in area of intersection of the two electrodes.

- Electrical energy is then absorbed by the manganese atoms which then release the energy as a spot of light similar to the glowing plasma effect in plasma panel.

- It requires more power than plasma panel.

- In this good color and gray scale difficult to achieve.

Light Emitting Diode (LED)

- In this display a matrix of multi-color light emitting diode is arranged to form the pixel position in the display. And the picture definition is stored in refresh buffer.

- Similar to scan line refreshing of CRT information is read from the refresh buffer and converted to voltage levels that are applied to the diodes to produce the light pattern on the display.

Liquid Crystal Display (LCD)

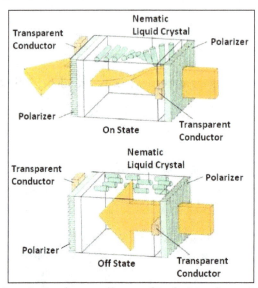

Light twisting shutter effect used in design of most LCD.

- It is generally used in small system such as calculator and portable laptop.

- This non emissive device produce picture by passing polarized light from the surrounding or from an internal light source through liquid crystal material that can be aligned to either block or transmit the light.

- The liquid crystal refreshes to fact that these compounds have crystalline arrangement of molecules then also flows like liquid.

- It consists of two glass plates each with light polarizer at right angles to each other sandwich the liquid crystal material between the plates.

- Rows of horizontal transparent conductors are built into one glass plate, and column of vertical conductors are put into the other plates.

- The intersection of two conductors defines a pixel position.

- In the ON state polarized light passing through material is twisted so that it will pass through the opposite polarizer.

- In the OFF state it will reflect back towards source.

- We applied a voltage to the two intersecting conductor to align the molecules so that the light is not twisted.

- This type of flat panel device is referred to as a passive matrix LCD.

- In active matrix LCD transistors are used at each (x, y) grid point.

- Transistor cause crystal to change their state quickly and also to control degree to which the state has been changed.

- Transistor can also serve as a memory for the state until it is changed.

- So transistor make cell ON for all time giving brighter display then it would be if it had to be refresh periodically.

Advantages of LCD Display

- Low cost

- Low weight

- Small size

- Low power consumption

Three Dimensional Viewing Devices

- The graphics monitor which are display three dimensional scenes are devised using a technique that reflects a CRT image from a vibrating flexible mirror.

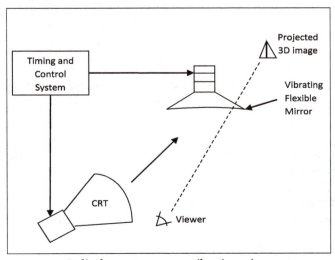

3D display system uses a vibrating mirror.

- Vibrating mirror changes its focal length due to vibration which is synchronized with the display of an object on CRT.

- The each point on the object is reflected from the mirror into spatial position corresponding to distance of that point from a viewing position.

- Very good example of this system is GENISCO SPACE GRAPH system, which use vibrating mirror to project 3D objects into a 25 cm by 25 cm by 25 cm volume. This system is also capable to show 2D cross section at different depth.

Application of 3D Viewing Devices

- In medical to analyze data from ultra-sonography.

- In geological to analyze topological and seismic data.

- In designing like solid objects viewing and 3D viewing of objects.

Stereoscopic and Virtual-reality Systems

Stereoscopic System

Stereoscopic views.

- Stereoscopic views does not produce three dimensional images, but it produce 3D effects by presenting different view to each eye of an observer so that it appears to have depth.

- To obtain this we first need to obtain two views of object generated from viewing direction corresponding to each eye.

- We can construct the two views as computer generated scenes with different viewing positions or we can use stereo camera pair to photograph some object or scene.

- When we see simultaneously both the view as left view with left eye and right view with right eye then two views is merge and produce image which appears to have depth.

- One way to produce stereoscopic effect is to display each of the two views with raster system on alternate refresh cycles.

- The screen is viewed through glasses with each lance design such a way that it act as a rapidly alternating shutter that is synchronized to block out one of the views.

Virtual Reality

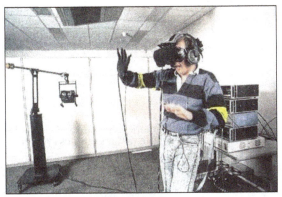

Virtual reality.

- Virtual reality is the system which produce images in such a way that we feel that our surrounding is what we are set in display devices but in actually it does not.

- In virtual reality user can step into a scene and interact with the environment.

- A head set containing an optical system to generate the stereoscopic views is commonly used in conjunction with interactive input devices to locate and manipulate objects in the scene.

- Sensor in the head set keeps track of the viewer's position so that the front and back of objects can be seen as the viewer "walks through" and interacts with the display.

- Virtual reality can also be produce with stereoscopic glass and video monitor instead of head set. This provides low cost virtual reality system.

- Sensor on display screen track head position and accordingly adjust image depth.

Raster Graphics Systems

Simple Raster Graphics System

- Raster graphics systems having additional processing unit like video controller or display controller.

- Here frame buffer can be anywhere in the system memory and video controller access this for refresh the screen.

- In addition to video controller more processors are used as co-processors to accelerate the system in sophisticated raster system.

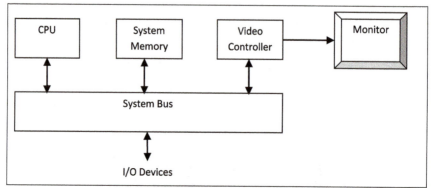

Architecture of a simple raster graphics system.

Raster Graphics System with a Fixed Portion of the System Memory reserved for the Frame Buffer.

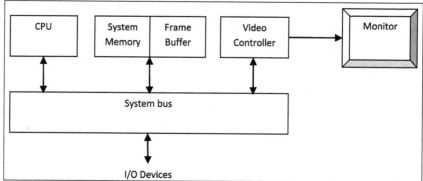

Architecture of a raster graphics system with a fixed portion of the system memory reserved for the frame buffer.

- A fixed area of the system memory is reserved for the frame buffer and the video controller can directly access that frame buffer memory.

- Frame buffer location and the screen position are referred in Cartesian coordinates.

- For many graphics monitors the coordinate origin is defined at the lower left screen corner.

- Screen surface is then represented as the first quadrant of the two dimensional systems with positive Xvalue increases as left to right and positive Y-value increases bottom to top.

Basic Refresh Operation of Video Controller

- Two registers are used to store the coordinates of the screen pixels which are X and Y.

- Initially the X is set to 0 and Y is set to Ymax.

- The value stored in frame buffer for this pixel is retrieved and used to set the intensity of the CRT beam.

- After this X register is incremented by one.

- This procedure is repeated till X becomes equals to Xmax.

- Then X is set to 0 and Y is decremented by one pixel and repeat above procedure.

- This whole procedure is repeated till Y is become equals to 0 and complete the one refresh cycle. Then controller reset the register as top –left corner i.e. X=0 and Y=Ymax and refresh process start for next refresh cycle.

- Since screen must be refreshed at the rate of 60 frames per second the simple procedure illustrated in figure cannot be accommodated by typical RAM chips.

- To speed up pixel processing video controller retrieves multiple values at a time using more numbers of registers and simultaneously refresh block of pixel.

- Such a way it can speed up and accommodate refresh rate more than 60 frames per second.

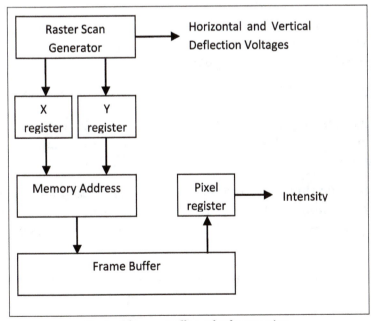

Basic video controller refresh operation.

Raster-graphics System with a Display Processor

- One way to designing raster system is having separate display coprocessor.

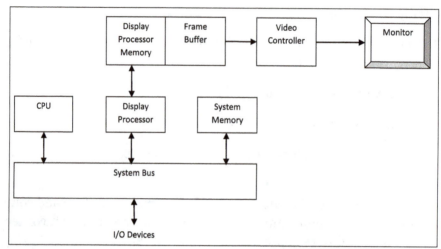

Architecture of a raster-graphics system with a display processor.

- Purpose of display processor is to free CPU from graphics work.

- Display processors have their own separate memory for fast operation.

- Main work of display processor is digitalizing a picture definition given into a set of pixel intensity values for store in frame buffer.

- This digitalization process is scan conversion.

- Display processor also performs many other functions such as generating various line styles (dashed, dotted, or solid). Display color areas and performing some transformation for manipulating object.

- It also interfaces with interactive input devices such as mouse.

- For reduce memory requirements in raster scan system methods have been devised for organizing the frame buffer as a line list and encoding the intensity information.

- One way to do this is to store each scan line as a set of integer pair one number indicate number of adjacent pixels on the scan line that are having same intensity and second stores intensity value this technique is called run-length encoding.

- A similar approach is when pixel. Intensity is changes linearly, encoded the raster as a set of rectangular areas (cell encoding).

- Disadvantages of encoding is when run length is small it requires more memory then original frame buffer.

- It also difficult for display controller to process the raster when many sort runs are involved.

Random-scan System

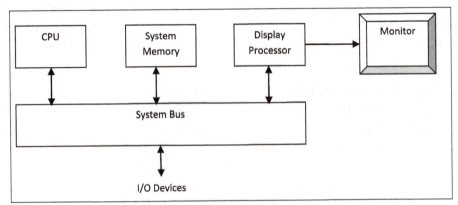

Architecture of a simple random-scan system.

- An application program is input & stored in the system memory along with a graphics package.

- Graphics commands in the application program are translated by the graphics package into a display file stored in the system memory.

- This display file is used by display processor to refresh the screen.

- Display process goes through each command in display file. Once during every refresh cycle.

- Sometimes the display processor in random scan system is also known as display processing unit or a graphics controller.

- In this system graphics platform are drawn on random scan system by directing the electron beam along the component times of the picture.

- Lines are defined by coordinate end points.

- This input coordinate values are converts to X and Y deflection voltages.

- A scene is then drawn one line at a time.

Progressive vs. Interlaced Scans

There are generally two types of scanning methods used in television broadcasting. They are progressive and interlaced scans used to display video. Televisions produce moving images that are broadcast from a studio to an antenna. This was common during the golden age of television, but nowadays cable and OTT streaming are more prevalent. Broadcast television is still widely available and free of charge.

These scanning methods are used to determine the technique for transmitting video frames. These refer to the transmission of signals that represent lines of resolution to a television screen display. Traditionally this used the CRT (Cathode Ray Tube), but now LCD (Liquid Crystal Display) are more common. The signals transmit patterns of how the CRT writes lines onto the television screen. The lines represent the video, and are written many times per second across the screen in the process called scanning.

The scanning rate is the repetition of how many times horizontal lines aka fields are written to the screen to display the video. It uses the same frequency as that of the power grid at 50 or 60 fields per second or Hz. Between 25 to 30 frames per second (fps) are sent. In North America, the monochrome (black and white) system uses 525 scan lines that are transmitted at a rate of 30 Hz, for a horizontal sweep frequency of 15,750 Hz (525 × 30). The color television system, also uses 525 scan lines, but the sweep frequency is adjusted to 15,734 Hz. This was done in order for both systems to remain compatible with each other for years to come.

Interlaced Scans

Interlaced scans transmits the frame as odd (1,3,5 ...) and even (2,4,6 ...) numbered lines for 1/60 of a second (in reference to 60 Hz). The process is repeated over and over and each series of lines displayed is what is called the field. Only half the frame is actually transmitted at a time, but it happens so quickly (1/60 of second) that it is not noticeable to the human eye. It happens fast enough to make viewers see the complete frame, but there may be some flickering.

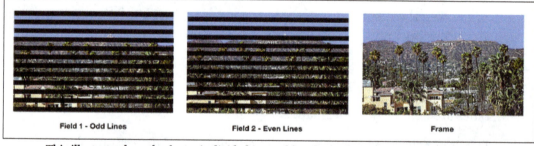

| Field 1 - Odd Lines | Field 2 - Even Lines | Frame |

This illustrates how the frame is divided into odd and even lines in interlaced scanning.

The cons of interlaced scanning are the movement within the frame can cause motion artifacts. This happens when the motion is really quick that it causes noticeable differences in the positions of the fields. An example of this is when you shoot sporting events with really fast motion, many artifacts can be generated. Viewers may also notice flickering on the screen of an interlaced display, like when watching TV from a satellite broadcast. This creates a combing effect (jagged edges), which can really affect image quality on screen. This means the frames are not entirely in sync with the actual motion. The interlacing can be so bad, but many systems use deinterlacing techniques to minimize this problem. It removes the combing effect by blurring the motion. The deinterlacing process is not perfect and it depends on how well the system was designed on the display or processing unit (e.g. cable box).

An example of combing in this video capture from Handbrake.
Notice the comb like jagged edges on the subject's hands.

A main reason for using interlaced scanning is to conserve bandwidth. By sending just half the frame at a time, it saves the amount of bandwidth needed for transmitting information on the network. You are not actually using less bandwidth per se. If your transmission channel is 8 MHz, it doesn't reduce to a lower value, you will still have 8 MHz. Instead think of it like this — doubling the frame rate of a video without consuming extra bandwidth.

The problem with requiring more bandwidth is that the greater the bandwidth, it becomes more expensive and complex to produce and broadcast content. An example is with interlacing on a PAL (Phase Alternating Line) system requires 50 fields per second (25 odd lines, 25 even lines). When interlaced, a half frame is sent every 1/50 of a second with less bandwidth requirements. If the full frame was sent, it could require another 8 MHz, thus increasing the need for more bandwidth.

Progressive Scans

In a progressive scan, the entire frame is transmitted at once. All the lines in frame are drawn at once to fill the screen. Progressive scans are more ideal for digital transmission compared to older interlaced scanning techniques. It became a technical standard for use with HD (High Definition) TV displays in the early 1990's.

Interlaced   Progressive

A comparison of interlaced and progressive. Progressive scans are more smoother and don't have the same problem with motion artifacting.

By transmitting the full frame at once, it reduces flicker and artifacts. The video will appear smoother, more realistic and high quality. This allows capturing stills from video without noticeable artifacts in the image. This is great for super slo-motion video that really captures the details. There is also no need to use intentional blurring (anti-aliasing) to minimize problems like combing. This is good for viewers since less flickering means less eye strain. Viewers can watch for much longer hours without catching eye fatigue.

Progressive video is more expensive but desired among independent filmmakers. This is because it has the look like that of film. The scanning technique results in the clearest images without worrying about too many artifacts. It also allows for better viewing of fast motion video like in action sequences in movies and sports.

Deinterlacing

Interlaced scanning was originally used in traditional analog SD (Standard Definition) broadcasts since it was more efficient in transmitting video. However it is not smooth despite being reliable. For the most part, OTA signals still use interlaced techniques for TV. This requires the use of deinterlacing to convert to progressive scanning when the signal is sent to the display.

Deinterlacing converts the interlaced video into a non-interlaced or progressive form. TV sets and computer monitors support progressive scanning, so they display much better video or digital output. This has been built-in to most modern DVD players, Blu-ray players, LCD/LED HDTV, digital projectors, TV set-top boxes, professional broadcast equipment and computer video players with varying levels of quality (they are not all the same).

Synopsis

The recording, playback and transmission of video used either progressive or interlaced techniques. Interlaced has its roots in the broadcasting industry and is still widely used because of its efficiency and reliability. Progressive is ideal for higher quality displays for smoother video output.

Our eyes are not really aware of the transitions that take place in our TV. On standard displays using interlaced scanning it should be fine, but flicker and artifacts are noticeable. It gets worse on progressive screens like computer monitors, so it requires deinterlacing first before it can be displayed. The overall advantage of progressive is image quality when it comes to video playback. However, interlaced displays are still suitable for video playback at a lower cost.

When shooting interlaced video, known issues are with motion artifacts. This requires more post editing of the content which takes up more time and costs. This is why editors need to deinterlace video. It is also required because most modern displays use progressive scanning.

Video broadcasts are traditionally interlaced.

When choosing displays like a TV, you will see the marketing as 720i, 1080p, 2160p, etc. The letter "i" denotes interlaced while "p" denotes progressive. The trend toward progressive displays is more prevalent now because of OTT streaming video-on-demand content and digital media (e.g. DVD, Blu-ray, etc.). Digital video signals are more attuned to progressive scanning methods. If you compare a progressive scan and interlaced image at 60 Hz, the progressive scan image appears much smoother. While interlaced video signals are still used in broadcasting, progressive displays that have deinterlacing features are the better choice for video output.

Graphics Input Devices

Input devices are those devices through which we can give the data and instructions to the computer. For Example– Mouse, Trackball, Keyboard, Light pen, etc.

Classification of Input Devices

- Manual data entry devices.
- Direct data entry devices.

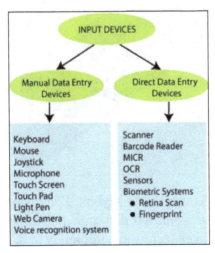

Manual Data Entry Devices

Manual input devices are those peripheral devices through which the user can enter the data manually (by hand) at the time of processing. It also includes:

1. Keyboard: It is the commonly used input device. It is designed to input text and characters. A keyboard contains approx. 108 keys. For Example– Alphanumeric keys, Numeric keys, Function key, and cursor key, etc.

Types of keys: These keys include:

- Alphanumeric keys: These are located in the center of the keyboard. These keys consist of alphabet (A-Z), Number (0-9), and symbols (@, #, $, %, ^, &, *, !, =, +).

- Numeric Keys: A part of keypad contains 17 numeric keys. In which we can include number up to 0-9, mathematics operator like +, -, /, *, and enter key.

- Function keys: These keys are placed at the top of the keyboard. In which we can include F1, F2 up-to F12. The function key performs many tasks according to the software.

- Cursor Keys: The cursor keys include Up, Down, Left, and Right. These are used to move the cursor on the screen.

Types of Keyboard: The type of keyboard is:

- Normal Keyboard: These are the commonly used keyboard. It is used by the user in their PCs. It contains 108 keys. The normal keyboards are connected to the CPU through the wire.

- Wireless Keyboard: The wireless keyboard connected to the computer without the wire. It works for a limited distance. It is more expensive than a normal keyboard. The user faces technical complexity in it.

- Ergonomic Keyboard: It gives the user comfort and ease during the typing; that's why it is called the "Ergonomic keyboard." This keyboard is used to increase the efficiency of the user. It also reduces wrist pain during typing.

Advantages of Keyboards:

- Easy to use.
- Enable fast data input.
- Well tried technology.

Disadvantages of Keyboards:

- Sometimes it is difficult to use.
- Need desk space to keep.

2. Mouse: It is used as a popular pointing device. It is used to create images, graphics as well as to click on any button or menu. The mouse has two or three buttons.

Functions of the mouse:

- Clicking
- Double Clicking
- Right Clicking

- Dragging

- Scrolling

Types of Mouse: There are three type of mouse are as follow:

- Mechanical Mouse

- Optical Mouse

- Wireless Mouse

1. Mechanical Mouse: This mouse has a rubber ball at the bottom, when we rotate the mouse on the surface than the rubber ball also rotates inside the shell. Now the sensors inside the mouse give a signal to the computer.

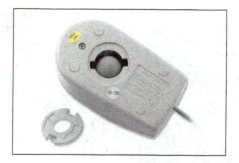

2. Optical Mouse: It is a type of Non-mechanical mouse. A light beam is emitted from the surface below it. Based on the light beam, the mouse determines the distance and speed of the object.

3. Wireless Mouse: This mouse communicates to the computer with the help of radio-frequency.

It has two main components:

- Transmitter: It is used to send the information of the mouse's speed and its click in the form of an electromagnetic signal.

- Receiver: It connects to the computer and used to receive the signals sent by the transmitter.

Advantages of Mouse:

- Easy to use

- Less Expensive

- The Cursor moves faster than the arrow keys of the keyboard.

Disadvantages of Mouse:

- Required flat surface to move

- Needs regularly cleaning

- Damaged easily

3. Joystick: It is a pointing device. It is used to play video games. It has a rounded ball at both ends. The joystick can be moved in all directions. The Joystick is similar to a mouse. It is also used in computer-aided designing (CAD).

Advantages of Joystick:

- Used in playing games.

- Fast Interface

- Easy to Navigate

Disadvantages of Joystick:

- Sometimes difficult to control

- Required hand Movement

- It is not robust

4. Microphone: The microphone was introduced by "Emile Berliner" in 1877. It is also called "Mic." The Microphone is used to take input in the form of audio. The microphone is plugged into the specific port of the sound card in the computer system. Some microphones are wireless.

5. Touch Screen: It is an Electronic Visual Display, which is used to detect the touch of finger and hand in its display area. It is most widely used with those computer machines that can interact with the user. For Example: Smartphones, Tablet, Etc.

Type of Touch Screen: The types of the touch screen are:

- Resistive: It is made up of hardened acrylic plastic. It is pressure sensitive. It has minimal clarity. It has a durability of 15 million touches.

- Capacitive: It is made up of glass with coating. It activates by human body electricity. It has the best clarity. It has a durability of 60 million touches.

- Surface Acoustic Wave (SAW): It is made up of a Glass with coating. SAW activates by wave absorption. It has medium clarity. It has a durability of 30 million touches.

Advantages of Touch Screen:

- Simple User Interface
- Speed
- Durability
- Improve Accessibility

Disadvantages of Touch Screen:

- Screen Size
- Sensitivity Issue
- Accidental Dialing

6. Touch Pad: It is a flat pad used in laptops on which we slide the finger to move the cursor. It is a touch-sensitive area. It is also called "Trackpad." It is used to translate the motion and position of the user's finger. It also includes two buttons:

- Left Click: It is used to select the option.
- Right Click: It is used to display the options on the screen.

Advantages:

- No Mouse Needed
- No need of a wire-like mouse

Disadvantages:

- Lacks of the scroll wheel
- Less sensitive than a mouse

7. Light Pen: It is a tool that is light sensitive. It is used to draw pictures and graphics on the computer screen. It is also used to select the objects. The pictures made by the light pen can be stored in the computer and can be improved as needed.

Advantages:

- It allows the user to select any object

- It does not have any coating

- Easy to Use

- Available in different colors

Disadvantages:

- Works only with CRT screens

- Not very accurate drawing

- Sensitive with dust

8. Web Camera: It is a hardware input device. It is a video camera that is used to transmit pictures or videos in real-time to a computer network. It is connected with laptops, or we can connect it with the computer through USB cable. It is also called a small digital camera.

Advantages:

- It can connect with people across the world

- Easy to use

- It uses both sound and video

Disadvantages:

- Poor Quality Images

- Limited Features

9. Voice Recognition System: It is also called the "Speech Recognition System." It is a computer software program that takes human speech as an input, converts that into digital form, and act on it. Voice recognition system is used to operate mobile phones through voice command. For Example: Google Assistant, SIRI (Apple) Etc.

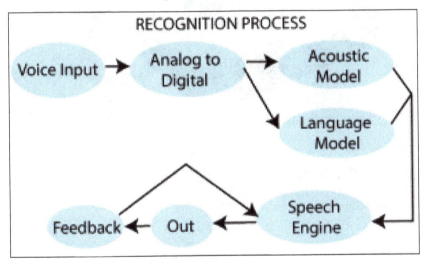

Advantages:

- Improves Efficiency

- Easy to use for anyone

- Easy to Understand

Disadvantages:

- Vocal Problems

- Requires more storage to store voice files

- Noise Interference

Direct Data Entry Devices

Direct data devices are those peripheral devices through which we can directly input the data from the source and transfer that to the computer system. It also includes:

1. Scanner: It is an input device. It is used to scan documents such as photographs. It is used to input any shape or written data on a page directly into the computer. Its main advantage is that the user does not have to type the information.

Advantages:

- High-Resolution Images

- Easy to handle

- Fast image analysis

- Image portability

Disadvantages:

- High Cost

- The Need for internet and power supply

- Difficult to manage large digital files

2. Barcode Reader: It is also known as "Price Scanner" or "Point-of-sale scanner." A barcode is a particular type of code. It contains a series of thick and thin lines, which are called "Bars." The bar contains the information. We can read the barcode through an optical scanner called "Barcode Reader." The user can connect the barcode reader with the computer through a serial cable.

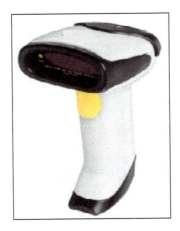

Advantages:

- Fast Speed

- Accuracy

- Portable

Disadvantages:

- Require a clear line of sight

- Expensive

3. MICR: It is also called "Magnetic Ink Character reader." It is widely used in the processing of cheques in the bank. MICR is used for reading magnetic ink printed characters. This machine is fast and automatic. There should be a nil chance of making mistakes.

Advantages:

- More secure than OCR

- More accurate than OCR

- Allow overwrite cheques

Disadvantages:

- Only a limited character set

- Expensive

4. OCR: It is also called "Optical Character Recognition." It is a technique which is used to read a special type of symbols, letters, or the numbers. The light source can read the characters. The OCR can read characters printed from typewriters, the character of the cash register, and the character of the credit card. The OCR fonts are stored on the computer.

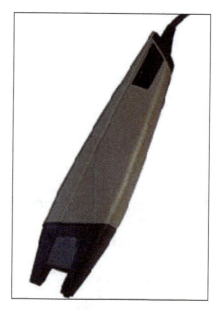

Advantages:

- Faster data entry

- Printed document converted into text files

Disadvantages:

- Cannot recognize all type of text

- Poor or Old documents cannot be recognized

5. Sensors: A Sensor can be treated as an input device that is used to detect and change the force, pressure, any other physical quantity, and sends the data to the computer.

Advantages of Sensors:

- Sensitivity

- Reliability

- High-Resolution

Disadvantages of Sensors:

- Affected by temperature and humidity

- Difficulties in designing

6. Biometric System: A biometric system is defined as an input system that is used to identify a person. A biometric machine can identify a person by face, eyes, voice, finger, or thumb impression. It is a secure system; it means no biometric data can be stolen.

Uses of Biometric System:

- Biometric Door Lock

- Biometric Attendance system

- Biometric ATM

A biometric system also includes:

- Finger Scanner: It is used to identify the person by his thumb or finger.

- Hand Scanner: It is used to identify the person by his palm impression.

Advantages of Biometrics:

- More secure than passwords

- Accuracy

- Uniqueness

Disadvantages of Biometrics:

- Costly

- Missing or injured body part problem

References

- Computer-graphics-tutorial: javatpoint.com, Retrieved 25, July 2020

- Types-of-computer-graphics: tutorialandexample.com, Retrieved 20, January 2020

- Difference-between-raster-vector: psprint.com, Retrieved 15, June 2020

- Progressive-vs-interlaced-182924800: medium.com, Retrieved 04, March 2020

- Input-devices-in-computer-graphics: tutorialandexample.com, Retrieved 13, August 2020

2

Hardware and Software

The physical components of a computer that can be touched are termed as hardware. The collection of instructions and procedures which are used to perform different tasks on a computer is known as computer software. This chapter has been carefully written to provide an easy understanding of the hardware and software aspects of computer graphics like open source vector graphics and open source games development software, etc.

Graphics Processing Unit

Graphics Processing Units (GPUs) are coprocessors that traditionally perform the rendering of 2-dimensional and 3-dimensional graphics information for display on a screen. In particular computer games request more and more realistic real-time rendering of graphics data and so GPUs became more and more powerful highly parallel specialist computing units. It did not take long until programmers realized that this computational power can also be used for tasks other than computer graphics. For example already in 1990 Lengyel, Reichert, Donald, and Greenberg used GPUs for real-time robot motion planning. In 2003 Harris introduced the term general-purpose computations on GPUs (GPGPU) for such non-graphics applications running on GPUs. At that time programming general-purpose computations on GPUs meant expressing all algorithms in terms of operations on graphics data, pixels and vectors. This was feasible for speed-critical small programs and for algorithms that operate on vectors of floating-point values in a similar way as graphics data is typically processed in the rendering pipeline.

The programming paradigm shifted when the two main GPU manufacturers, NVIDIA and AMD, changed the hardware architecture from a dedicated graphics-rendering pipeline to a multi-core computing platform, implemented shader algorithms of the rendering pipeline in software running on these cores, and explicitly supported general-purpose computations on GPUs by offering programming languages and software development tool chains.

An Introduction to Modern GPUs

Graphics processing units have evolved to coprocessors of a size larger than typical

CPUs. While CPUs use large portions of the chip area for caches, GPUs use most of the area for arithmetic logic units (ALUs). The main concept that both NVIDIA and AMD GPUs use to exploit the computational power of these ALUs is executing a single instruction stream on multiple independent data streams (SIMD). This concept is known from CPUs with vector registers and instructions operating on these registers. For example, a 128-bit vector register can hold four single-precision floating-point values; an addition instruction operating on two such registers performs four independent additions in parallel. Instead of using vector registers, GPUs use hardware threads that all execute the same instruction stream on different sets of data. NVIDIA calls this approach to SIMD computing "single instruction stream, multiple threads (SIMT)". The number of threads required to keep the ALUs busy is much larger than the number of elements inside vector registers on CPUs. GPU performance therefore relies on a high degree of data-level parallelism in the application.

To alleviate these requirements on data-level parallelism, GPUs can also exploit task-level parallelism by running different independent tasks of a computation in parallel. This is possible on all modern GPUs through the use of conditional statements. Some recent GPUs support the exploitation of task-level parallelism also through concurrent execution of independent GPU programs. Each of the independent tasks again needs to involve a relatively high degree of data-level parallelism to make full use of the computational power of the GPU, but exploitation of task-level parallelism gives the programmer more flexibility and extends the set of applications that can make use of GPUs to accelerate computations.

NVIDIA GPUs

In 2006 NVIDIA introduced the Compute Unified Device Architecture. Today all of NVIDIA's GPUs are CUDA GPUs. CUDA is not a computer architecture in the sense of a definition of an instruction set and a set of architectural registers; binaries compiled for one CUDA GPU do not necessarily run on all CUDA GPUs. More specifically, NVIDIA defines different CUDA compute capabilities to describe the features supported by CUDA hardware. The first CUDA GPUs had compute capability 1.0. In 2011 NVIDIA released GPUs with compute capability 2.1, which is known as "Fermi" architecture.

A CUDA GPU consists of multiple so-called streaming multiprocessors (SMs). The threads executing a GPU program, a so-called kernel, are grouped in blocks. Threads belonging to one block all run on the same multiprocessor but one multiprocessor can run multiple blocks concurrently. Blocks are further divided into groups of 32 threads called warps; the threads belonging to one warp are executed in lock step, i.e., they are synchronized. As a consequence, if threads inside one warp diverge via a conditional branch instruction, execution of the different branches is serialized. On GPUs with compute capability 1.x all streaming multiprocessors must execute the same kernel. Compute capability 2.x supports concurrent execution of different kernels on different streaming multiprocessors.

Each streaming multiprocessor contains several so-called CUDA cores, 8 per SM in compute capability 1.x , 32 per SM in compute capability 2.0 and 48 per SM in compute capability 2.1. One could think that for example a reasonable number of threads per SM is 8 for compute-capability-1.x GPUs or 48 for computecapability-2.1 GPUs. In fact it needs many more threads to fully utilize the ALUs; the reason is that concurrent execution of many threads on one SM is used to hide arithmetic latencies and up to some extent also memory access latencies. For compute capability 1.x NVIDIA recommends to run at least 192 or 256 threads per SM. To fully utilize the power of compute-capability-2.x GPUs even more threads need to run concurrently on one SM. For applications that involve a very high degree of data-level parallelism it might now sound like a good idea to just run as many concurrent threads as possible. The problem is that the register banks are shared among threads; the more threads are executed the fewer registers are available per thread. Finding the optimal number of threads running concurrently on one streaming multiprocessor is a crucial step to achieve good performance.

Aside from registers, each thread also has access to various memory domains. Each streaming multiprocessor has several KB of fast shared memory accessible by all threads on this multiprocessor. This memory is intended to exchange data between the threads of a thread block, latencies are as low as for register access but throughput depends on access patterns. The shared memory is organized in 16 banks. If two threads within the same half-warp (16 threads) load from or store to different addresses on the same memory bank in the same instruction, these requests are serialized. Such requests to different addresses on the same memory bank are called bank conflicts. Graphics cards also contain several hundred MB up to a few GB of device memory. Each thread has a part of this device memory dedicated as so called local memory. Another part of the device memory is global memory accessible by all threads. Access to device memory has a much higher latency than access to shared memory or registers. Additionally, each thread has cached read-only access to constant memory and texture and surface memory. Loads from constant cache are efficient if all threads belonging to a half-warp load from the same address; if two threads within the same half-warp load from different addresses in the same instruction, throughput decreases by a factor equal to the number of different load addresses. Another decision (aside from the number of threads per SM) that can have huge impact on performance is what data is kept in which memory domain. Access from threads to different memories is depicted in Figure.

Communication between CPU and GPU is done by transferring data between the host memory and the GPU device memory or by mapping page-locked host memory into the GPU's address space. Asynchronous data transfers between page-locked host memory and device memory can overlap with computations on the CPU. For some CUDA devices since compute capability 1.1 they can also overlap with computations on the GPU. Since CUDA 4.0 NVIDIA simplifies data exchange between host memory and device memory of Fermi GPUs by supporting a unified virtual address space. The unified virtual address space is particularly interesting in conjunction with peer-to-peer memory access between multiple GPUs. This technique makes it possible to access the memory of one GPU directly from another GPU without data transfers through host memory.

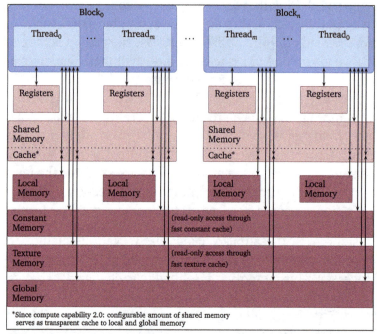

Access to different memories from threads on NVIDIA CUDA devices. Light-red memories are fast, dark-red memories are parts of device memory with high-latency access.

AMD GPUs

The hardware and software technologies that allow programmers to use AMD GPUs for general-purpose computations are called AMD Accelerated Parallel Processing (APP) formerly known as ATI Stream. Each APP device consists of multiple so-called compute units, each compute unit contains multiple stream cores, which, in turn, contain multiple processing elements. Multiple instances of a GPU program (kernel) are executed concurrently on different data, one such instance of a kernel is called a work-item. Multiple work-items are executed by all stream cores of one compute unit in lock step one such group of work items executed together is called wavefront. The number of work-items in a wavefront is hardware dependent. The programmer decides how many work-items are scheduled to one compute unit in a so-called workgroup. Best performance is obtained if this number is a multiple of the size of a wavefront.

In principle different compute units can execute different kernels concurrently. However, the number of different kernels running on one APP device may be limited. All stream cores of one compute element execute the same instruction sequence consisting of very-large-instruction-word (VLIW) arithmetic instructions, control-flow instructions and memory load and store instructions. The up to four or five (depending on the device) instructions inside a VLIW instruction word are co-issued to the processing elements.

Similar to NVIDIA GPUs, AMD GPUs have various memories with different visibility to work-items and different latencies and throughputs. The private memory is specific to each work-item and is kept in a register file with very fast access. Work-items inside one workgroup, i.e. running on the same compute unit, can communicate through local memory. This "local memory" is not a part of the device memory as on NVIDIA GPUs. In fact it is very similar to what NVIDIA calls shared memory, a relatively small memory with fast access for efficient exchange of data between work-items. Access to local memory is about an order of magnitude faster than access to device memory. Furthermore all work-items executing in one context have access to the global device memory and cached read-only access to a part of the device memory called constant memory.

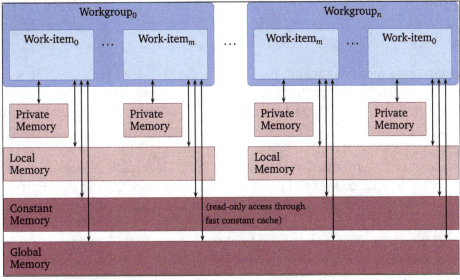

Access to different memories from work-items on AMD APP devices. Light-red memories are fast; dark-red memories are parts of device memory with high-latency access.

Access from work-items to different memories is depicted in Figure. Communication with the host is done through DMA transfers between host and device memory. Computation on both the CPU and the GPU can overlap with DMA transfers.

Programming GPUs in High-level Languages

With the CUDA architecture NVIDIA introduced language extensions to the C programming language that allowed to write programs that are partially executed on the GPU. The resulting programming language is called "C for CUDA". Note that depending on the compute capability some restrictions apply for the part of the program that is executed by the GPU, for example compute capability 1.x does not support recursive function calls.

The first software-development tool that AMD offered for general-purpose computation on GPUs was called Close-to-Metal (CTM) which gave low-level access to the native instruction set of the GPU. High-levellanguage support was first offered in the ATI

Stream SDK v1 with the ATI Brook+ language, which is based on BrookGPU developed at Stanford University.

Both solutions, C for CUDA and Brook+ could only be used to implement software for the respective manufacturer's GPUs. As a more portable approach both NVIDIA and AMD now also support the OpenCL programming language and API developed by the Khronos group. This programming language is designed for development of software for parallel computations on arbitrary heterogeneous systems. Two versions of the language have been released, OpenCL 1.0 in November 2008 and OpenCL 1.1 in June 2004.

Today the recommended way to program NVIDIA GPUs is using either C for CUDA or OpenCL for CUDA. AMD recommends OpenCL as high-level programming language for their GPUs in their latest Accelerated Parallel Processing SDK.

The compilation process is very similar for all of the high-level languages. In a first step the compiler separates the parts of the program that run on the CPU from the parts that run on the GPU. The CPU part is further compiled using native C or C++ compilers for the respective host architecture. The GPU part is first translated to an intermediate low-level language. For NVIDIA this language is called PTX, for AMD it is called IL. The advantage of this intermediate language is that it is somewhat device independent. More specifically, PTX code is compatible across minor revisions of the compute capability; IL code is forward compatible. The GPU driver contains a just-in-time compiler for this intermediate language. Code that needs to run on GPUs with different hardware capabilities can thus be translated only to intermediate language, final compilation to binary code is performed by the respective driver. This last compilation step can also be done offline to produce binaries for a specific GPU architecture.

Programming GPUs in Assembly

Most software today is written in high-level languages, but some areas of computing still employ hand optimized assembly routines to achieve best performance. One of these areas is high-performance computing – in computations that run for weeks or months even small performance gains are typically worth the effort of implementing parts of the software in assembly. Now that GPUs explicitly support applications in high-performance computing one would expect that the manufacturers also provide assemblers. However, this is not the case. Until the CUDA 4.0 toolkit was released in May 2011, NVIDIA offered neither an assembler nor a disassembler for their GPUs, an assembler is still not provided by NVIDIA. To fill this gap, van der Laan reverse-engineered the binary format and developed the cubin utilities consisting of the disassembler decuda and the assembler cudasm.

For the Fermi GPUs (compute capability 2.0 and 2.1) NVIDIA includes the cuobjdump disassembler in the CUDA 4.0 toolkit. An assembler for Fermi GPUs is being developed by the asfermi project. AMD documents the instruction-set architecture of their recent GPUs, for example the Radeon R600 series, the Radeon R700 series, and the Evergreen series. AMD does not document the complete ELF format of the binaries and does not provide an assembler for their GPUs. Similar to NVIDIA, community projects work on assemblers that support different families of AMD GPUs.

GPU Performance Bottlenecks

What makes GPUs a very interesting computing platform for many algorithms is their pure computing power. For example, an NVIDIA GTX 295 graphics card containing two GT200b GPUs can dispatch a total of 745 billion single-precision floating-point operations per second. For comparison, all 4 cores of a 2.4 GHz Intel Core 2 Quad CPU can dispatch a total of 57.6 billion single-precision floating-point operations, more than one order of magnitude less. One might thus expect that GPUs speed up computations by a factor of 10 or more, but as the examples in the following sections show this is not the case for many applications. The reason is that in order to make use of the computational power of GPUs, applications need to fulfill two conditions:

1. The degree of data-level parallelism required to keep hundreds of threads busy is much larger than the degree of data-level parallelism that is required for the SIMD implementations of current CPUs. For example, keeping 192 threads on each of the 60 multiprocessors of 2 GPUs on an NVIDIA GTX 295 graphics card busy needs 11520 independent data streams. Keeping the 4 cores of a CPU busy working on 128-bit vector registers needs just 16 such independent streams. Less data-level parallelism typically requires multiple threads to work on the same data which involves communication and thread synchronization overhead.

2. GPU performance depends on memory-access patterns much more than CPU performance does. The reason is that GPUs spend most of their chip area on ALUs while CPUs spend a large part of the chip area on fast caches that reduce load and store latencies. Computations that can keep the active set of data in the available registers benefit from the large computational power of the ALUs but the high latencies of device-memory loads and stores typically incur huge performance penalties in applications that cannot. Some applications can use the shared memory on NVIDIA GPUs or the local memory on AMD GPUs as cache, Fermi GPUs make this easy by using a configurable amount of shared memory as transparent cache. If the same data is required by all threads this is indeed a very good solution. However, if each thread requires different data in cache (for example register content temporarily spilled to memory) the amount of shared memory per thread is typically too small. Compilers therefore use device memory for register spills. Another way to deal with high memory latencies is to run more threads and thus hide the latencies. Note that this comes at the price of a smaller number of registers per thread and even higher requirements on data-level parallelism.

Another potential bottleneck is data transfer between host memory and device memory. All modern graphics cards are connected through PCI Express. Throughput rates highly depend on the version of PCI Express, and the number of lanes. For example the theoretical throughput of PCI Express 2.0 with 16 lanes (commonly denoted x16) is 8 GB/s in both directions. The throughput obtained in practice is considerably lower and depends on the size of data packets transmitted over the bus. More serious than throughput limitations can be the latency incurred by data transfers over PCI Express, at least for applications that require frequent communication and cannot interleave communication with computations.

With these limitations in mind it is interesting to see that GPU advertisements and also various scientific papers claim speedups by a factor of 100 and more of software running on a GPU compared to software running on a CPU. In most of the cases a careful look at how these speedups were achieved reveals that the CPU implementation is far from state of the art—for example it does not use the SIMD computing capabilities of modern CPUs—and the CPU implementation is not set up to run on multiple cores.

Despite these misleading comparisons found in many places, GPUs are very powerful computing devices and with careful optimization GPUs can speed up many computations considerably compared to the same computations running on a CPU.

GPUs as Cryptographic Coprocessors

Cryptographic computations such as encryption and decryption, hashing, signature generation, and signature verification rely on high performance in software for many applications. Furthermore most of the algorithms involved can be implemented in relatively small code size and it is feasible to hand-optimize code on the assembly level. This is why for example AES and RSA encryption were among the algorithms that were implemented using shader instructions of the graphics rendering pipeline of traditional GPUs.

When using GPUs for cryptographic computations one should keep in mind that GPUs and graphics drivers are not designed for computations on sensitive data and should be used for such computations only with precaution. For instance, on various graphics cards it is possible for a computing kernel to read out parts of the memory content left behind by a previously executed kernel. Keeping cryptographic keys in these parts of the memory can be used to speed up computations. On the other hand this can also be a serious security threat in multi-user environments if one user manages to launch a GPU kernel that reads out the key of another user. In environments where data in GPU memory can be protected, for example on a single-user server, or with careful protections to avoid memory readout, modern GPUs can be used as powerful cryptographic coprocessors for throughput-oriented applications.

AES on GPUs

In particular the possibility to implement the Advanced Encryption Standard (AES), the most widely used symmetric encryption algorithm, on GPUs has attracted a lot of attention. AES is a block cipher with supported key sizes of 128, 192 and 256 bits and a block size of 128 bits. Most implementations focus on AES with 128- bit keys. In this setting the key is first expanded into 11 round keys $K_0, \ldots, K_{11}$. Each 128-bit input block (state) is then transformed in 10 rounds, each round involving one of the 11 round keys. The first round key Ko is xored to the block before the first round. The most common implementation technique for AES, operates on 32-bit words and uses 4 lookup tables To, T1, T2, and T3 of size 1 KB (256 32-bit words) each. The 128-bit state is represented as 4 such 32-bit words. The operations of one round of AES in C notation is given in Listing.

- Listing: One round of AES encryption in C, the 128-bit input state is in 32-bit unsigned integers y0, y1, y2, y3, the output state is in 32-bit unsigned integers z0, z1, z2, z3; the 128-bit round key is in 32-bit unsigned integers k0, k1, k2, k3.

z0	= To[y0 >> 24	]	^ T1[(y1 >> 16)	& 0xff] \
	^ T2[(y2 >> 8) & 0xff	]	^ T3[y3	& 0xff] ^ k0;
z1	= To[y1 >> 24	]	^ T1[(y2 >> 16)	& 0xff] \
	^ T2[(y3 >> 8) & 0xff	]	^ T3[y0	& 0xff] ^ k1;
z2	= To[y2 >> 24	]	^ T1[(y3 >> 16)	& 0xff] \
	^ T2[(y0 >> 8) & 0xff	]	^ T3[y1	& 0xff] ^ k2;
z3	= To[y3 >> 24	]	^ T1[(y0 >> 16)	& 0xff] \
	^ T2[(y1 >> 8) & 0xff	]	^ T3[y2	& 0xff] ^ k3;

To achieve the required degree of parallelism, GPU implementations of AES typically either consider many independent streams that are encrypted in parallel or they use a parallel mode of operation such as ECB or CTR that allows to encrypt blocks of a single stream independently. The most important decision to make for high-performance AES encryption on GPUs is how to use the available memory domains. CPU implementations store lookup tables and expanded keys in RAM, after some rounds of AES the tables will be in level-1 cache and lookups are fast. On most GPUs a straight-forward adaptation of this approach— placing tables and expanded keys in device memory—will incur high latency penalties because access to device memory is uncached (except for NVIDIA Fermi GPUs where part of the shared memory is used as transparent cache). A better approach is to place the lookup tables in the fast shared memory of NVIDIA GPUs or the local memory of AMD GPUs. Recall that loads from shared memory on NVIDIA GPUs can be as fast as register access but that throughput and latency depend on the access pattern. AES table lookups have an unpredictable access pattern, so one must expect penalties due to memory-bank conflicts. One solution to avoid these penalties is to store multiple copies of the lookup tables in the fast memory such that each entry is available on each memory bank. If shared memory is not large enough to hold these copies of the tables, it may still be possible to store copies of only one of the tables and obtain entries of the other tables through rotations. The best combination of optimization techniques depends on the target GPU.

Not only the decision about location and layout of the lookup tables is important, also handling of the round keys influences performance. This is relatively easy if one big stream is encrypted in a parallel mode of operation. In this case all threads use the same key and it can be stored in constant memory. Unlike lookups from the tables, the round keys are accessed in a completely predictable pattern; they are broadcasted to all threads which is exactly what the constant memory is made for. The situation is different for the encryption of many independent streams under different keys. If each thread needs different round keys, there is not enough fast memory on most GPUs to store all these round keys. Instead of loading round keys from slow device memory it may be a better choice to expand the key on the fly. Again, the best solution highly depends on the specific target GPU.

A completely different approach to implement AES is bitslicing. This technique was first introduced for the Data Encryption Standard (DES) by Biham in and has also been used for various AES implementations. The idea of this technique is transposition of data: Instead of storing a 128-bit state in, e.g., 4 32-bit registers, it uses 128 registers, 1 register per bit. This representation of data allows to simulate a hardware implementation, logical gates become bit-logical instructions. For just one computation this is not efficient, but if all n bits of registers are used to perform computations on n independent streams, this can be very efficient. Note that on top of the high degree of parallelism required for GPU computations, bitslicing requires another factor of n of parallelism, n being the register width.

In Yang and Goodman describe different implementations of AES for AMD GPUs. Their bitsliced implementation aims at key search so keys need to be expanded into round keys on the fly. On an AMD HD 2900 XT GPU this implementation performs encryption of one block under 145 million keys per second, this corresponds to a throughput of 18.5 Gbit/s. For the lookup-table-based implementation they report an AES encryption throughput of 3.5 Gbit/s on an AMD HD 2900 XT GPU.

The implementation by Manavski uses a lookup-table-based approach to achieve a peak throughput of 8.28 Gbit/s on an NVIDIA 8800 GTX graphics card (G80 GPU); to achieve this peak throughput at least 8 MB of data need to be encrypted under the same key. This implementation exploits parallelism inside AES, 4 threads perform the transformation of one 128-bit block. Harrison and Waldron report a throughput of 15.423 Gbit/s for their lookup-table based implementation of AES on an NVIDIA G80 GPU. This peak performance is achieved for input messages of ≥ 65 MB, overhead from data transfers to and from the GPU is not included in the benchmarks. Both the implementation achieve a significantly lower throughput when data transfers are included in the benchmarks: 2.5 Gbit/s and 6.9 Gbit/s.

Two more recent papers report speeds beyond 30 Gbit/s on NVIDIA GPUs. Osvik, Bos, Stefan, and Canright described an implementation of AES with 128-bit keys that achieves 30.9 Gbit/s throughput on one GPU of an NVIDIA GTX 295 graphics card (containing 2 GT200b GPUs). The implementation interleaves data transfers with computations by using page-locked host memory. Interleaving data transfers with kernel execution was not possible for the GPUs used for benchmarking. This throughput is achieved for encryption under one key in constant memory but the paper also describes an implementation with on-the-fly key schedule suitable for key-search applications, that achieves a throughput of 23.8 Gbit/s. Jang, Han, Han, Moon, and Park present a GPU-accelerated SSL proxy. For the AES implementation included in this proxy they report 32.8 Gbit/s on an NVIDIA GTX 285 graphics card (GT200b GPU), not including data transfers. They also report detailed performance numbers of AES encryption in the non-parallel CBC mode for different numbers of independent streams on an NVIDIA GTX 580 graphics card (GF110 GPU).

Note that these high throughputs of AES on GPUs can only be achieved by performing AES encryption on thousands of blocks in parallel. This amount of data-level parallelism can certainly be found for some database applications or when writing large amounts of data to an encrypted hard disk. The encryption of typically small Internet packages in applications that do not just need high throughput but also low latency will still do better with a CPU-based approach, not only when using CPUs that support AES in hardware. For example the bitsliced implementation for Intel processors encrypts 1500-byte packets in 7.27 cycles per byte on a 2668 MHz Intel Core i7 920 CPU. This corresponds to a throughput of more than 11.7 Gbit/s on 4 cores.

Asymmetric Cryptography on GPUs

Also asymmetric cryptographic primitives can be accelerated by laying off the computations from the CPU to the GPU. As for symmetric primitives like AES one way to obtain the necessary degree of parallelism is to consider operations on many independent messages. However, there is another source for parallelism inherent in the algorithms. Most state-of-the art asymmetric algorithms involve operations on large integers, for example RSA signature generation is the computation of $m^d \bmod n$, where m, d and n are integers of 1024 bits or larger. Arithmetic on such integers, in particular multiplication, squaring and modular reduction needs to be decomposed in many operations on machine words. Elliptic-curve cryptography involves modular arithmetic on integers of smaller size typically between 160 bits and 256 bits but arithmetic on those integers still decomposes into many operations on machine words. For example when using a multiplier with 32-bit output, schoolbook multiplication of two 256-bit integers requires 256 multiplications of 16-bit limbs and 240 additions of the 32-bit multiplication outputs. Most of these operations are independent and can be done in parallel by multiple threads. Exploiting such parallelism inside one computation has some obvious advantages. If multiple threads process one input stream together, fewer independent input streams are required to make use of the computational power of the GPU. This makes GPU computations attractive also for applications that require low latency rather than high throughput. Furthermore, when multiple threads carry out one computation together the overall amount of data involved in the computations is smaller; this can be used to fit all data into memory domains that offer low-latency access. However, exploiting data-level parallelism inside computations like big-integer multiplication comes with the disadvantage that it involves overhead from thread synchronization and exchange of data between treads.

Several papers describe implementations of RSA on modern graphics cards. Szerwinski and Güneysu describe a CUDA implementation that performs 813 modular exponentiations (RSA encryption) of 1024-bit integers on a NVIDIA 8800 GTS graphics card. This paper furthermore reports a throughput of 104.3 modular exponentiations for 2048-bit RSA encryption. Harrison and Waldron focus on RSA decryption and report 5536.75 RSA-1024 decryptions per second on an NVIDIA 8800 GTX graphics card. This computation can make use of the Chinese Remainder Theorem to perform arithmetic on half-size integers. The RSA implementation included in the SSL proxy can perform for example 74732 RSA1024 decryptions or 12044 RSA-2048 decryptions per second on an NVIDIA GTX 580 graphics card. What is particularly interesting about this implementation is that it does not purely focus on throughput but also needs to keep the latency low enough for the application in the SSL proxy. For RSA-1024 the latency is at 3.8 ms, for RSA-2048 it is 13.83 ms.

To put this into perspective to what is currently possible on CPUs, the eBACS benchmarking project reports, for example, more than 11000 1024-bit integer exponentiations per second on all 6 cores of an AMD Phenom II X6 1090T. Again, this speed does not require the large number of independent parallel computations that GPU implementations need and although it is much slower from a pure throughput perspective it may be the better choice for applications that do not process multiple messages in parallel.

Also elliptic-curve cryptography has been implemented on GPUs. Szerwinski and Güneysu report 1412 scalar multiplications per second on the NIST P-224 elliptic curve on an NVIDIA 8800 GTS graphics card. On the same curve but the more recent NVIDIA GTX 285 graphics card Antão, Bajard, and Sousa report 9990 scalar multiplications per second. More than an order of magnitude slower at significantly lower security is the implementation of scalar multiplication on an elliptic-curve over a binary field. Cohen and Parhi report only 96.5 scalar multiplications per second.

Elliptic-curve scalar multiplication has received more attention on CPUs, for example reports 226872 cycles for a scalar multiplication on a 255-bit elliptic curve on an Intel Xeon E5620 CPU running at 2.4 GHz. This corresponds to more than 40000 scalar multiplication per second on all four cores. Even faster speeds for CPU implementations for scalar multiplication on elliptic curves with efficiently computable endomorphisms. These comparative numbers may suggest that GPU implementations of elliptic-curve cryptography cannot compete with state-of-the-art CPU implementations, not even in throughput-oriented applications. However, the next section describes implementations of elliptic-curve operations on GPUs for cryptanalysis that outperform CPU implementations. The reason that there are no faster GPU implementations targeting constructive applications may be that there are simply not many applications that require only throughput and can ignore latency.

An asymmetric cryptosystem that appears to be much better suited for implementation on GPUs than elliptic-curve cryptography or RSA is NTRU. The central operation for encryption and decryption is convolution which can be carried out by many threads without significant communication or synchronization due to its parallel structure. Hermans, Vercauteren, and Preneel describe an implementation of NTRU with a set of parameters that aims at the 256-bit security level. This implementation is able to perform 218000 encryption operations per second on an NVIDIA GTX 280 graphics card (GT200 GPU).

GPUs in Cryptanalysis

Cryptanalytical computations are in many ways similar to cryptographic computations. In many cases breaking a cryptographic system means executing the same or very similar computations that are used in the constructive use of the cryptosystem. One example is brute-force key recovery of symmetric ciphers that simply performs encryption with many different keys. Another example is hash-function collision search with the computationally most expensive part being computing hashes. An example in the cryptanalysis of asymmetric systems is Pollard's rho algorithm to solve the discrete logarithm problem (DLP). Again the computationally most expensive part are the same or very similar operations in the same mathematical structures that are involved in the legitimate use of the DLP-based system.

In three very important points cryptanalytical computations are different from cryptographic computations and all three make them even better suited for GPUs. First they typically involve an arbitrary amount of datalevel parallelism, the same computations are carried out on huge amounts of independent data; this is exactly the sort of computations that GPUs are best at. Second many of these computations do not care about latency, they are purely throughput oriented. Third there is no confidential data involved that needs to be protected, one could say that the opposite is true, revealing the confidential data is the target of the computation.

The most obvious applications of GPUs for cryptanalysis are attacks against symmetric encryption and hash functions. Various commercial solutions for password recovery already include GPU implementations to speed up the computations. These tools typically try out many different passwords from a given word list and either compare with given hash values or derive symmetric keys from a list of known passphrases to recover the content of encrypted files.

The power of GPUs was also used by the winner of Engineyard's SHA-1 programming contest: The task was to find an input to SHA-1 that has minimal Hamming distance to a given hash value. Lange reports that code by Bernstein is able to compute more than 328 million hashes per second on an NVIDIA GTX 295 graphics card. Each of these hashes required computation of only one 64-byte block of input, so this corresponds to a throughput of more than 167 Gbit/s. As a comparison, all four cores of a 2.4 GHz Intel Core 2 Quad Q6600 CPU involved in the same computation computed 47 million hashes per second. Also the SHA-3 candidates have been implemented on GPUs, password recovery being the most obvious application. Bos and Stefan describe implementations of all of the SHA-3 round-2 candidates on NVIDIA GT200 GPUs. The reported throughputs reach from 0.9 Gbit/s for Cubehash 16/1 up to 36.8 Gbit/s for Blake-32 and BMW-256 on one GPU of an NVIDIA GTX 295 graphics card. Again to put this into perspective, on a recent CPU, the Intel Core i7-2600K, hashing with Blake-32 takes 6.68 cycles/byte, this corresponds to a throughput of 16.29 Gbit/s.

These applications in password recovery are quite straightforward, but GPUs have also been used for cryptanalysis of asymmetric systems. One of the most famous problems closely related to the RSA cryptosystem is the factorization of large numbers. A critical step inside the factorization of large RSA numbers with the number-field sieve is the factorization of many smaller numbers using the elliptic-curve factorization method (ECM). Bernstein, Chen, Cheng, Lange and Yang describe an implementation of ECM for 280-bit numbers. This implementation running on both GT200b GPUs of an NVIDIA GTX 295 graphics card outperforms a state-of-the-art CPU implementation running on all 4 cores of an Intel Core 2 Quad Q9550 by a factor of more than 2.8. The GPU implementation tries 400.7 curves per second, the CPU implementation 142.17 curves per second. A much higher ECM throughput for slightly smaller numbers is reported. For example for 210-bit numbers a GTX 295 graphics card is reported to try 4928 curves per second. Although these numbers are not as impressive as the speedups achieved by using GPUs in symmetric cryptanalysis the results show that GPUs can also be used to speed up elliptic-curve arithmetic.

This is confirmed for elliptic curves over binary fields. As part of a large effort to solve Certicom's elliptic-curve discrete-logarithm-problem (ECDLP) challenge ECC2K-130 this paper presents an implementation of Pollard's rho algorithm for GT200b GPUs. On the two GPUs inside the GTX 295 graphics card this implementation is able to perform 63 million Pollard rho iterations per second. As a comparison, the CPU implementation computing the same iteration function performs 22.45 million iterations per second on all 4 cores of an Intel Core 2 Extreme Q6850 CPU.

GPUs have also been considered for solving the discrete-logarithm problem on elliptic curves over large prime fields. The implementation targets an ECDLP on a 109-bit prime curve and is reported to "have generated about 320.000 points/second" on an NVIDIA 8800 GTS graphics card with a G92 GPU. This probably means 320000 iterations per second, but it is unclear what the exact performance of the implementation is.

Malware Detection on GPUs

Similar to cryptographic applications, malware-detection software is expected to operate in the background with as little influence on the system's performance as possible. A large computational task of virus detection is pattern matching of byte sequences found in files with known signatures of malware. This task is highly parallel, so it is an application that can run at high speed on GPUs.

Seamans and Alexander describe an implementation of parallel virus signature matching for NVIDIA GPUs. Researchers integrated this implementation into the ClamAV virus scanner and compare the performance of this implementation running on an NVIDIA GTX 7800 graphics card to the original CPU implementation running on an unspecified 3-GHz Intel Pentium 4 CPU; researcher do not specify the number of CPU cores used for this comparison. The speedup obtained by running the pattern matching on the GPU depends on the number of matches because matches need to be communicated back to the CPU. If no matches are found the GPU implementation is 27 times faster than the CPU implementation; this factor drops to 17 at a match rate of 1% and further to 11 at a match rate of 50%.

Vasiliadis and Ioannidis describe an implementation of virus-signature pattern matching targeting more recent NVIDIA GPUs. Their implementation filters out clean, unsuspicious regions, it is included as a preprocessing step into the ClamAV [18] virus scanner. Researchers achieve a 100-times higher throughput with this approach running on an NVIDIA GTX295 graphics card compared to the CPU-only virus scanner running on 1 core of an Intel Xeon E5520 CPU. Compared to the CPU implementation running on 8 cores of 2 CPUs the speedup is still 10-fold.

The approach of using the GPU as a coprocessor for malware detection is not purely academic. In December 2009 Kaspersky announced that they incorporated an implementation of the "similarity service" for NVIDIA Tesla cards into their infrastructure. The press release [38] does not give much detail but claims a 360-times speedup of the GPU implementation running on an NVIDIA Tesla S1070 compared to the a CPU implementation running on a 2.6 GHz Intel Core 2 Duo processor. This comparison does not give details about the number of CPU cores used, it also does not say whether the speedup is obtained from running the GPU code on one or all four GPUs included in the Tesla S1070.

Signature matching is also one of the main performance bottlenecks of network-intrusion-detection systems. Consequently GPUs can also be used to speed up such systems. This was first described by Jacob and Brodley who use a traditional GPGPU approach targeting the NVIDIA 6800 GT graphics card. They conclude that with their

GPU pattern-matching extension to the open-source intrusion detection system Snort "there was no appreciable speedup in packet processing under normal-load conditions". A more efficient approach targeting the NVIDIA 8600 GT graphics card. Vasiliadis, Antonatos, Polychronakis, Markatos, and Ioannidis present a GPU pattern-matching extension of Snort that increases the overall Snort throughput capacity by a factor of 2 compared to CPU-only Snort running on a 3.4 GHz Intel Pentium 4 processor. Vasiliadis, Polychronakis, and Ioannidis describe a Snort-based intrusion detection solution that exploits parallelism on multiple levels. The system makes use of multiple GPUs and multiple CPU cores and copes with a network throughput of 5.2 GBit per second. This performance number was achieved on a system with two NVIDIA GTX 480 graphics cards and two Intel Xeon E5520 CPUs. The pure pattern-matching step reaches a peak performance of more than 70 GBit per second on the two graphics cards.

Malware Targeting GPUs

GPUs can not only be used to accelerate malware detection, malware itself can also use GPUs to hide from virus scanners. Vasiliadis, Polychronakis, and Ioannidis describe an implementation of a malware unpacker running on an NVIDIA GPU. The complete malware package consists of two parts, the unpacker running on the GPU and the actual malware that runs on the CPU. These two parts communicate through host memory mapped into the GPU's address space.

Unpackers are one of the most common techniques to hide malware from scanners: The malware code is packed or encrypted in some way and gets unpacked (decrypted) only when it is actually executed. The advantage from the malware researcher's perspective of using GPU code for the unpacker is twofold as it offers better protection against detection by both static and dynamic malware-detection systems. Static systems try different known unpacking techniques to recover the original malware. This becomes harder if the computational power of the GPU is used for computationally more expensive unpacking algorithms. Dynamic unpacking tools use the unpacker that is included in the malware, for example inside a sandbox or virtual machine. At least existing dynamic tools do not support GPU binaries and would thus fail.

As a second step also describes GPU-assisted run-time polymorphism on the function level. The malware binary is never fully decrypted, only the currently executed function resides in memory, when returning from a function call the function is encrypted again and the next function context is decrypted.

The implementations are still just a proof of concept and there have been no reports of real-world malware using the GPU to hide from scanners. Some of the claimed advantages of using the GPU to hide malware can obviously be addressed by malware-detection tools also using the GPU. Others will require better tools for static and dynamic analysis of GPU code. It will be interesting to see whether or how much GPUs become a new battlefield in the everlasting fight between malware and malware detection.

Open Source Vector Graphics Software

The vector graphics software allows users to use mathematical commands to design computer images. It will enable you to create high-definition Illustrations. With vector images, you can create programs without compromising the quality aspect.

Who makes Use of Vector Graphics Software?

Graphic designers make use of online vector graphics tools. The designers that mostly make use of this tool are as follows:

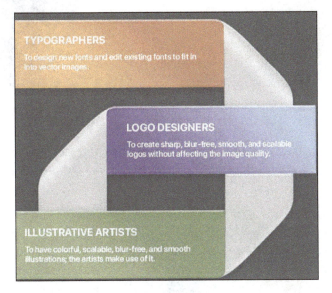

What are the Features of Vector Graphics Software?

The prominent features of Vector graphics software are as follows:

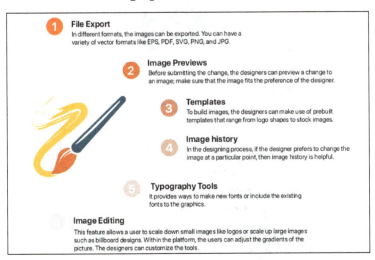

Purpose of Vector Graphics Software

For graphic creation, the businesses make use of vector graphics.

What are the Benefits of Vector Graphics Software?

In designing, the main advantages of vector graphics software are as follows:

In the market, you will come across various types of Vector Graphics Software. Some would be commercial, open-source, free or cloud-based. In this piece of writing, by getting the insights of the free and open-source vector graphics tools, you will come to know how you can add value to your graphics business. Have a look of the Comparison chart of free and open-source Vector Graphics software.

Software	Devices Supported	Business Size	Prominent Features
YouiDraw	Windows, Mac, Linux, Web-based	S M	Import/Export, Logo Creator, Object Creation, Object Manipulation, File Formats
Synfig Studio	Windows, Mac, Linux	S M L Freelancer	3D Objects, Animations & Transitions, Collaboration Tools, Media Library, Search/Filter, Modeling, Customizable
Inkscape	Windows, Mac, Linux, Web-based	S M	Logo Creator, Object Creation, Object Manipulation, Rendering, File Formats, Text Support
Vectr	Windows, Mac, Linux, Web-based	S M	Import/Export, Object Creation, Object Manipulation, Rendering, File Formats, Text Support
Gravit Designer	Windows, Mac, Linux, Web-based	S M Freelancer	Import/Export, Logo Creator, Object Creation, Object Manipulation, Rendering, File Formats, Text Support, Typography
Skencil	Windows, Mac, Linux, Web-based	S M	Import/Export, Object Creation, Object Manipulation, Rendering, File Formats
LibreOffice Draw	Windows, Mac, Linux	S M Freelancer	Collaboration, Database Creation, Document Creation, File Sharing, Presentation Tools, Project Management, Real time for higher productivity

Free and Open-Source Vector Graphics Software

YouiDraw

YouiDraw is the open-source vector graphics software that provides a variety of customizable textured brushes to the users. This free vector drawing tool offers modern tools like a pencil for the plain line or sketchy and different color options.

With different color and border size, users can shape new text. This tool is easy to use, very convenient and simple online drawing tool. Its logo design includes lots of features like quick styles, freehand logo tools, graphic templates, and vector logo effects.

The typical users of this software are Startups, agencies, enterprises, and SMEs. It works on HTML5 canvas with Google Drive. Anywhere or anytime, you can access your work. You will find this tool a powerful vector graphic design solution on the web. In various environments, you can express your style and creativity. The software can be integrated with almost all web applications.

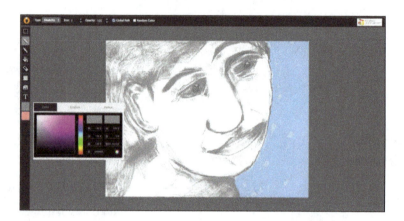

About YouiDraw:

- Drawing: It serves as a powerful vector graphic design solution on the web. You can express your style and creativity with this feature.

- Logo Creator: It creates high-quality vector graphics, icons, website elements, HTML5 logos, and buttons.

- Painter: You can work with dozens of customizable brushes, paper textures that seem to be real.

- Template & Style: The different styles and templates graphics will help in improving work efficiency. You will enjoy gradient, simple, and artistic styles.

- Tools: To point edit mode, straight line and curve arc, you can use a pen, pencil, brush, and switch elements.

- Text and shapes: With text button, you can create a shape into canvas, rectangle, ellipse, convex, concave, gear, round-corner rectangle.

- Transform: You can change the size, scale, and position, rotate, skew for the desired shape or text.

- Shape combine: It holds five different combine mode: Union, Intersect, Exclude, divide, and subtract.

Synfig Studio

Synfig Studio is powerful 2D animation open-source vector graphics software. It works with high dynamic range imaging. You will find that it holds the ability to design the animation in the front-end and at a later time render it with the backend.

With less resources and people, it supports a multitude of layers of different types. You can apply real-time effects to layers or a group of layers. This free vector graphics tool allows experienced animators to create high-quality animations. You can apply gradients, geometric, fractal, distortions, filters, fractal, and transformation to your animations as it supports a multitude of layers. You can enjoy fast and efficient animation with this app.

About Synfig Studio:

- Vector Tweening: It provides powerful tools to have full control of your vector artwork. Automatically, it calculates in-between frames.

- Layers and filters: It offers 50+ layers to create artwork and animation. You can choose from various layer types like geometric, filters, gradients, distortions, transformations, and fractals.

- Bones: With bitmap images, you can create pattern images. The bone system allows you to control your vector artwork.

- Advanced Controls: You can create sophisticated character puppets and other types of dynamic structures. Directly or through mathematical expressions, you can link parameters of various layers.

- Cross Platforms: It is a cross-platform that works on Windows, OS X, Mac, and Linux.

- Sound support: You can sync sounds music and narration to your videos with this feature.

Inkscape

If you are looking for powerful and free vector graphics software, then Inkscape is an ideal choice for you. For Linux, Windows, and macOS, this app works as a professional vector graphics editor. The interface of this software is transparent, stable, and consistent. The users get various tooltips along with useful information from this versatile and flexible software. Design professionals and hobbyists create a wide variety of graphics like icons, logos, illustrations, maps, diagrams, and web graphics from this open-source vector drawing tool.

With the add-ons feature, the users can customize the functionality of this tool. The graphic designers will find it a hugely adaptable and excellent tool. This tool produces highly professional vector graphics documents. You will find a fast and easy interface.

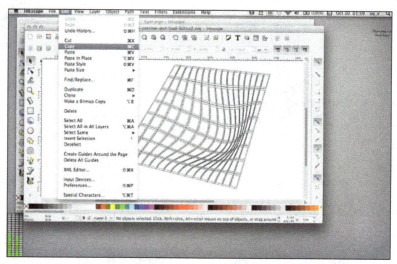

About Inkscape:

- Import/Export: It can import and export various file formats that include SVG, AI, PDF, PS, PNG, and EPS.

- Object Creation: It provides various tools for drawing and shapes. You will get embedded bitmaps, text tool, and clones.

- Object manipulation: It works on transformations, Z-order operations that include raising and lowering, grouping objects, layers, and alignment and distribution commands.

- Fill and stroke: You will get color selector, color picker tool, copy/paste style, pattern fills, path makers, dashed strokes, and the gradient editor.

- File formats: It follows SVG format file generation and editing. For export and conversions, it commands line options.

- Create and edits: You can create and edit graphics, logos, diagrams, cartoons, and illustrations that you can scale to a larger or smaller size.

- Vector images: You can convert slogans and easy designs into vector images. You will find the method easy and fast.

Vectr

You can quickly and intuitively create vector graphics with this free vector drawing software known as Vectr. This software is quick to learn and easy to use. Being cross-platform, you can use this app on the web or download to your desktop. In real-time, your work will be automatically saved and synchronized.

This simple yet powerful tool allows users to create and edit beautiful designs, cards, brochures, presentations, website mock-ups, 2D graphics, and blur-free logos. Due to its user-friendly interface, the primary users will find this tool perfect. You can work with shapes, text, and multiple layers with this app. You should try Vectr if you are looking for simple and free vector software that supports collaboration. It is easy to learn and use. This app holds the potential to be the best web-based vector creation tool.

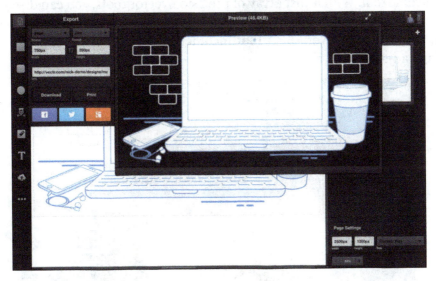

About Vectr:

- Tools: You can create custom shapes and add text with the pen, pencil, and text tools.

- Real-Time sharing: It allows for real-time collaboration in which you can create and edit designs live.

- Scalable: It scales designs to any size without losing clarity.

- Cross-platform: It can be used on the web or download to your desktop. Across all platforms, the work can be performed.

- 2D graphic: It is used to create 2D graphics and graphics for business cards, greeting cards, websites, illustrations, resumes, brochures, posters, presentations, and icons.

- Import and edit SVGs: It imports and edit SVGs and bitmaps that can be used as a background. It imports in AI, EPS, PNG, and JPEG file formats.

- Multiple layers: This app supports multiple layers and pages that allow you to organize your project.

Gravit Designer

Gravit Designer is one of the best free vector graphics editors that provides necessary tool sets to the designers. It is a versatile tool that helps in creating solutions. This app is intuitive and holds powerful vector toolset. You will find advanced and intuitive dashboard, customizable interface, advanced editing tools, and drag-and-drop functionality.

This app works on all platforms. You can open the full power of your creativity with this fast and flexible tool. With a vast array of precision vector tools, you can discover a new world of creativity. You can edit images for posting, print or larger design project. With this tool, you will enjoy everything that includes image and photo editing from color and lighting adjustments, filters and blending.

About Gravit Designer:

- Smart shapes: For fast and flexible geometric shape creation, it provides smart shape primitives with magic control points.

- Powerful aligning: It provides align to edges and center points of the selection. It aligns to page limits.

- Dashboard: The advanced and supportive dashboard allows its users to set the width and height of the documents.

- Intuitive interface: The customizable, clean, intuitive interface allows users to navigate and explore Gravit designer seamlessly.

- Web and App UI: For web and mobile user, you can create mockups and wire-frames to share styles, master pages, symbols, overrides.

- Brand visuals and imagery: This professional vector editing tool provides so many options to create icons, branding, logos, illustrations, and stand-out objects.

- Social Media: You can design stunning images for social media like Facebook, Twitter, and Pinterest.

- Built-in templates and libraries: In no time you can create flyers, banners, business cards, and other collateral.

- Advanced typography: You can gain control over typography like font styles, line, character, paragraph spacing.

- Import/export options: With versatile import and export options, you can import and edit PDF, EPS, Adobe Illustrator, Sketch file formats; and export multi-page PDF documents.

- Reusable design elements and styles: It embraces a fast and efficient design process. Throughout the entire design process, you can quickly select and change the font family.

- Transform and organize objects: With sub-pixel precision, you can scale, rotate, skew, and move design elements. You can organize your designs into pages and groups.

Skencil

Skencil is the flexible and powerful free interactive vector drawing application. Shapes like rectangles, ellipses, and curves are used for skencil drawing that can be filled and stroked. It has unlimited undo history.

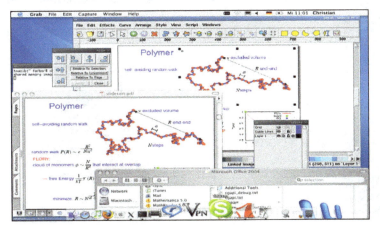

This open-source vector graphics editor is implemented in a very high-level and inter-preted language known as Python. Formerly, this app was known as Sketch and holds the quality of bending a text along a path. You will find this tool intensive, user-friendly, and of higher level.

About Skencil:

- Drawing Primitives: It includes rectangles, external images, EPS images, text, ellipses, and Bézier Curves.

- Export filters: This app writes the drawing to various file formats. For its format, adobe illustrator, PDF and SVG files; this online vector graphics editor holds filters.

- Import filters: It allows this tool to read different file formats. It has import filters for Adobe Illustrator files, Corel CMX, scalable vector graphics, and its file format.

- Blend groups: It automatically updates interpolations of arbitrary objects.

- External images: JPEG and PNG are the external images' properties for raster image that Python Imaging Library can read.

- Text along a path: It bends text along a way with EPS (Encapsulated PostScript) files.

LibreOffice-Draw

LibreOffice-Draw is the open-source vector graphics software that allows you to produce anything from a quick sketch to an elaborate plan. This tool acts as a means to communicate with graphics and diagrams. For creating technical drawings and general posters, you can use this tool with a maximum page size of 300cm by 300cm.

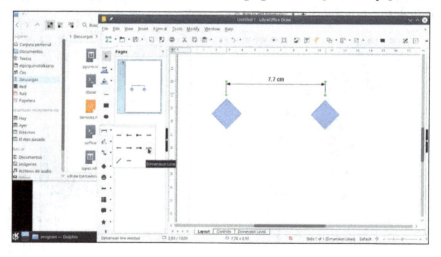

This free application is included in the LibreOffice suite that is developed by the Document Foundation. You can create simple and complex drawings and can export the same in the standard image formats. In your pictures, you can insert tables, charts, formulas, and other types of items. With this software, you can have a wide variety of graphical images. As per your preference, style, and formatting box you can arrange tools and in just one click you can put all your graphics styles.

About LibreOffice -Draw:

- Vector Graphics: By using lines and curves, it creates vector graphics that are defined by mathematical vectors.

- 3D Objects: In LibreOffice Draw, this tool can create simple 3D objects such as cubes, spheres, and cylinders. It modifies the light source of the objects.

- Connect Objects: To show the relationship between objects; you can connect objects with distinct lines known as "connectors."

- Grid and Snap Lines: In your drawing, you can align objects with the help of visual cues. You can snap an object to a snap line and grid line.

- Graphic File Formats: It can export many graphic file formats like BMP, GIF, PNG, and JPG.

- Gallery: It includes images, sounds, animations, and other types of items that can be inserted and used in your drawings.

- Displaying Dimensions: To calculate and display linear dimensions, you can use dimensions lines.

- Geometric elements: It stores and displays an image as an assembly of simple elements that include lines, polygons, and circles.

- Smart Connectors: You can effortlessly build flowcharts, organization charts, and network diagrams with intelligent connectors. It allows the conversion of images to a range of image and document formats with the help of a powerful engine.

Open Source Games Development Software

The video gaming industry is intriguing, and it is flourishing in an accelerated pace with new apps entering the market every day. Statista reports that there are more than 2.5 billion online gamers worldwide. The escalating internet, easy accessibility to virtual games even from the remote locations, user-friendliness of the software, and quick navigation facilities are the major factors driving the growth of this industry.

The most interesting fact is that 80% of the total revenue earned from online gaming industry belongs to software sales. Modern web technologies and the recent browser technologies are contributing towards the creation of high quality & stunning games, and to distribute those games to different gaming sources. The combination of new desktop technologies and their native OS counterparts have geared up the usage of advanced game development software programs. These programs are continually marking their presence in the industry to make it possible to develop better and more powerful games that can efficiently run on any standard-compliant web browser. They are not just simple card games or multi-player social games based on Flash that have been played earlier. Games today include; 3D action shooters, RPGs, PlayStation-based games, and many more.

Credit goes to the JavaScript technology and new APIs, which have been facilitating the development of games that can run on different browsers without compromising. These majorly include the browsers on HTML 5 powered devices based on Firefox OS.

What are the Different Forms of Virtual Games?

There are many fantasy sports, video games, animation solutions, AR, VR, and MR application programming, online casino games, land-based casino games, race betting, and sweepstakes. Hence, we have categorized online games into the following types:

- Commercial PC or Xbox games – This type of video games are played on personal computers. They are more diverse and include user-determined hardware and software. They generally have higher capacity in input, video and audio output processing.

- Console Games – Console games are a form of interactive multimedia entertainment. They comprise manipulated images and sound generated by the gaming console and can display them on the Television or a similar audio-video system. The game is usually managed and controlled with a handheld device called controller, connected to the console system.

- Indie Games – Indie games are independent video games, and they are most often created without the publisher's financial support. These are innovative games and mostly rely on digital distribution.

- Mobile Games – Mobile games are played on feature phones, smartphones, tablets, PDA, smartwatch, graphics calculator, and a portable media player. These games are usually downloaded from the app stores and the portals of the mobile operators.

The first ever video game was developed during the 1950s, but needed mainframe computers and was unavailable to the general public. PONG is one of the earliest arcade video games and was the first ever publicly available game for the public featuring two-dimensional graphics of the table tennis sports game. It was originally developed by Atari and has been released in 1972.

The year 1970 pioneered the commercialization of the game development practices. It was the time when first-generation video game consoles and home computers were invented, and single-developer game development started due to low cost and low capabilities of the computer machines.

Pong Machine

Game Development in the 21st Century

During the 1990s, heightened expectations for better consumer experience and increased computer processing power has lead to the creation of mainstream console or a PC game. The average price of developing a video game slightly increased from US$1 to 4 million in 2000 to over $5 million in 2006, and then over $20 million by 2010.

Today, games are not played just for fun. There are thousands of games available on gaming consoles like PS4, Mac, Windows, Nintendo Switch, Xbox One, and so on. Gamers acquire new knowledge and sophisticated skills too. Games and simulations are also serving as a powerful hands-on tool to impart practical and technical skills. Interestingly, the virtual gaming market is also likely to touch 90 billion US dollars as revenue by the year 2020.

What is the Most Popular Type of Online Games?

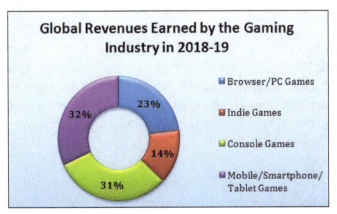

According to a leading report, mobile/smartphone/tablet games take the lead followed by console games. Indie games are slowly taking a back seat while people are still fascinated with the Browser/PC games.

What are the Most Played Gaming Genres?

When we talk about the gaming genres, they can be simple board games, card games, action games, and strategy games. As per a recent survey related to activity gaming, the list given below shows the percentage of different gaming genres as per their popularity among the gamers. Action games are at the top of the list, as four in ten players prefer this genre of gaming followed by sports and battle-royale games.

Game Software Architecture

Today, video gaming makes up a $100 billion global industry and nearly two-thirds of the household members in America play video games regularly. Apart from a gamut of development platforms launched recently, video games have been thrilling the gamers in a variety of ways right from arcade systems, to home consoles, to handheld consoles till mobile devices. Let us check what the concept of game software architecture holds for the game developers.

- Coding and Programming.

- Game Engine (Rendering your 3D model, game logic and play music).

- Art (Drawing 3D model, texturing and animation).

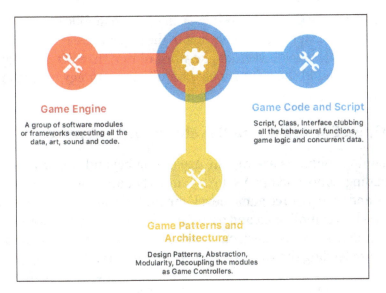

- Sound/Audio Engine.

- Story, Design (GamePlay, and Level Design).

- Rendering & Vision-Input Engine.

- Optimization (Using fewer resources for creating a better game).

- I/O Devices (such as Mouse, keyboard, speaker, monitor, etc.)

- Drivers/Device APIs and DLL Files.

Leading Trends in Game Development Software Industry in 2019

The gaming demographics is widened and time-killing nature of mobile games is fascinating most players to combat even the complex games. Let us check what more the coming year is going to hold for the game lovers and what interesting things it is brining for recent day's game developers.

- Fortnite and PUBG (Player Unknown's Battlegrounds) games have offered mobile players an opportunity to play these games at multiple platforms. PUBG has created a new milestone with getting over 200 million downloads worldwide. Its revenue growth is almost 166%, as reported by the leading news portal Business Today.

- Mobile game developers are constantly suffered by the toxicity in the gaming communities. Cyber-bulling is playing a major role to infect gaming communities across, PC, mobile and console. However, the Fair Play Alliance was created to combat this with hosting a summit during Game Development Council.

- AR is becoming more popular than VR, as it requires lower hardware. ARKit and ARCore are making it easier for mobile game developers for generating AR experiences for mobile.

- 'Game Discovery Challenge' is increasing for the mobile game developers to get their game discovered by the players in the app stores. Hence, they are combining the organic growth vectors like word of mouth, SEO, ASO (app store optimization) to build the effective user acquisition strategy to reach more number of users.

Free and Open Source Game Development Software

Today, the gaming solutions are rapidly expanding beyond the proprietary operating systems, including Linux and open source games that are being released regularly. The advent of free and open source game development software solutions have made gaming architecture less complicated and easily affordable for the developers and game development companies. Let us check out some of the best free and open source software solutions that are leading the game development industry.

Godot Engine	godotengine.org
GDevelop	gdevelop-app.com
Cocos2d-x	cocos2d-x.org
DeltaEngine	deltaengine.net
Starling	gamua.com/starling
Panda3D	www.panda3d.org
MonoGame	www.monogame.net
Superpowers	superpowers-html5.com/index.en.html

The following comparison chart will help you understand quickly each of the software solutions at a glance.

Name of Software	Deployment	Device Supported	Business Size	Software Features
Godot Enigine	Open-API	Windows, Mac, Linux	Small, Medium, Large, Free-lancer	• Debug & Optimize • Drag & Drop • Marketplace Integrations • Physics Editor • Script Editor • Visuals • Workflow

Gdevelop	Open-API, On-Premise	Windows, Mac, Linux	Small, Medium, Freelancer	• Characters & Animation • Drag & Drop • Image Editor • Marketplace Integrations • Object Editor • Physics Engine • Script Engine • Tilesets • Visuals • Workflow
Cocos2d-x	Open-API	Windows, Web-based	Small, Medium, Large	• Character & Animation • Debug & Optimize • Drag 7 Drop • Object Editor • Scene Editor • Script Editor • Visuals
DeltaEngine	Open-API	Windows, Web-based	Small, Medium, Large	• Characters & Animation • Drag & Drop • Image Editor • Marketplace Integrations • Object Editor • Scene Editor • Script Editor • Visuals
Starling	Open-API	Windows, Web-based	Small, Medium, Large	• Characters & Animation • Debug & Optimize • Drag & Drop • Image Editor • Object Editor • Physics Editor • Script Editor • Workflow

Panda3D	Open-API	Windows, Web-based	Small, Medium, Large	• Characters & Animation • Debug & Optimize • Image Editor • Marketplace Integrations • Physics Editor • Scene Editor • Script Editor • Visuals
MonoGame	Open-API	Windows, Web-based	Small, Medium, Large	• Characters & Animation • Debug & Optimize • Image Editor • Marketplace Integrations • Object Editor • Scene Editor • Tilesets • Workflow
Superpowers	Open-API	Windows, Web-based	Small, Medium, Large	• Characters & Animation • Debug & Optimize • Drag & Drop • Marketplace Integrations • Object Editor • Physics Editor • Script Editor • Workflow

Godot Engine

Godot Engine is a free and open source 2D and 3D game engine that is compatible with the cross-platform application. It operates on Linux, MacOS, Windows, BSD and Haiku (both 32 and 64-bit). It is licensed as per MIT license and can create the games targeting PC, web and mobile platforms. The Godot Engine software is written in C, C++ language and the stable version 3.1.1 of this software is released in April 2019.

Features:

- Godot software offers the visual editor with full of sophisticated tools to create fabulous 2D and 3D games.

- Timeline based visual animator facilitates frame-based or cut-out animation for rigs and sprites.

- The software has powerful profilers and debuggers. It can also debug a game running on mobile devices.

- It provides friendly C++ API for optimizing parts of the game or extends any part of the gaming engine.

- It offers uncluttered UI with the context-sensitive editors.

- Unique 2D shooter Stereobreak, Shipwreck, ChromeTrip, and DeepSixed are some of the popular games created using this software.

GDevelop

GDevelop is another reliable open source, cross-platform game creator that unleashes one's creativity to create any game. The software runs on Windows, macOS and most recent Linux distributions. The stable version of the software is GDevelop 5, and it is tailored for fast and intuitive game making.

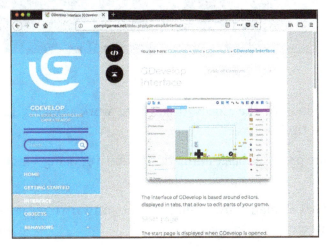

Features:

- The GDevelop software requires one simple click to add the object to the game or a particular scene – video objects and text objects both.

- Shape Painters facilitate drawing custom shapes on the screen.

- Facilities of debugger and performance profiler given in the game.

- Sound effect generation with Jfxe and designing your assets with Piskel.

- RPG-like maps with the Tiled map objects are the most important product of this software.

Cocos2d-x

Cocos2d-x is the world's leading game development tool that comes in a unified package. It is cross-platform game development software written in C++ language. The stable version 3.17.1 of the software is released on December 18, 2018, and its latest version is v2.0.5. Cocos2d-x software is MIT licensed and contains many branches i.e. Cocos2d-objc, Cocos2d-x, Cocos2d-html5 and Cocos2d-XNA.

Features:

- All the versions of the Cocos2d software work utilizing the basic primitive known as 'sprite'.

- The software provides basic animation primitives using a set of actions and timers.

- Common GUI elements are included in the software like labels, text boxes, buttons, menus etc.

- Modern C++ API is facilitated with end number of functionalities.

- The software can be installed on OS X, Windows, Linux and is deployable to deploy to iOS, Android, OS X, Windows, and even game consoles.

- Hardest Game Ever 2, DQMSL, Tiny Village, Badland, Small Street, Tiny Tower, are some of the popular games built on this platform.

DeltaEngine

An open source application engine – DeltaEngine is popularly known for writing 2D and 3D applications or games quickly and easily using .NET-based Visual Editor. The software is compatible with C#, C++, Objective-C, Java, and JavaScript languages, and the apps are built to run compatibly on Android, iOS, Windows Phone, Windows 8, HTML5. The initial version of the software is version 1.0 and the community edition that was last released in 2014.

Features:

- The Delta Engine software offers a unified way to support physical simulation. Most 2D and 3D codes are interchangeable.

- The Delta Engine software supports 3D features like 3D model importing and particle effect editor.

- Specific tools are provided in the software itself to create most contents like Images, Sound, Music and 3D Models that are saved directly.

- The software supports the integration of the external libraries and frameworks like Spine – the 2D Sprite animation library.

- Star Chronicles and Delta Force: Black Hawk Down are popular games based on this software.

Starling

Staring is a cross-platform, free and open source game engine that can be downloaded and used straight away. It is a Gamua-based product that is a leading company and consistently facilitating different types of gaming platforms like Flox and Sparrow, in addition to Starling. It is a 2D game development framework that supports both mobile and desktop platforms. The latest version of the software is Starling 2.5.1.

Features:

- Starling software is the most batter-saving program for the devices on which its games are used.

- Though it is a 2D engine, it can facilitate the transition between **scenes** flipping playing cards realistically using the 3D magic.

- Fast process of rendering textures with special effects is facilitated like bullet holes in the wall and footprints in the snow.

- The software supports classic Bitmap Fonts and TrueType fonts.

- Different blend modes are promoted like dynamic highlights and glowing fire to create special effects.

- Several filters are provided for modifying the look of your display objects.

- Angry Birds Friends, and Incredipede are popular games based on this software.

Panda3D

Panda3D is yet another popular open source framework for 3D rendering and game development. It is written on C++ and Python and runs on Microsoft Windows, Linux, MacOS, FreeBSD operating systems. The initial release of the software happened in the year 2002, and stable version 1.10.3 of the software was released on May 19, 2019. This game engine is licensed as per Revised BSD license.

Features:

- Panda3D can run on any platform when it is combined with the appropriate platform support code.

- The software includes command-line tools to process and optimize source assets.

- It includes pstats, i.e., an over-the-network profiling system designed to help the users to understand the usage of their frame time.

- The software facilitates rapid prototyping with no complicated initialization code.

- It comes with the out-of-the-box support for many popular third-party libraries like Assimp model loader, OpenAL, FMOD sound libraries, Bullet physics engine, and so on.

- Toontown Online, and Pirates of the Caribbean Online are popular games built on this software.

MonoGame

MonoGame is a free and open source C# based game development framework. It supports Windows, Windows Phone, Android, iOS, tvOS, MacOS, PlayStation, Linux, Vita, Xbox One, and Nintendo Switch and is licensed as per Microsoft Public License. The stable version 3.7.1 of this software is released on December 18, 2018.

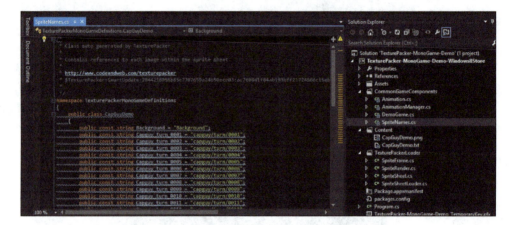

- MonoGame software is the evolution of XNA Touch started by Jose Antonio Farias and Silver Sprite by Bill Reiss.

- The software attempts to implement the XNA 4 API fully.

- It is a Windows and web-based software based on open API solutions.

- Device orientation, accelerometer sensor, and multi-touch gesture points are some new features in the framework.

- The software provides an excellent textual format for the ease of editing.

- It holds a compiled and optimized binary format for the runtime usage.

- Skulls of the Shogun, Bastion, TowerFall, and Transistor (video game) are some of the popular games built on this software.

SuperPowers

SuperPowers software is created for Windows, and it is the best example of the real-time collaboration of free and open source 2D and 3D indie gaming software. It runs on Windows Vista/7/8/8.1/10 (32-Bit/64-Bit). It can be exported to Windows, OS X, and Linux, Android or iOS. The stable version of the software is SuperPowers 5.3.0.

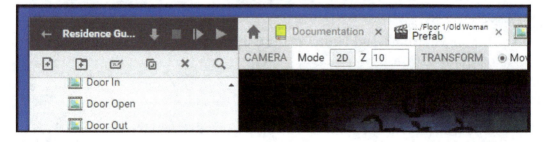

- SuperPowers software comes with a host of plug-ins and is a downloadable HTML5 app.

- There is a bunch of asset editors to make games using TypeScript.

- Easy and well-laid GUI interface helps the new-age developers to learn game development quickly.

- Built-in library of games and examples inspire beginners with this robust platform.

Unity

Unity is a popular real-time 3D development platform. It lets users create, manage and monetize captivating games. Unity is known for its flexible structure and close-to-cinematic visuals in real-time. One can create games that feature built-in area lights, volumetrics, reflections, high-quality shadows, advanced materials and more. It lets user develop games on beautiful dark themed User Interface.

Features:

- Game developers can modify or remove the splash screen.

- Users get insights about the performance of their game with real time data on crashes and user feedback.

- It can store the whole project on cloud servers.

- ad monetization solution for mobile games.

- Simplify in app purchase.

- Unity Learn Premium is designed to impart advanced learning and skills to users. It is a program by which users can learn and master real-time 3D development.

- It provides a platform to build: Console and PC Games, Mobile Games, Instant Games and AR/VR Games.

- Unity offers rich visuals and art tools that are required to build games.

- It's Mobile Games Development Platform assists you to create device-ready content and all types of mobile games.

- It uses the bleeding-edge technology and live-ops services to ensure high visibility, reliable performance and revenue growth.

- Customizable and ultra-slim runtime.

3

Plane Geometry in Computer Graphics

The study of 2-dimensional shapes is known as plane geometry. Few fundamental concepts of plane geometry are Euclidean geometry, 2D geometry, points and lines, ellipse, 2D viewing, etc. The diverse types of plane geometry in computer graphics have been thoroughly discussed in this chapter.

Euclidean Geometry

Euclidean geometry is the study of geometrical shapes and figures based on different axioms and theorems. It is basically introduced for flat surfaces. It is better explained especially for the shapes of geometrical figures and planes. This part of geometry was employed by Greek mathematician Euclid, who has also described it in his book, Elements. Therefore this geometry is also called Euclid geometry.

The axioms or postulates are the assumptions which are obvious universal truths, they are not proved. Euclid has introduced the geometry fundamentals like geometric shapes and figures in his book elements and has stated 5 main axioms or postulates. Here, we are going to discuss the definition of euclidean geometry, its elements, axioms and five important postulates.

The excavations at Harappa and Mohenjo-Daro depict the extremely well-planned towns of Indus Valley Civilization (about 3300-1300 BC). The flawless construction of Pyramids by the Egyptians is yet another example of extensive use of geometrical techniques used by the people back then.

The development of geometry was taking place gradually, when Euclid, a teacher of mathematics, at Alexandria in Egypt, collected most of these evolutions in geometry and compiled it into his famous treatise, which he named 'Elements'.

Euclidean Geometry is considered as an axiomatic system, where all the theorems are derived from the small number of simple axioms. Since the term "Geometry" deals with things like points, line, angles, square, triangle, and other shapes, the Euclidean Geometry is also known as the "plane geometry". It deals with the properties and relationship between all the things.

Non-Euclidean is different from Euclidean geometry. There is a difference between these two in the nature of parallel lines. In Euclid geometry, for the given point and line, there is exactly a single line that passes through the given points in the same plane and it never intersects.

Euclid's Elements

Euclid's Elements is a mathematical and geometrical work consisting of 13 books written by ancient Greek mathematician Euclid in Alexandria, Ptolemaic Egypt. Further, the 'Elements' was divided into thirteen books which popularized geometry all over the world. As a whole, these Elements is a collection of definitions, postulates (axioms), propositions (theorems and constructions), and mathematical proofs of the propositions.

Book 1 to 4th and 6th discuss plane geometry. He gave five postulates for plane geometry known as Euclid's Postulates and the geometry is known as Euclidean geometry. It was through his works, we have a collective source for learning geometry; it lays the foundation for geometry as we know now.

Euclidean Axioms

Here are the seven axioms given by Euclid for geometry:

- Things which are equal to the same thing are equal to one another.

- If equals are added to equals, the wholes are equal.

- If equals are subtracted from equals, the remainders are equal.

- Things which coincide with one another are equal to one another.

- The whole is greater than the part.

- Things which are double of the same things are equal to one another.

- Things which are halves of the same things are equal to one another.

Euclid's Five Postulates

Before discussing Euclid's Postulates let us discuss a few terms as listed by Euclid in his book 1 of the 'Elements'. The postulated statements of these are:

- Assume the three steps from solids to points as solids-surface-lines-points. In each step, one dimension is lost.

- A solid has 3 dimensions, the surface has 2, the line has 1 and point is dimensionless.

- A point is anything that has no part, a breadthless length is a line and the ends of a line point.

- A surface is something which has length and breadth only.

It can be seen that the definition of a few terms needs extra specification.

Euclid's Postulate 1

"A straight line can be drawn from anyone point to another point." This postulate states that at least one straight line passes through two distinct points but he did not mention that there cannot be more than one such line. Although throughout his work he has assumed there exists only a unique line passing through two points.

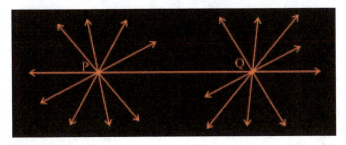

Euclid's Postulate 2

"A terminated line can be further produced indefinitely." In simple words what we call a line segment was defined as a terminated line by Euclid. Therefore this postulate means that we can extend a terminated line or a line segment in either direction to form a line. In the figure given below, the line segment AB can be extended as shown to form a line.

Euclid's Postulate 3

"A circle can be drawn with any centre and any radius." Any circle can be drawn from the end or start point of a circle and the diameter of the circle will be the length of the line segment.

Euclid's Postulate 4

"All right angles are equal to one another." All the right angles (i.e. angles whose measure is 90°) are always congruent to each other i.e. they are equal irrespective of the length of the sides or their orientations.

5th Euclid Postulate

If a straight line falling on two straight lines makes the interior angles on the same side of it taken together less than two right angles, then the two straight lines, if produced indefinitely, meet on that side on which the sum of angles is less than two right angles.

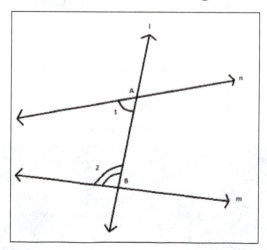

In the given diagram, the sum of angle 1 and angle 2 is less than 180°, so lines n and m will meet on the side of angle 1 and angle 2. Now let us focus on the equivalent version of Euclid's fifth postulate given by John Playfair. As per him:

"In a plane, given a line and a point not on it, at most one line parallel to the given line can be drawn through the point". In simple words, the above statement can be written as:

'For every line l and for every point P not lying on l, there exists a unique line m passing through P and parallel to l'.

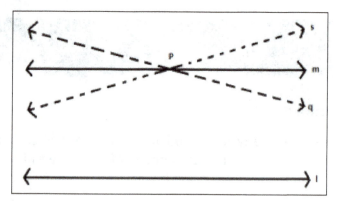

In the above figure, consider line l and a point P not lying on l. Now, we know that an infinite number of lines can pass through a given point. Thus, infinite lines can pass through point P. But, are all the lines parallel to line l or are some of them parallel to line l or are none of them parallel to line l? According to Playfair there is only line passing through P which will be parallel to the line l.

Draw any line passing through point P, say lines. If you draw a transversal cutting lines s and l and passing through point P, you can see that on one of the sides, the sum of co-interior angles will be less than 180° thus both the lines will meet in that direction. There is only one possibility, i.e. line m, in which the sum of the co-interior angles if exactly 180° on both sides. Hence, in this case, both lines will never meet.

Thus, we can observe that this axiom by itself is not inevitably (or logically) equivalent to the Euclidean parallel postulate as there are geometries under which one is true, and the other is not. Still, each of these can be used to prove the other in the presence of the remaining axioms which give Euclidean geometry; therefore, they are said to be equivalent in terms of absolute geometry.

2D Geometry

Points and Lines

- Point plotting is done by converting a single coordinate position furnished by an application program into appropriate operations for the output device in use.

- Line drawing is done by calculating intermediate positions along the line path between two specified endpoint positions.

- The output device is then directed to fill in those positions between the end points with some color.

- For some device such as a pen plotter or random scan display, a straight line can be drawn smoothly from one end point to other.

- Digital devices display a straight line segment by plotting discrete points between the two endpoints.

- Discrete coordinate positions along the line path are calculated from the equation of the line.

- For a raster video display, the line intensity is loaded in frame buffer at the corresponding pixel positions.

- Reading from the frame buffer, the video controller then plots the screen pixels.

- Screen locations are referenced with integer values, so plotted positions may only approximate actual line positions between two specified endpoints.

- For example line position of (12.36, 23.87) would be converted to pixel position (12, 24).

- This rounding of coordinate values to integers causes lines to be displayed with a stair step appearance ("the jaggies"), as represented in figure.

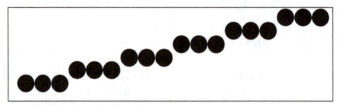

Stair step effect produced when line is generated as a series of pixel positions.

- The stair step shape is noticeable in low resolution system, and we can improve their appearance somewhat by displaying them on high resolution system.

- More effective techniques for smoothing raster lines are based on adjusting pixel intensities along the line paths.

- For raster graphics device-level algorithms discuss here, object positions are specified directly in integer device coordinates.

- Pixel position will referenced according to scan-line number and column number which is illustrated by following figure.

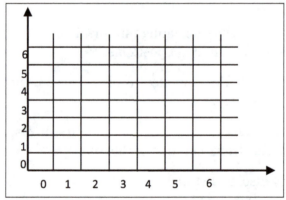

Pixel positions referenced by scan-line number and column number.

- To load the specified color into the frame buffer at a particular position, we will assume we have available low-level procedure of the form setpixel (x, y).

- Similarly for retrieve the current frame buffer intensity we assume to have procedure getpixel(x, y).

Line Drawing Algorithms

- The Cartesian slop-intercept equation for a straight line is "$y = mx + b$" with 'm' representing slop and 'b' as the intercept.

- The two endpoints of the line are given which are say (x_1, y_1) and (x_2, y_2).

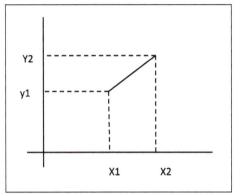

Line path between endpoint positions.

- We can determine values for the slope m by equation: m = (y2 − y1)/(x2 − x1).

- We can determine values for the intercept b by equation: b = y1 − m ∗ x1.

- For the given interval Δx along a line, we can compute the corresponding y interval Δy as: Δy = m ∗ Δx.

- Similarly for Δx: Δx = Δy/m.

- For line with slop |m| < 1, Δx can be set proportional to small horizontal deflection voltage and the corresponding vertical deflection voltage is then set proportional to Δy which is calculated from above equation.

- For line with slop |m| > 1, Δy can be set proportional to small vertical deflection voltage and the corresponding horizontal deflection voltage is then set proportional to Δx which is calculated from above equation.

- For line with slop m = 1, Δx = Δy and the horizontal and vertical deflection voltages are equal.

DDA Algorithm

DDA stands for Digital Differential Analyzer. It is an incremental method of scan conversion of line. In this method calculation is performed at each step but by using results of previous steps. Suppose at step i, the pixels is (x_i, y_i).

$$y_i = mx_{i+b}$$

Next value will be

$$y_{i+1} = m_{xi+1} + b$$

$$m = \frac{\Delta y}{\Delta x}$$

$$y_{i+1} - y_i = \Delta y$$

$$y_{i+1} - x_i = \Delta x$$

$$y_{i\,1} = y_i + \Delta y$$

$$\Delta y = m\Delta x$$

$$y_{i+1} = y_i + m\Delta x$$

$$\Delta x = \Delta y / m$$

$$x_{i+1} = x_i + \Delta x$$

$$x_{i+1} = x_i + \Delta y / m$$

Case1: When $|M| < 1$ then (assume that $x_1 2$),

$$x = x_1, y = y_1 \text{ set } \Delta x = 1$$

$$y_{i+1} = y_{1+m}, \quad x = x+1$$

Until $x = x_2$

Case2: When $|M| < 1$ then (assume that $y_1 2$)

$$x = x_1, y = y_1 \text{ set } \Delta y = 1$$

$$x_{i+1} = \frac{1}{m}, \quad y = y+1$$

Until $y \rightarrow y_2$

Advantage:

- It is a faster method than method of using direct use of line equation.

- This method does not use multiplication theorem.

- It allows us to detect the change in the value of x and y ,so plotting of same point twice is not possible.

- This method gives overflow indication when a point is repositioned.

- It is an easy method because each step involves just two additions.

Disadvantage:

- It involves floating point additions rounding off is done. Accumulations of round off error cause accumulation of error.

- Rounding off operations and floating point operations consumes a lot of time.

- It is more suitable for generating line using the software. But it is less suited for hardware implementation.

DDA Algorithm

Step 1: Start Algorithm.

Step 2: Declare x_1, y_1, x_2, y_2, dx, dy, x, y as integer variables.

Step 3: Enter value of x_1, y_1, x_2, y_2.

Step 4: Calculate dx = x_2-x_1.

Step 5: Calculate dy = y_2-y_1.

Step 6: If ABS (dx) > ABS (dy):

Then step = abs (dx)

Else

Step 7: x_{inc}=dx/step:

y_{inc}=dy/step

assign x = x_1

assign y = y_1

Step 8: Set pixel (x, y).

Step 9: x = x + x_{inc}:

y = y + y_{inc}

Set pixels (Round (x), Round (y))

Step 10: Repeat step 9 until x = x_2.

Step 11: End Algorithm.

Example: If a line is drawn from (2, 3) to (6, 15) with use of DDA. How many points will needed to generate such line?

Solution: P_1 (2,3) P_{11} (6,15)

$x_1 = 2$

$y_1 = 3$

$x_2 = 6$

$y_2 = 15$

$dx = 6 - 2 = 4$

$dy = 15 - 3 = 12$

$m = \dfrac{dy}{dx} = \dfrac{12}{4}$

For calculating next value of x takes $x = x + \dfrac{1}{m}$

$P_1(2,3)$ point plotted

$P_2(2\frac{1}{3},4)$ point plotted

$P_3(2\frac{2}{3},5)$ point not plotted

$P_4(3,6)$ point plotted

$P_5(3\frac{1}{3},7)$ point not plotted

$P_6(3\frac{2}{3},8)$ point not plotted

$P_7(4,9)$ point plotted

$P_8(4\frac{1}{3},10)$ point not plotted

$P_9(4\frac{2}{3},11)$ point not plotted

$P_{10}(5,12)$ point plotted

$P_{11}(5\frac{1}{3},13)$ point not plotted

$P_{12}(5\frac{2}{3},14)$ point not plotted

$P_{13}(6,15)$ point plotted

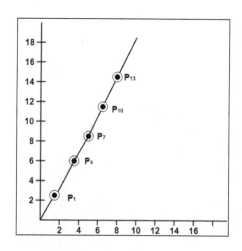

Program to Implement DDA Line Drawing Algorithm

```c
#include<graphics.h>

#include<conio.h>

#include<stdio.h>

void main()

{

    intgd = DETECT ,gm, i;

    float x, y,dx,dy,steps;

    int x0, x1, y0, y1;

    initgraph(&gd, &gm, "C:\\TC\\BGI");

    setbkcolor(WHITE);

    x0 = 100 , y0 = 200, x1 = 500, y1 = 300;

    dx = (float)(x1 - x0);

    dy = (float)(y1 - y0);

    if(dx>=dy)

            {

        steps = dx;

    }

    else

            {

        steps = dy;

    }

    dx = dx/steps;

    dy = dy/steps;

    x = x0;

    y = y0;

    i = 1;

    while(i<= steps)

    {
```

```
        putpixel(x, y, RED);

        x += dx;

        y += dy;

        i=i+1;

    }

    getch();

    closegraph();

}
```

Output:

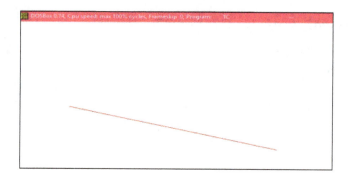

Symmetrical DDA

The Digital Differential Analyzer (DDA) generates lines from their differential equations. The equation of a straight line is:

$$\frac{dy}{dx} = \frac{\Delta y}{\Delta x}$$

The DDA works on the principle that we simultaneously increment x and y by small steps proportional to the first derivatives of x and y. In this case of a straight line, the first derivatives are constant and are proportional to Δx and Δy. Therefore, we could generate a line by incrementing x and y by $\epsilon \Delta x$ and $\epsilon \Delta y$, where ϵ is some small quantity. There are two ways to generate points:

- By rounding to the nearest integer after each incremental step, after rounding we display dots at the resultant x and y.

- An alternative to rounding the use of arithmetic overflow: x and y are kept in registers that have two parts, integer and fractional. The incrementing values, which are both less than unity, are repeatedly added to the fractional parts and whenever the results overflows, the corresponding integer part is incremented.

The integer parts of the x and y registers are used in plotting the line. In the case of the symmetrical DDA, we choose ε=2-n, where 2n-1≤max (|Δx|,|Δy|)<2π.

A line drawn with the symmetrical DDA is shown in fig:

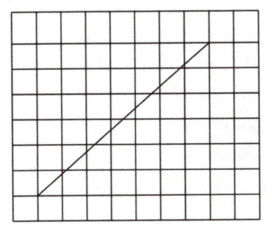

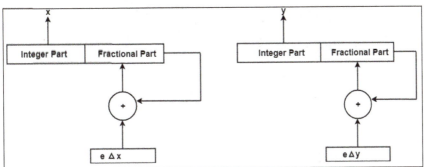

Organization of symmetrical DDA.

Example: If a line is drawn from (0, 0) to (10, 5) with a symmetrical DDA.

- How many iterations are performed?

- How many different points will be generated?

Solutions: Given: P¹ (0,0) P² (10,5)

$$x^1 = 0$$
$$y^1 = 0$$
$$x^2 = 10$$
$$y^2 = 5$$
$$dx = 10 - 0 = 10$$
$$dy = 5 - 0 = 0$$
$$m = \frac{y_2 - y_1}{x_2 - x_1} = \frac{5 - 0}{10 - 0} = \frac{5}{10} = 0.5$$

P^1 (0,0) will be considered starting points

P^3 (1,0.5)	point not plotted
P^4 (2, 1)	point plotted
P^5 (3, 1.5)	point not plotted
P^6 (4,2)	point plotted
P^7 (5,2.5)	point not plotted
P^8 (6,3)	point plotted
P^9 (7,3.5)	point not plotted
P^{10} (8, 4)	point plotted
P^{11} (9,4.5)	point not plotted
P^{12} (10,5)	point plotted

Following Figure show line plotted using these points:

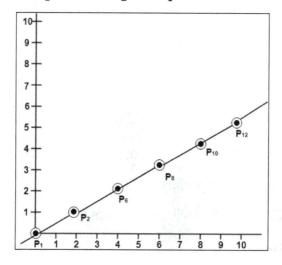

Bresenham's Algorithm

Bresenham is a scientist and is popular for his contributions to line drawing and circle drawing procedures, and few others, which are not of our interest. Assume a line with slope <1, the same discussion that we had during DDA procedure is still valid here, i.e. sample the line along x-axis at unit x-intervals if the line slopes are <=1 otherwise sample the line along y-axis.

Let's start our assumptions with a line whose slope <1 i.e. the line is more inclined towards x-axis, so it is obvious to sample the line along x-axis at unit xintervals and compute the corresponding y values. Also that to compute next points on a line, we always starts with a known point on the line and tries computing the next unknown point on the line using recursive equations. So the next x i.e. $x_{k+1} = x_{k+1}$ and the next y i.e. y_{k+1} is to be computed. Let the known plotted point on the line be (x_k, y_k).

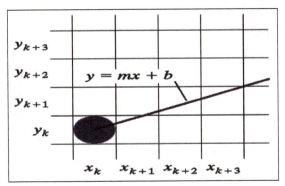

Before we get into the derivation lets understand the underlying principle of Bresenham's procedure. To compute the next point on the line (X_{k+1}, Y_{k+1}), a value called 'decision parameter' is computed. Based on the result a pixel is chosen for plotting.

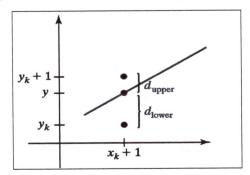

As shown in the figure above let the line shown be the theoretical line and we need to find the best possible approximation for this by computing Bresenham's line. For the next X position, X_{k+1}, the corresponding Y value could not be plotted as the position (X_{k+1}, y) does not exist on the monitor. We have to choose between Y_k and Y_{k+1}. i.e. next position to be plotted is either (X_{k+1}, Y_k) or (X_{k+1}, Y_{k+1}). Now how do we decide among the two choices. The answer is, compute the vertical difference between the possible pixel position and the position on the true theoretical line which is.

Let d_{lower} be the vertical difference between the position (y) on theoretical line and the lower pixel (y_k) and d_{upper} be the vertical difference between the position (y) on theoretical line and the upper pixel (y_{k+1}). As evident if d_{lower} is $< d_{upper}$ the theoretical line is closer to the lower pixel so choose position (X_{k+1}, Y_k) otherwise choose position. The difference between d_{lower} and d_{upper} is considered as 'decision parameter', as the sign of the difference operation helps us decide what y coordinate position is to be chosen for the next x.

- 'Decision parameter' referred to as pk helps us decide which of the pixels is to be chosen

- Whichever pixel position is close to the theoretical line, that pixel is chosen i.e. next X is $X_{k+1} = X_k+1$, and next Y is $Y_{k+1}=Y_k$ or Y_k+1 depending on the sign of pk.

Let's derive those recursive equations of the Bresenham's procedure. To start with we use slope-intercept form of line equation. Having known the position (x_k,y_k) on the line, the next x position would be x_{k+1}. From the slope-intercept form of line equation, for the next x position we have,

$$y = mx_{k+1} + c$$

Now compute d_{upper} and d_{lower} as,

$$d_{upper} = y_k + 1 - y$$
$$d_{lower} = y - y_k$$

Substituting for y the first equation we get,

$$d_{upper} = y_{k+1} - mx_{k+1} - c$$
$$d_{lower} = mx_{k+1} + c - y_k$$
$$d_{lower} - d_{upper} = 2mx_{k+1} - 2y_k + 2c - 1$$

Now replace m $\dfrac{\Delta y}{\Delta x}$ with and cross multiplying the terms with the equation we have,

$$\Delta x\left(d_{lower} - d_{upper}\right)$$
$$= 2\Delta y x_{k+1} - 2\Delta x y_k + \Delta x\left(2c-1\right)$$

In the above step it is interesting to observer that division due to dy/dx is avoided by cross multiplying dy/dx with the equations,

$$P_k = 2\Delta y x_{k+1} - 2\Delta x y_k + \Delta x\left(2c-1\right)$$

Because $\Delta x(2C-1)$ is a constant with Δx and C being constants for a given line with end points we can replace $\Delta x(2C-1)$ with a constant say 'b'.

$$P_{k+1} = 2\Delta y k_{k+1} - 2\Delta x y_{k+1} + b$$

Now taking the difference between P_k and P_{k+1} we get,

$$P_{k+1} - P_k$$
$$= 2\Delta y\left(x_{k+1} - x_k\right) - 2\Delta x\left(y_{k+1} - y_k\right)$$
$$P_{k+1} = P_k + 2\Delta y\left(x_{k+1} - x_k\right) - 2\Delta x\left(y_{k+1} - y_k\right)$$
$$P_k + 1 = P_k + 2\Delta y - 2\Delta x\left(y_{k+1} - y_k\right)$$

Now the sign of P_k is to be checked.

Case (i): If pk <=0 the lower pixel (X_k+1, Y_k) is to be plotted, i.e. next x is X_k+1 and next y is Y_k. Therefore $y_{k+1}=y_k$. Now the previous equation for P_k+1 reduces to,

$$P_{k+1} = P_k + 2\Delta y$$

Case (ii): If pk >0 the upper pixel $(Xk+1, Yk+1)$ is to be plotted, Therefore next y, $y_{k+1}=y_k+1$, now substituting for y_{k+1} in the equation for P_{k+1} we get,

$$P_{k+1} = P_k + 2\Delta y - 2\Delta x$$

The initial decision parameter po is computed as below (use the following eq.)

$$p_k = 2\Delta y x_k - 2\Delta x y_k + 2\Delta y + \Delta x(2c-1)$$

Replace k with 0 and compute c as shown.

$$y_0 = mx_0 + c$$

$$y_0 = \frac{\Delta y}{\Delta x} x_0 + c$$

$$c = y_0 - \frac{\Delta y}{\Delta x} x_0$$

$$p_0 = 2\Delta y x_0 - 2\Delta x y_0 + 2\Delta y$$

$$+ \Delta x \left(2y_0 - 2\frac{\Delta y}{\Delta x} x_0 - 1 \right)$$

$$p_0 + 2\Delta y x_0 - 2\Delta x y_0 + 2\Delta y$$

$$+ \Delta x \left(2y_0 - 2\frac{\Delta y}{\Delta x} x_0 - 1 \right)$$

$$p_0 + 2\Delta y x_0 - 2\Delta x y_0 + 2\Delta y + 2\Delta x y_0$$

$$- 2\Delta y x_0 - \Delta x$$

$$p_0 = 2\Delta y - \Delta x$$

If the point on the theoretical line is equidistant from either of the possible pixel locations then either of the pixels could be plotted. Now the algorithm steps can be summarized as follows for the case when $|m| <= 1$.

- Input the two end points.

- Compute Po.

- Check cases depending on the sign of Po.

- Continue with the next decision parameters till the end of the line is reached.

All this is well only for lines with slopes <1. What about other line types? Now let's summarize the equations as below:

When $|m|<=1$

$$P_0 = 2\Delta y - \Delta x$$

Case (i): If pk<=0 the lower pixel (X_k+1, Y_k) is to be plotted.

$$y_{k+1} = y_k \text{ and } P_{k+1} = P_k + 2\Delta y$$

Case (ii): If $p_k > 0$ the upper pixel (X_k+1, Y_k+1) is to be plotted.

$$y_{k+1} = y_k + 1 \text{ and } P_{k+1} = P_k + 2\Delta y - 2\Delta x$$

When $|m|>1$

The roles of X and y get reversed.

$$p_0 = 2\Delta x - \Delta y$$

Case (i): If $p_k <= 0$ the lower pixel (X_k+1, Y_k) is to be plotted,

If $p_k <= 0$ the left pixel (X_k, Y_k+1) is to be plotted.

$$x_{k+1} = x_k \text{ and } p_{k+1} = p_k + 2\Delta x$$

Case (ii): If $p_k > 0$ the right pixel (X_k+1, Y_k+1) is to be plotted.

$$x_{k+1} = x_k + 1 \text{ and } p_{k+1} = p_k + 2\Delta x - 2\Delta y$$

	✓ Compute absolute values of $\Delta x, \Delta y$			
	$|m|<=1, (P_0=2\Delta y-\Delta x)$		$|m|>1, (P_0=2\Delta x-\Delta y)$	
m +ve	$P_k<=0$	$P_k>0$	$P_k<=0$	$P_k>0$
	$X_{k+1}=X_k+1$	$X_{k+1}=X_k+1$	$X_{k+1}=X_k$	$X_{k+1}=X_k+1$
	$Y_{k+1}=Y_k$	$Y_{k+1}=Y_k+1$	$Y_{k+1}=Y_k+1$	$Y_{k+1}=Y_k+1$
	$P(X_{k+1},Y_k)$	$P(X_k+1,Y_k+1)$	$P(X_k,Y_k+1)$	$P(X_k+1,Y_k+1)$
	$P_{k+1}=P_k+2\Delta y$	$P_{k+1}=P_k+2\Delta y-2\Delta x$	$P_{k+1}=P_k+2\Delta x$	$P_{k+1}=P_k+2\Delta x-2\Delta y$
m -ve	$P_k<=0$	$P_k>0$	$P_k<=0$	$P_k>0$
	$X_{k+1}=X_k+1$	$X_{k+1}=X_k+1$	$X_{k+1}=X_k$	$X_{k+1}=X_k+1$
	$Y_{k+1}=Y_k$	$Y_{k+1}=Y_k-1$	$Y_{k+1}=Y_k-1$	$Y_{k+1}=Y_k-1$
	$P(X_{k+1},Y_k)$	$P(X_k+1,Y_k-1)$	$P(X_k,Y_k-1)$	$P(X_k+1,Y_k-1)$
	$P_{k+1}=P_k+2\Delta y$	$P_{k+1}=P_k+2\Delta y-2\Delta x$	$P_{k+1}=P_k+2\Delta x$	$P_{k+1}=P_k+2\Delta x-2\Delta y$

Parallel Execution of Line Algorithms

- The line-generating algorithms we have discussed so far determine pixel positions sequentially.

- With parallel computer we can calculate pixel position along a line path simultaneously by dividing work among the various processors available.

- One way to use multiple processors is partitioning existing sequential algorithm into small parts and compute separately.

- Alternatively we can go for other ways to setup the processing so that pixel positions can be calculated efficiently in parallel.

- Important point to be taking into account while devising parallel algorithm is to balance the load among the available processors.

- Given np number of processors we can set up parallel Bresenham line algorithm by subdividing the line path into np partitions and simultaneously generating line segment in each of the subintervals.

- For a line with slope $0 < m < 1$ and left endpoint coordinate position $(x0, y0)$, we partition the line along the positive x direction.

- The distance between beginning x positions of adjacent partitions can be calculated as: $\Delta xp = (\Delta x + np - 1)/$. Where Δx is the width of the line. And value for partition with Δxp is computed using integer division.

- Numbering the partitions and the processors, as 0, 1, 2, up to np-1, we calculate the starting x coordinate for the kth partition as: $xk = x0 + k\Delta xp$

- To apply Bresenham's algorithm over the partitions, we need the initial value for the y coordinate and the initial value for the decision parameter in each partition.

- The change Δyp in the y direction over each partition is calculated from the line slope m and partition width Δxp:

  $\Delta yp = m\Delta x$

- At the kth partition, the starting y coordinate is then.

- $yk = y0 + round(k\Delta yp)$.

- The initial decision parameter for Bresenham's algorithm at the start of the kth subinterval is obtained from Equation:

  $$p_k = 2\Delta y x_k - 2\Delta x y_k + 2\Delta y + 2\Delta x b - \Delta x$$

$$p_k = 2\Delta y(x_0 + k\Delta xp) - 2\Delta x\left(y_0 + round(k\Delta y_p)\right) + 2\Delta y + 2\Delta x\left(y_0 - \frac{\Delta y}{\Delta x}x_0\right) - \Delta x$$

$$p_k = 2\Delta yx_0 - 2\Delta yk\Delta x_p - 2\Delta xy_0 - 2\Delta x round(k\Delta y_p) + 2\Delta y + 2\Delta xy_0 - 2\Delta yx_0 - \Delta x$$

$$p_k = 2\Delta yk\Delta x_p - 2\Delta x round(k\Delta y_p) + 2\Delta y - \Delta x$$

- Each processor then calculates pixel positions over its assigned subinterval.

- The extension of the parallel Bresenham algorithm to a line with slope greater than 1 is achieved by partitioning the line in the y direction and calculating beginning x values for the positions.

- For negative slopes, we increment coordinate values in one direction and decrement in the other.

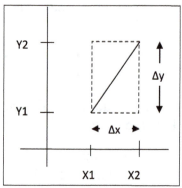

Bounding box for a line with coordinate extents Δx and Δy.

- Another way to set up parallel algorithms on raster system is to assign each processor to a particular group of screen pixels.

- With sufficient number of processor we can assign each processor to one pixel within some screen region.

- This approach can be adapted to line display by assigning one processor to each of the pixels within the limit of the bounding rectangle and calculating pixel distance from the line path.

- The number of pixels within the bounding rectangle of a line is $\Delta x \times \Delta y$.

- Perpendicular distance d from line to a particular pixel is calculated by:

$$d = Ax + By + C$$

Where,

$$A = -\Delta y / linelength$$
$$B = -\Delta x / linelength$$
$$C = (x_0\Delta y - y_0\Delta x) / linelength$$

With,

$$\text{linelength} = \sqrt{\Delta x^2 + \Delta y^2}$$

- Once the constant A, B, and C have been evaluated for the line each processors need to perform two multiplications and two additions to compute the pixel distance d.

- A pixel is plotted if d is less than a specified line thickness parameter.

- Instead of partitioning the screen into single pixels, we can assign to each processor either a scan line or a column a column of pixels depending on the line slope.

- Each processor calculates line intersection with horizontal row or vertical column of pixels assigned to that processor.

- If vertical column is assign to processor then x is fix and it will calculate y and similarly is horizontal row is assign to processor then y is fix and x will be calculated.

- Such direct methods are slow in sequential machine but we can perform very efficiently using multiple processors.

Mid-Point Algorithm

Mid-point algorithm is due to Bresenham which was modified by Pitteway and Van Aken. Assume that you have already put the point P at x, y coordinate and the slope of the line is $0 \le k \le 1$ as shown in the following illustration.

Now you need to decide whether to put the next point at E or N. This can be chosen by identifying the intersection point Q closest to the point N or E. If the intersection point Q is closest to the point N then N is considered as the next point; otherwise E.

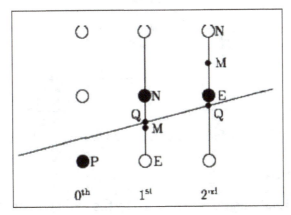

To determine that, first calculate the mid-point Mx + 1, y + ½. If the intersection point

Q of the line with the vertical line connecting E and N is below M, then take E as the next point; otherwise take N as the next point. In order to check this, we need to consider the implicit equation:

$$Fx, y = mx + b - y$$

For positive m at any given X,

- If y is on the line, then Fx, y = 0.
- If y is above the line, then Fx, y < 0.
- If y is below the line, then Fx, y > 0.

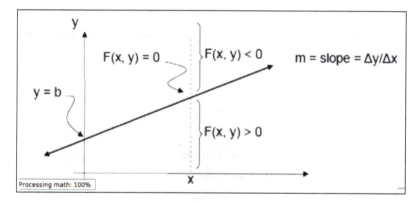

Circle

A circle is defined as the set of points that are all at a given distance r from a center position say (xc , yc).

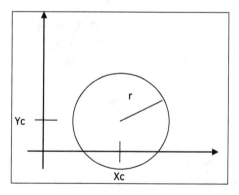

Circle with center coordinates (xc , yc) and radius r.

Properties of Circle

- The distance relationship is expressed by the Pythagorean theorem in Cartesian coordinates as: $(x - x_c)^2 + (y - y_c)^2 = r^2$.

- We could use this equation to calculate circular boundary points by increment-ing 1 in x direction in every steps from xc − r to xc + r and calculate correspond-ing y values at each position as:

$$(x-x_c)^2 + (y-y_c)^2 = r^2$$
$$(y-y_c)^2 = r^2 - (x-x_c)^2$$
$$(y-y_c) = \pm\sqrt{r^2 - (x-x_c)^2}$$
$$y = y_c \pm \sqrt{r^2 - (x_c-x)^2}$$

- But this is not best method for generating a circle because it requires more number of calculations which take more time to execute.

- And also spacing between the plotted pixel positions is not uniform as shown in figure below:

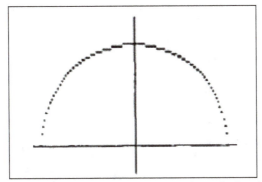

Positive half of circle showing non uniform spacing bet calculated pixel positions.

- We can adjust spacing by stepping through y values and calculating x values whenever the absolute value of the slop of the circle is greater than 1. But it will increases computation processing requirement.

- Another way to eliminate the non-uniform spacing is to draw circle using polar coordinates 'r' and 'θ'.

- Calculating circle boundary using polar equation is given by pair of equations which is as follows.

$$x = x_c + r\cos\theta$$
$$y = y_c + r\sin\theta$$

- When display is produce using these equations using fixed angular step size circle is plotted with uniform spacing.

- The step size 'θ' is chosen according to application and display device.

- For a more continuous boundary on a raster display we can set the step size at 1/r. This plot pixel position that are approximately one unit apart.

- Computation can be reduced by considering symmetry city property of circles. The shape of circle is similar in each quadrant.

- We can obtain pixel position in second quadrant from first quadrant using reflection about y axis and similarly for third and fourth quadrant from second and first respectively using reflection about x axis.

- We can take one step further and note that there is also symmetry between octants. Circle sections in adjacent octant within one quadrant are symmetric with respect to the 450 line dividing the two octants.

- This symmetry condition is shown in figure below where point (x, y) on one circle sector is mapped in other seven sector of circle.

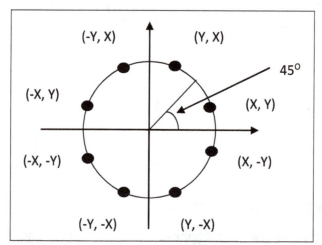

Symmetry of circle.

- Taking advantage of this symmetry property of circle we can generate all pixel position on boundary of circle by calculating only one sector from x = 0 to x = y.

- Determining pixel position along circumference of circle using any of two equations shown above still required large computation.

- More efficient circle algorithm is based on incremental calculation of decision parameters, as in the Bresenham line algorithm.

- Bresenham's line algorithm can be adapted to circle generation by setting decision parameter for finding closest pixel to the circumference at each sampling step.

- The Cartesian coordinate circle equation is nonlinear so that square root evaluations would be required to compute pixel distance from circular path.

- Bresenham's circle algorithm avoids these square root calculations by comparing the square of the pixel separation distance.

A method for direct distance comparison to test the midpoint between two pixels to determine if this midpoint is inside or outside the circle boundary. This method is easily applied to other conics also. Midpoint approach generates same pixel position as generated by bresenham's circle algorithm. The error involve in locating pixel positions along any conic section using midpoint test is limited to one half the pixel separation.

Mid-Point Circle Algorithm

The mid-point circle drawing algorithm is an algorithm used to determine the points needed for rasterizing a circle. We use the mid-point algorithm to calculate all the perimeter points of the circle in the first octant and then print them along with their mirror points in the other octants. This will work because a circle is symmetric about its centre.

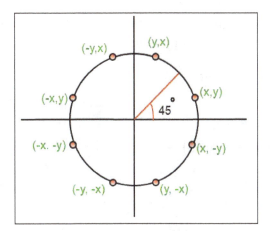

The algorithm is very similar to the Mid-Point Line Generation Algorithm. Here, only the boundary condition is different. For any given pixel (x, y), the next pixel to be plotted is either $(x, y+1)$ or $(x-1, y+1)$. This can be decided by following the steps below.

- Find the mid-point p of the two possible pixels i.e $(x-0.5, y+1)$.

- If p lies inside or on the circle perimeter, we plot the pixel $(x, y+1)$, otherwise if it's outside we plot the pixel $(x-1, y+1)$.

Boundary Condition: Whether the mid-point lies inside or outside the circle can be decided by using the formula.

Given a circle centered at $(0,0)$ and radius r and a point $p(x,y)$,

$F(p) = x^2 + y^2 - r^2$,

if $F(p)<0$, the point is inside the circle,

F(p)=0, the point is on the perimeter,

F(p)>0, the point is outside the circle.

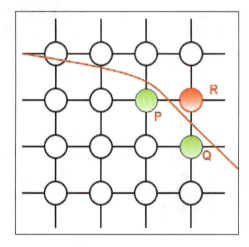

We denote F(p) with P. The value of P is calculated at the mid-point of the two contending pixels i.e. (x-0.5, y+1). Each pixel is described with a subscript k.

$$P_k = \left(x_k - 0.5\right)^2 + \left(y_k - 1\right)^2 - r^2$$

Now,

$$x_{k+1} = x_k \text{ or } x_{k-1}, y_{k=1} = y_k + 1$$

$$\therefore P_{k+1} = \left(x_{k+1} - 0.5\right)^2 + \left(y_{k+1} + 1\right)^2 - r^2$$

$$= \left(x_{k+1} - 0.5\right)^2 + \left[\left(y_{k+1} + 1\right) + 1\right]^2 - r^2$$

$$= \left(x_{k+1} - 0.5\right)^2 + \left(y_k + 1\right)^2 + 2\left(y_k + 1\right) + 1 - r^2$$

$$= \left(x_{k+1} - 0.5\right)^2 + \left[-\left(x_k - 0.5\right)^2 + \left(x_k - 0.5\right)^2\right] + \left(y_k + 1\right)^2 - r^2 + \left(y_k + 1\right) + 1$$

The first point to be plotted is (r, 0) on the x-axis. The initial value of P is calculated as follows:

$$P1 = \left(r - 0.5\right)^2 + \left(0 + 1\right)^2 - r^2$$

$$= 1.25 - r$$

$$= 1 - r \left(\text{When rounded off}\right)$$

Examples:

Input: Centre -> (0, 0), Radius -> 3

Output: (3, 0) (3, 0) (0, 3) (0, 3)

(3, 1) (-3, 1) (3, -1) (-3, -1)

(1, 3) (-1, 3) (1, -3) (-1, -3)

(2, 2) (-2, 2) (2, -2) (-2, -2)

(x1,y1) is initioally printed before the loop: (3,0) (3,0) (0,3) (0,3)							
k	P_k	X_k	Y_k	P_{k+1}	X_{k+1}	Y_{k+1}	Output
1	-2	3	0	-1	3	1	(3,1) (-3,1) (3,-1) (-3,-3) (1,3) (-1,3) (1,-3) (-1,-3)
2	-1	3	1	2	2	2	(2,2) (-2,2) (2,-2) (-2,-2)
3	2	2	2				Break from loop

Input: Centre -> (4, 4), Radius -> 2

Output: (6, 4) (6, 4) (4, 6) (4, 6)

(6, 5) (2, 5) (6, 3) (2, 3)

(5, 6) (3, 6) (5, 2) (3, 2)

```c
// C program for implementing
// Mid-Point Circle Drawing Algorithm
#include<stdio.h>


// Implementing Mid-Point Circle Drawing Algorithm
void midPointCircleDraw(int x_centre, int y_centre, int r)
{
    int x = r, y = 0;


    // Printing the initial point on the axes
    // after translation
    printf("(%d, %d) ", x + x_centre, y + y_centre);


    // When radius is zero only a single
    // point will be printed
    if (r > 0)
```

```
{
        printf("(%d, %d) ", x + x_centre, -y + y_centre);

        printf("(%d, %d) ", y + x_centre, x + y_centre);

        printf("(%d, %d)\n", -y + x_centre, x + y_centre);

}


// Initialising the value of P

int P = 1 - r;

while (x > y)

{

        y++;


        // Mid-point is inside or on the perimeter

        if (P <= 0)

                P = P + 2*y + 1;


        // Mid-point is outside the perimeter

        else

        {

                x--;

                P = P + 2*y - 2*x + 1;

        }


        // All the perimeter points have already been printed

        if (x < y)

                break;


        // Printing the generated point and its reflection

        // in the other octants after translation
```

```
            printf("(%d, %d) ", x + x_centre, y + y_centre);

            printf("(%d, %d) ", -x + x_centre, y + y_centre);

            printf("(%d, %d) ", x + x_centre, -y + y_centre);

            printf("(%d, %d)\n", -x + x_centre, -y + y_centre);


        // If the generated point is on the line x = y then
        // the perimeter points have already been printed
        if (x != y)
        {
                printf("(%d, %d) ", y + x_centre, x + y_centre);

                printf("(%d, %d) ", -y + x_centre, x + y_centre);

                printf("(%d, %d) ", y + x_centre, -x + y_centre);

                printf("(%d, %d)\n", -y + x_centre, -x + y_centre);

        }

    }

}


// Driver code
int main()
{
    // To draw a circle of radius 3 centred at (0, 0)
    midPointCircleDraw(0, 0, 3);
    return 0;

}
```

Output:

        (3, 0) (3, 0) (0, 3) (0, 3)

        (3, 1) (-3, 1) (3, -1) (-3, -1)

        (1, 3) (-1, 3) (1, -3) (-1, -3)

        (2, 2) (-2, 2) (2, -2) (-2, -2)

Bresenham's Circle Generation Algorithm

Scan-Converting a circle using Bresenham's algorithm works as follows: Points are generated from 90° to 45°, moves will be made only in the +x & -y directions as shown in fig:

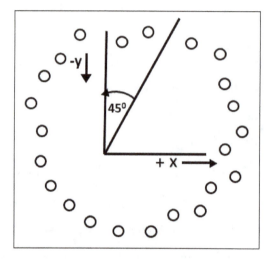

The best approximation of the true circle will be described by those pixels in the raster that falls the least distance from the true circle. We want to generate the points from 90° to 45°. Assume that the last scan-converted pixel is P1 as shown in fig. Each new point closest to the true circle can be found by taking either of two actions:

- Move in the x-direction one unit.

- Move in the x- direction one unit & move in the negative y-direction one unit.

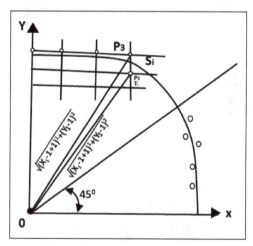

Let D (S_i) is the distance from the origin to the true circle squared minus the distance to point P_3 squared. D (T_i) is the distance from the origin to the true circle squared minus the distance to point P_2 squared. Therefore, the following expressions arise.

Let D (S_i) is the distance from the origin to the true circle squared minus the distance to point P_3 squared. D (T_i) is the distance from the origin to the true circle squared minus the distance to point P_2 squared. Therefore, the following expressions arise.

$$D(S_i) = (x_{i-1}+1)^2 + y_{i-1}^2 - r^2$$
$$D(T_i) = (x_{i-1}+1)^2 + (y_{i-1}-1)^2 - r^2$$

Since D (S_i) will always be +ve & D (T_i) will always be -ve, a decision variable d may be defined as follows:

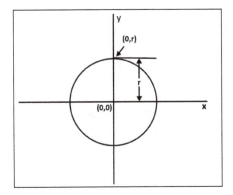

$$d_i = D\ (S_i) + D\ (T_i)$$

Therefore,

$$d_i = (x_{i-1}+1)^2 + y_{i-1}^2 - r^2 + (x_{i-1}+1)^2 + (y_{i-1}-1)^2 - r^2$$

From this equation, we can drive initial values of d_i as,

If it is assumed that the circle is centered at the origin, then at the first step x = 0 & y = r.

Therefore,

$$d_i = (0+1)^2 + r^2 - r^2 + (0+1)^2 + (r-1)^2 - r^2$$
$$= 1 + 1 + r^2 - 2r + 1 - r^2$$
$$= 3 - 2r$$

Thereafter, if d_i<0, then only x is incremented.

$$x_{i+1} = x_{i+1} \qquad d_{i+1} = d_i + 4x_i + 6$$

& if $d_i \geq 0$, then x & y are incremented.

$$x_{i+1} = x_{i+1} \qquad y_{i+1} = y_i + 1$$
$$d_{i+1} = d_i + 4\ (x_i - y_i) + 10$$

Bresenham's Circle Algorithm

Step 1: Start Algorithm.

Step 2: Declare p, q, x, y, r, d variables.

    p, q are coordinates of the center of the circle

    r is the radius of the circle

Step 3: Enter the value of r.

Step 4: Calculate d = 3 - 2r.

Step 5: Initialize   x=0

    &nbsy= r

Step 6: Check if the whole circle is scan converted.

    If x > = y

    Stop

Step 7: Plot eight points by using concepts of eight-way symmetry. The center is at (p, q). Current active pixel is (x, y).

    putpixel (x+p, y+q)

    putpixel (y+p, x+q)

    putpixel (-y+p, x+q)

    putpixel (-x+p, y+q)

    putpixel (-x+p, -y+q)

    putpixel (-y+p, -x+q)

    putpixel (y+p, -x+q)

    putpixel (x+p, -y-q)

Step 8: Go to step 6.

Step 9: Stop Algorithm.

Example: Plot 6 points of circle using Bresenham Algorithm. When radius of circle is 10 units. The circle has centre (50, 50).

Solution: Let r = 10 (Given)

Step 1: Take initial point (0, 10).

$$d = 3 - 2r$$

$$d = 3 - 2 * 10 = -17$$

$$d < 0 \therefore d = d + 4x + 6$$

$$= -17 + 4 (0) + 6$$

$$= -11$$

Step 2: Plot (1, 10).

$$d = d + 4x + 6 \; (\because d < 0)$$

$$= -11 + 4 (1) + 6$$

$$= -1$$

Step 3: Plot (2, 10).

$$d = d + 4x + 6 \; (\because d < 0)$$

$$= -1 + 4 \times 2 + 6$$

$$= 13$$

Step 4: Plot (3, 9) d is > 0 so x = x + 1, y = y - 1

$$d = d + 4 (x-y) + 10 \; (\because d > 0)$$

$$= 13 + 4 (3-9) + 10$$

$$= 13 + 4 (-6) + 10$$

$$= 23-24=-1$$

Step 5: Plot (4, 9).

$$d = -1 + 4x + 6$$

$$= -1 + 4 (4) + 6$$

$$= 21$$

Step 6: Plot (5, 8).

$$d = d + 4 (x-y) + 10 \; (\because d > 0)$$

$$= 21 + 4 (5-8) + 10$$

$$= 21-12 + 10 = 19$$

So P_1 (0,0)$\Rightarrow$(50,50).

$\quad$ P_2 (1,10)$\Rightarrow$(51,60)

$\quad$ P_3 (2,10)$\Rightarrow$(52,60)

$\quad$ P_4 (3,9)$\Rightarrow$(53,59)

$\quad$ P_5 (4,9)$\Rightarrow$(54,59)

$\quad$ P_6 (5,8)$\Rightarrow$(55,58)

Program to Draw a Circle Using Bresenham's Circle Drawing Algorithm

```
#include <graphics.h>

#include <stdlib.h>

#include <stdio.h>

#include <conio.h>

#include <math.h>


    void     EightWaySymmetricPlot(int xc,int yc,int x,int y)
    {
    putpixel(x+xc,y+yc,RED);
    putpixel(x+xc,-y+yc,YELLOW);
    putpixel(-x+xc,-y+yc,GREEN);
    putpixel(-x+xc,y+yc,YELLOW);
    putpixel(y+xc,x+yc,12);
    putpixel(y+xc,-x+yc,14);
    putpixel(-y+xc,-x+yc,15);
    putpixel(-y+xc,x+yc,6);
    }


    void BresenhamCircle(int xc,int yc,int r)
    {
```

```
int x=0,y=r,d=3-(2*r);

EightWaySymmetricPlot(xc,yc,x,y);


while(x<=y)
 {
  if(d<=0)
          {
    d=d+(4*x)+6;
  }
  else
   {
    d=d+(4*x)-(4*y)+10;
    y=y-1;
  }
   x=x+1;
   EightWaySymmetricPlot(xc,yc,x,y);
  }
}


int  main(void)
{
/* request auto detection */
int xc,yc,r,gdriver = DETECT, gmode, errorcode;
/* initialize graphics and local variables */
 initgraph(&gdriver, &gmode, "C:\\TURBOC3\\BGI");


 /* read result of initialization */
 errorcode = graphresult();
```

```
    if (errorcode != grOk)   /* an error occurred */

{

    printf("Graphics error: %s\n", grapherrormsg(errorcode));

    printf("Press any key to halt:");

    getch();

    exit(1); /* terminate with an error code */

}

    printf("Enter the values of xc and yc :");

    scanf("%d%d",&xc,&yc);

    printf("Enter the value of radius  :");

    scanf("%d",&r);

    BresenhamCircle(xc,yc,r);


    getch();

    closegraph();

    return 0;

}
```

Output:

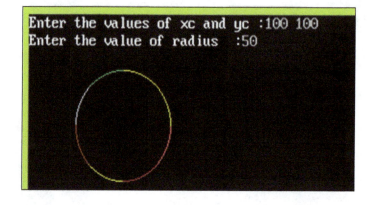

Ellipse

Loosely stated, an ellipse is an elongated circle. Therefore, elliptical curves can be generated by modifying circle-drawing procedures to take into account the different dimensions of an ellipse along the major and minor axes.

Properties of Ellipses

An ellipse is defined as the set of points such that the sum of the distances from two fixed positions (foci) is the same for all points. If the distances to the two foci from any point P = (x, y) on the ellipse are labeled d_1 and d_2, then the general equation of an ellipse can be stated as:

$d_1 + d_2$ = constant

Expressing distances d_1 and d_2 in terms of the focal coordinates $F_1 = (x_1, y_1)$ and $F_2 = (x_2, y_2)$, we have,

$$\sqrt{\left((x-x_1)^2+(y-y_1)^2\right)}+\sqrt{\left((x-x_2)^2+(y-y_2)^2\right)}=\text{constant} \longrightarrow A$$

By squaring this equation, isolating the remaining radical, and then squaring again, we can rewrite the general ellipse equation in the form:

$$Ax^2 + By^2 + Cxy + Dx + Ey + F = 0 \longrightarrow B$$

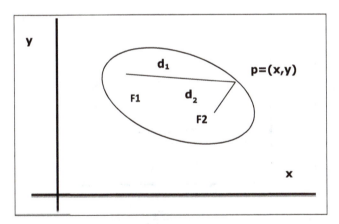

Where the coefficients A, B, C, D, E, and F are evaluated in terms of the focal coordinates and the dimensions of the major and minor axes of the ellipse. The major axis is the straight line segment extending from one side of the ellipse to the other through the foci. The minor axis spans the shorter dimension of the ellipse, bisecting the major axis at the halfway position (ellipse center) between the two foci.

An interactive method for specifying an ellipse in an arbitrary orientation is to input the two foci and a point on the ellipse boundary. With these three coordinate positions, we can evaluate the constant in A. Then, the coefficients in B can be evaluated and used to generate pixels along the elliptical path.

Ellipse equations are greatly simplified if the major and minor axes are oriented to align with the coordinate axes. In figure, we show an ellipse in "standard position" with major and minor axes oriented parallel to the x and y axes. Parameter r_x for this example labels the semi major axis, and parameter r_y labels the semi minor axis. The equation of the ellipse shown in figure can be written in terms of the ellipse center co-ordinates and parameters r_x and r_y as:

$$\left((x-x_c)/r_x\right)^2 + \left((y-y_c)/r_y\right)^2 = 1 \xrightarrow{\hspace{2cm}} C$$

Using polar coordinates r and θ, we can also describe the ellipse in standard position with the parametric equations,

$$x = x_c + r_x \cos\theta$$
$$y = y_c + r_y \sin\theta$$

Symmetry considerations can be used to further reduce computations. An ellipse in standard position is symmetric between quadrants, but unlike a circle, it is not symmetric between the two octants of a quadrant. Thus, we must calculate pixel positions along the elliptical arc throughout one quadrant, and then we obtain positions in the remaining three quadrants by symmetry,

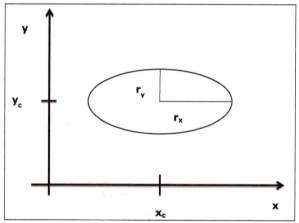

Ellipse centered at$(x_c, y_c)$with semimajor axis r_x and semiminor axis r_y.

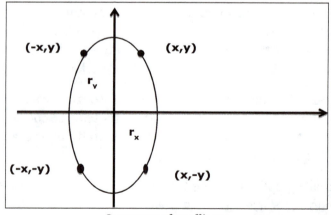

Symmetry of an ellipse.

DDA Algorithm

To write an algorithm to generate an ellipse using the Digital Differential Analyzer Algorithm (DDA). Equation to the ellipse is,

$$\left((x-xc)/r_x\right)^2 + \left((y-yc)/r_y\right)^2 = 1$$

Where (xc,yc) - center of the ellipse. r_x- x radius of ellipse, r_y-y radius of ellipse.

- START

- Get the centre (xc,yc),x radius (rx) and y radius (ry) of the ellipse.

- The polar co-ordinates on an ellipse are:

x=xc+rxcosθ

y=yc+r y sinθ

- Plot the point(x,y) corresponding to the values of θ where 0<=θ<=360.

- STOP

Midpoint Ellipse Algorithm

Our approach here is similar to that used in displaying a raster circle. Given parameters r_x, r_y and (x_c, y_c), we determine points (x,y) for an ellipse in standard position centered on the origin, and then we shift the points so the ellipse is centered at (x_c, y_c). If we wish also to display the ellipse in nonstandard position, we could then rotate the ellipse about its center coordinates to reorient the major and minor axes. For the present, we consider only the display of ellipses in standard position.

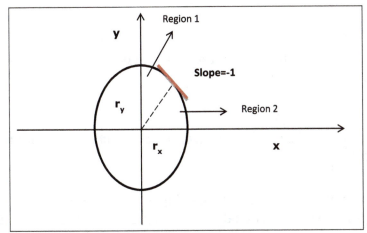

Ellipse processing regions. Over region 1, the magnitude of the ellipse slope is less than 1; over region 2, the magnitude of the slope is greater than 1.

The midpoint ellipse method is applied throughout the first quadrant in two parts. Figure shows the division of the first quadrant according to the slope of an ellipse with rx<ry. We process this quadrant by taking unit steps in the x direction where the slope of the curve has a magnitude less than 1, and taking unit steps in the y direction where the slop has a magnitude greater than 1.

Regions 1 and 2 can be process in various ways. We can start at position $(0, r_y)$ and step clockwise along the elliptical path in the first quadrant, shifting from unit steps in x to unit steps in y when the slope becomes less than -1. Alternatively, we could start at $(r_x, 0)$ and select points in a counterclockwise order, shifting from unit steps in y to unit steps in x when the slope becomes greater than -1. With parallel processors, we could calculate pixel positions in the two regions simultaneously. As an example of a sequential implementation of the midpoint algorithm, we take the start position at $(0, r_y)$ and step along the ellipse path in clockwise order throughout the first quadrant.

We define an ellipse function from C with $(x_c, y_c) = (0,0)$ as,

$$f_{ellipse}(x,y) = r_y^2 x^2 + r_x^2 y^2 - r_x^2 r_y^2$$

This has the following properties:

$$f_{ellipse}(x, y) \quad \begin{array}{l} <0 \text{ if}(x, y) \text{ is inside the ellipse boundary} \\ =0 \text{ if}(x, y) \text{ is on the ellipse boundary} \\ >0 \text{if}(x, y) \text{ is outside the ellipse boundary} \end{array}$$

Thus, the ellipse function $f_{ellipse}(x, y)$ serves as the decision parameter in the midpoint algorithm. At each sampling position, we select the next pixel along the ellipse path according to the sign of the ellipse function evaluated at the midpoint between the two candidate pixels.

Midpoint Ellipse Algorithm

- Input rx, ry and ellipse center (xc, yc), and obtain the first point on an ellipse centered on the origin as:

  $(x_0, y_0) = (0, r_y)$

- Calculate the initial value of the decision parameter in region 1 as:

- $p1_0 = r_y^2 - r_x^2 r_y + (1/4)r_x^2$

  At each xk position in region 1, starting at k = 0, perform the following test: If plk< 0, the next point along the ellipse centered on (0, 0) is (xk+1, yk) and,

  $p1_{k+1} = p1_k + 2r_y^2 x_{k+1} + r_y^2$

Otherwise, the next point along the circle is $(x_k + 1, y_k - 1)$,

$$p1_{k+1} = p1_k + 2r^2_y x_{k+1} - 2r^2_x y_{k+1} r^2_y$$

with,

$$2r^2_y x_{k+1} = 2r^2_y x_k + 2r^2_y$$

$$2r^2_x y_{k+1} = 2r^2_x y_k - 2r^2_x$$

and continue until $2r^2_y x \geq 2r^2_x y$.

- Calculate the initial value of the decision parameter in region 2 using the last point (x0, y0) calculated in region 1 as:

$$p2_0 = r^2_y \left(x_0 + (1/2) \right)^2 + r^2_x \left(y_0 - 1 \right)^2 - r^2_x r^2_y$$

- At each yk position in region 2, starting at k = 0, perform the following test: If p2k>0, the next point along the ellipse centered on (0, 0) is (xk, yk-1) and,

$$p2_{k+1} = p2_k - 2r^2_x y_{k+1} + r^2_x$$

Otherwise, the next point along the circle is $(x_k + 1, y_k - 1)$ and,

$$p2_{k+1} = p2_k + 2r^2_y x_{k+1} - 2r^2_x y_{k+1} + r^2_x$$

Using the same incremental calculations for x and y as in region 1.

- Determine symmetry points in the other three quadrants.

- Move each calculated pixel position (x, y) onto the elliptical path centered on(xc, yc) and plot the coordinate values:

$$x = x + x_c \quad y = y + y_c$$

- Repeat the steps for region 1 until $2r^2_y x \geq 2r^2_x y$.

Example: Given input ellipse parameters $r_x = 8$ and $r_y = 6$, we illustrate the steps in the midpoint ellipse algorithm by determining raster positions along the ellipse path in the first quadrant. Initial values and increments for the decision parameter calculations are:

$$2r^2_y x = 0 \left(\text{with increment } 2r^2_y = 72 \right)$$

$$2r^2_x y = 2r^2_x r_y \left(\text{withincrement} - 2r^2_x = -128 \right)$$

For region 1: The initial point for the ellipse centered on the origin is $(x_o, y_o) = (0, 6)$and the initial decision parameter value is,

$$p1_0 = r^2_y - r^2_x ry + (1/4)r^2_x = -332$$

Successive decision parameter values and positions along the ellipse path are calculated using the midpoint method as,

k	$p1_k$	(x_{k+1}, y_{k+1})	$2r^2_y x_{k+1}$	$2r^2 xyk+1$
0	-332	(1,6)	72	768
1	-224	(2,6)	144	768
2	44	(3,6)	216	768
3	208	(4,5)	288	640
4	-108	(5,5)	360	640
5	288	(6,4)	432	512
6	244	(7,3)	504	384

We now move out of region 1, since $2r^2_y x > 2r^2_x y$

For region 2, the initial point is $(x_0, y_0) = (7,3)$ and the initial decision parameter is,

$$p2_0 = f(7+(1/2),2) = -151$$

The remaining positions along the ellipse path in the first quadrant are then calculated as,

k	$P2_k$	(x_{k+1}, y_{k+1})	$2r^2_y x_{k+1}$	$2r^2_x y_{k+1}$
0	-151	(8,2)	576	256
1	233	(8,1)	576	128
2	745	(8,0)	-	-

References

- Euclidean-geometry, maths: byjus.com, Retrieved 19, February 2020

- Computer-graphics-dda-algorithm: javatpoint.com, Retrieved 29, May 2020

- Line-generation-algorithm, computer-graphics: tutorialspoint.com, Retrieved 10, March 2020

- Mid-point-circle-drawing-algorithm: geeksforgeeks.org, Retrieved 16, January 2020

- Computer-graphics-bresenhams-circle-algorithm: javatpoint.com, Retrieved 25, June 2020

- Computer-graphics-first-module-second: ercankoclar.com, Retrieved 17, April 2020

4

3D Computer Graphics

The graphics that use a representation of three dimensional geometric data stored in a computer in order to perform calculations is termed as 3D. The concepts explained in this chapter will help in gaining a better perspective about 3D computer graphics as well as 3D geometry modelling and 3D transformations.

3D computer graphics (in contrast to 2D computer graphics) are graphics that utilize a three-dimensional representation of geometric data that is stored in the computer for the purposes of performing calculations and rendering 2D images. Such images may be for later display or for real-time viewing.

Despite these differences, 3D computer graphics rely on many of the same algorithms as 2D computer vector graphics in the wire frame model and 2D computer raster graphics in the final rendered display. In computer graphics software, the distinction between 2D and 3D is occasionally blurred; 2D applications may use 3D techniques to achieve effects such as lighting, and primarily 3D may use 2D rendering techniques. 3D computer graphics are often referred to as 3D models. Apart from the rendered graphic, the model is contained within the graphical data file.

3D Viewing

Viewing in 3D involves the following considerations:

- We can view an object from any spatial position, eg.

  - In front of an object,

  - Behind the object,

  - In the middle of a group of objects,

  - Inside an object, etc.

- 3D descriptions of objects must be projected onto the flat viewing surface of the output device.

- The clipping boundaries enclose a volume of space.

Viewing Pipeline

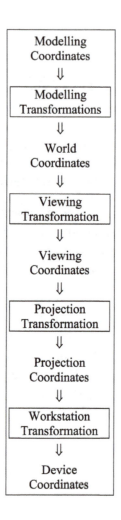

```
Modelling
Coordinates
    ⇓
Modelling
Transformations
    ⇓
World
Coordinates
    ⇓
Viewing
Transformation
    ⇓
Viewing
Coordinates
    ⇓
Projection
Transformation
    ⇓
Projection
Coordinates
    ⇓
Workstation
Transformation
    ⇓
Device
Coordinates
```

Explanation:

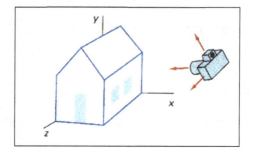

Modelling Transformation and Viewing Transformation can be done by 3D transformations. The viewing-coordinate system is used in graphics packages as a reference for specifying the observer viewing position and the position of the projection plane.

Projection operations convert the viewing-coordinate description to coordinate positions on the projection plane. (Involve clipping, visual-surface identification, and surface-rendering) Workstation transformation maps the coordinate positions on the projection plane to the output device.

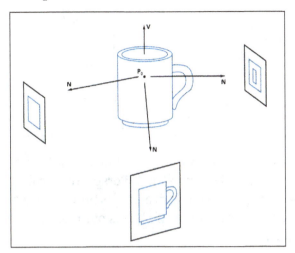

Viewing Transformation

Conversion of objection descriptions from world to viewing coordinates is equivalent to a transformation that superimposes the viewing reference frame onto the world frame using the basic geometric translate-rotate operations:

- Translate the view reference point to the origin of the world-coordinate system.

- Apply rotations to align the xv, yv, and zv axes (viewing coordinate system) with the world xw, yw, zw axes, respectively.

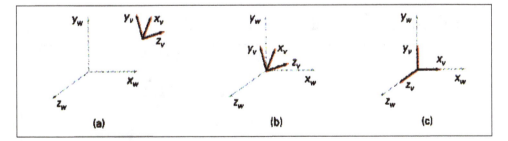

Projections

There are 2 basic projection methods:

- Parallel Projection transforms object positions to the view plane along parallel lines. A parallel projection preserves relative proportions of objects. Accurate views of the various sides of an object are obtained with a parallel projection. But not a realistic representation.

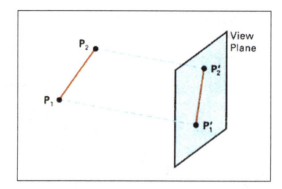

- Perspective Projection transforms object positions to the view plane while converging to a center point of projection. Perspective projection produces realistic views but does not preserve relative proportions. Projections of distant objects are smaller than the projections of objects of the same size that are closer to the projection plane.

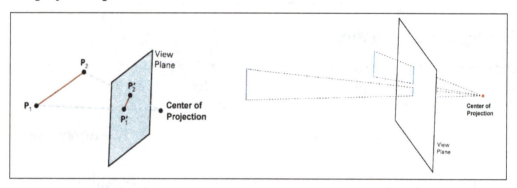

Parallel Projection

Classification: Orthographic Parallel Projection and Oblique Projection.

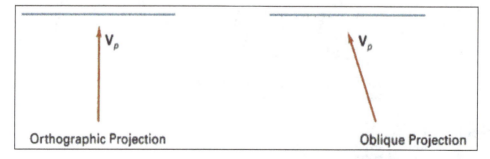

- Orthographic parallel projections are done by projecting points along parallel lines that are perpendicular to the projection plane.

- Oblique projections are obtained by projecting along parallel lines that are NOT perpendicular to the projection plane.

Some special Orthographic Parallel Projections involve Plan View (Top projection), Side Elevations, and Isometric Projection.

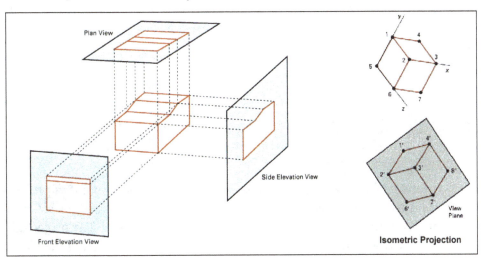

The following results can be obtained from oblique projections of a cube:

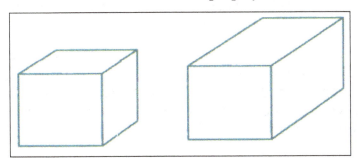

Perspective Projection

View Volumes

- View window: A rectangular area in the view plane which controls how much of the scene is viewed. The edges of the view window are parallel to the xv and yv viewing axes.

- View volume: Formed by the view window and the type of projection to be used. Only those objects within the view volume will appear in the generated display. So we can exclude objects that are beyond the view volume when we render the objects in the scene.

- A finite view volume is obtained by bounding with front plane and backplane (or the near plane and the far plane). Hence a view volume is bounded by 6 planes => rectangular parallelepiped or a frustum, for parallel projection and perspective projection respectively.

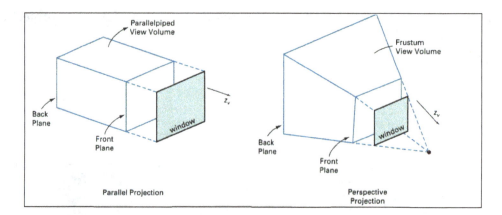

- Perspective effects depend on the positioning of the center point of projection. If it is close to the view plane, perspective effects are emphasised, ie. closer objects will appear larger than more distant objects of the same size. The projected size of an object is also affected by the relative position of the object and the view plane.

- 'Viewing' a static view: The view plane is usually placed at the viewing-coordinate origin and the center of projection is positioned to obtain the amount of perspective desired.

- 'Viewing' an animation sequence: Usually the center of projection point is placed at the viewing-coordinate origin and the view plane is placed in front of the scene. The size of the view window is adjusted to obtain the amount of scene desired. We move through the scene by moving the viewing reference frame (ie. the viewing coordinate system).

Clipping

The purpose of 3D clipping is to identify and save all surface segments within the view volume for display on the output device. All parts of objects that are outside the view volume are discarded. Thus the computing time is saved.

3D clipping is based on 2D clipping. To understand the basic concept we consider the following algorithm:

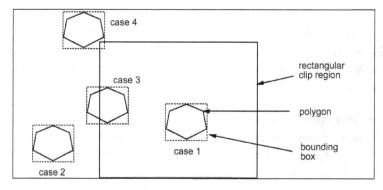

Polygon Clipping

Assuming the clip region is a rectangular area,

- The rectangular clip region can be represented by xmin, xmax, ymin and ymax.

- Find the bounding box for the polygon: ie. the smallest rectangle enclosing the entire polygon.

- Compare the bounding box with the clip region (by comparing their xmin, xmax, ymin and ymax).

- If the bounding box for the polygon is completely outside the clip region (case 2), the polygon is outside the clip region and no clipping is needed.

- If the bounding box for the polygon is completely inside the clip region (case 1), the polygon is inside the clip region and no clipping is needed.

- Otherwise, the bounding box for the polygon overlaps with the clip region (cases 3 and 4) and the polygon is likely to be partly inside and partly outside of the clip region. In that case, we clip the polygon against each of the 4 border lines of the clip region in sequence as follows:

  ○ Using the first vertex as the current vertex. If the point is in the inside of the border line, mark it as 'inside'. If it is outside, mark it as 'outside'.

  ○ Check the next vertex. Again mark it 'inside' or 'outside' accordingly.

  ○ Compare the current and the next vertices. If one is marked 'inside' and the other 'outside', the edge joining the 2 vertices crosses the border line.

  ○ In this case, we need to calculate where the edge intersects the border (ie. intersection between 2 lines).

  ○ The intersection point becomes a new vertex and we mark it as 'synthetic'.

  ○ Now we set the next vertex as the current vertex and the following vertex as the next vertex, and we repeat the same operations until all the edges of the polygon have been considered.

  ○ After the whole polygon has been clipped by a border, we throw away all the vertices marked 'outside' while keeping those marked as 'inside' or 'synthetic' to create a new polygon.

  ○ We repeat the clipping process with the new polygon against the next border line of the clip region.

- This clipping operation results in a polygon which is totally inside the clip region.

Hardware Implementations

Most graphics processes are now implemented in graphics chip sets. Hardware systems are now designed to transform, clip, and project objects to the output device for either 3D or 2D applications. In a typical arrangement, each of the individual chips in a chip set is responsible for geometric transformations, projection transformation, clipping, visible-surface identification, surface-shading procedure, octree representation processing, or ray-tracing etc., in a pipe-line way.

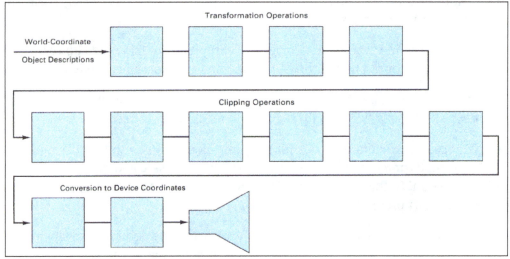

A hardware implementation of three-dimensional viewing operations using 12 chips for the coordinate transformations and clipping operations.

3D Geometric Modeling

3D models represent a 3D object using a collection of points in 3D space, connected by various geometric entities such as triangles, lines, curved surfaces, etc. Being a collection of data (points and other information), 3D models can be created by hand, algorithmically (procedural modeling), or scanned.

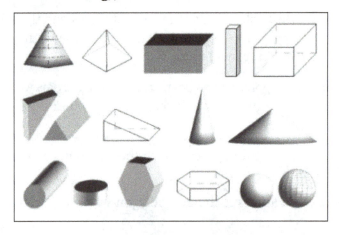

3D models are widely used anywhere in 3D graphics. Actually, their use predates the widespread use of 3D graphics on personal computers. Many computer games used pre-rendered images of 3D models as sprites before computers could render them in real-time.

Representation

Almost all 3D models can be divided into two categories:

- Solid: These models define the volume of the object they represent (like a rock). These are more realistic, but more difficult to build. Solid models are mostly used for nonvisual simulations such as medical and engineering simulations, for CAD and specialized visual applications such as ray tracing and constructive solid geometry.

- Shell/boundary: These models represent the surface, e.g. the boundary of the object, not its volume (like an infinitesimally thin eggshell). These are easier to work with than solid models. Almost all visual models used in games and film are shell models.

Compared to 2D Methods

3D photorealistic effects are often achieved without wireframe modeling and are sometimes indistinguishable in the final form. Some graphic art software includes filters that can be applied to 2D vector graphics or 2D raster graphics on transparent layers. Advantages of wireframe 3D modeling over exclusively 2D methods include:

- Flexibility, ability to change angles or animate images with quicker rendering of the changes.

- Ease of rendering, automatic calculation and rendering photorealistic effects rather than mentally visualizing or estimating.

- Accurate photorealism, less chance of human error in misplacing, overdoing, or forgetting to include a visual effect.

Disadvantages compare to 2D photorealistic rendering may include a software learning curve and difficulty achieving certain photorealistic effects. Some photorealistic effects may be achieved with special rendering filters included in the 3D modeling software. For the best of both worlds, some artists use a combination of 3D modeling followed by editing the 2D computer-rendered images from the 3D model.

Object Representations

Fundamentally an object is modelled in either of the two ways:

- Surface modeling (boundary representation).

- Solid Modeling (Space-partitioning representation).

Surface Modeling: Here we try to model only the outer surface / skin of the object that encloses the object, i.e., we ignore the inside of it assuming that the inside is empty space. Example techniques: Mesh, splines, NURBS, sweep representations.

Solid Modeling: Here we try to model the outside as well as inside of the object. Example techniques: Constructive Solid Geometry (CSG), Octrees, BSP Trees.

Just because the inside of an object is of less interest in general, it is the surface modeling that we will use often, but only when it is really necessary to model the inside we will go for solid modeling. It is also unnecessary and wastage of resources to model the inside of an object, when we never have something to do with the inside.

Polygonal/Mesh Modeling

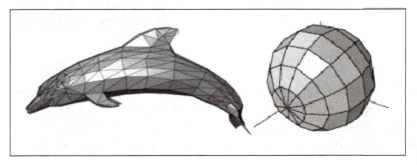

Let's look at the figures above, each of them are modelled using mesh. A Mesh is a collection of connected polygonal faces / polygons. i.e., we try to approximate the shape of an object by set of connected polygons. The process of modeling a surface using a collection of triangles is called triangulation or tessellation. If you observe the fish shape above, it is all triangles, but the sphere object is made up of quadrilaterals for its entire shape except for top and bottom parts which use triangles.

Consider the standard shapes as shown here, a standard Cube and a Cylinder. A cube has 6 polygonal faces that can be easily modelled using 6 connected polygons, while cylinder has one single curved surface which can be modelled using many thin connected polygonal strips as shown. So it can be inferred that with polygonal mesh modeling, surfaces that are flat are best modelled, while spherical or curved or other irregular surfaces can only be approximated. So cube is best modelled while cylindrical surface is approximated. The word 'approximation' is used while modeling non-flat surfaces because, we never get the true underlying surface using meshes, for instance, look at the sphere model above, its shape is only approximated by many connected polygons. The more the number of polygons used to model the better is the approximation to the underlying smoother surface. The essence is that we are trying to use flat planar polygons to model non-flat smoother/curved surfaces, the net effect is 'approximation'.

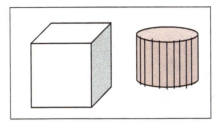

To construct or represent a shape using a polygonal Mesh, we need to start with vertices, connect them with edges, join edges to for polygons, connect many polygons to form a face/surface of the object. Observe the figure below.

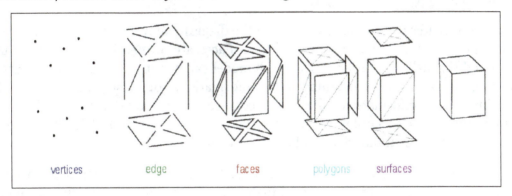

vertices   edge   faces   polygons   surfaces

Polygonal mesh data is represented by the data structure comprising of vertices, edges, faces, surfaces, surface normals. As shown in the figure below, mesh data is entered into various lists like, vertex list, edge list, surface / face list, normal list.

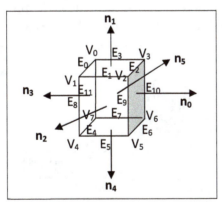

Vertex List – $\{V_0\ (x_0,y_0,z_0),\ V_1\ (x_1,y_1,z_1),\ V_2,\ ......,\ V_7(x_7,y_7,z_7)\}$

Edge List – $\{E_0 – (V_0V_1),$

$E_1 - (V_1V_2)$

$E_2 - (V_2V_3)$

$-------E_{11} – (V_0V_7)\},$

Face List – {S_0 (E_2, E_9, E_6, E_{10}),

$\quad$ S_1 (E_0, E_1, E_2, E_3),

$\quad$ S_2 (E_5, E_9, E_1, E_8),

$\quad$ S_3 (E_4, E_{11}, E_0, E_8),

$\quad$ S_4 (E_4, E_5, E_6, E_7),

$\quad$ S_5 (E_7, E_{10}, E_3, E_{11})}

Normal List – { n_0, n_1, n_2, n_3, n_4, n_5}

Consider a standard unit cube as shown in the diagram above. Vertices are where few or more edges meet. Edges connect vertices. Faces are formed by planes containing edges and Normals are for faces. The mesh model can be represented through various lists as given: Vertex list containing vertex information, Edge List (12 edges, E_0 to E_{11}) containing Edge information, where each edge connects two vertices, Face list (6 in number from S_0 to S_5), containing list of surfaces / faces, Normal List (6, from n_0 to n_5 one for each face) containing normal vector information.

It is important to store normal vector information for a face in the normal list. A normal is the direction perpendicular and outward to the plane of the polygon. This data is important because the orientation of a face towards the light source is better understood from its normal vector. It is also useful to compute the angle between the viewing direction and the direction of light source, which is a clue to compute the intensity of the pixel at point of incidence. These lists mentioned comprise the geometric information of the mesh model. Along with this we can also store attribute information (color, texture etc.,) in separate lists.

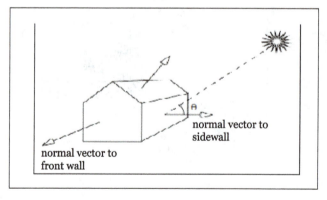

normal vector to sidewall

normal vector to front wall

Splines

These are purely mathematical modeling tools that can be used to model planar, or non-planar or curvy or irregular surfaces. Splines are used in automotive design, CAD etc., Splines are fundamentally space curves, and when they are extended in two different directions, they form spline surfaces. With spline surfaces we can model, flowing cloth, water bodies, wrap a spline surface around another object and much more. Spline curves give utmost flexibility to designers to design/model shapes of their choice. There are a variety of splines viz:

- Hermite Splines,

- Cardinal Splines,

- Bezier Splines,

- Basis Splines,

- NURBS (Non-Uniform Rational Basis Splines).

Any composite curve formed with polynomial sections satisfying specified continuity conditions at the boundary of the pieces. If the above definition is closely observed, it is evident that, a spline curve is formed by joining many smaller curves end to end to form a single continuous smoothly flowing spline curve, and at each joint the curve satisfies specified continuity conditions. Each of the smaller curves is a polynomial function, so the spline curve is a polynomial curve.

Spline Terminology

- Parametric forms,

- Control Points,

- Convex Hull,

- Boundary conditions,

- Order and degree,

- Approximating,

- Interpolating,

- Blending functions,

- Local Control,

- Basis,

- Cox-De Boor recurrence relations.

Spline curves are represented in parametric form, which uses a parameter U that varies in the range 0 to 1.

P (u) = (x (u), y (u), z (u)) where the parameter u varies from 0 to 1.

For a cubic spline:

$$x(u) = a_x u^3 + b_x u^2 + c_x u + d_x$$

$$y(u) = a_y u^3 + b_y u^2 + c_y u + d_y \quad 0 \leq u \leq 1$$

$$z(u) = a_z u^3 + b_z u^2 + c_z u + d_z$$

$$P(u) = au^3 + bu^2 + cu + d$$

The curve P (U) is a cubic parametric curve, and is a function of x(u), y(u), z(u), each of which is a cubic parametric polynomial curve by itself. And coefficients, a (a_x, a_y, a_z), b(b_x, b_y, b_z) and c (c_x, c_y, c_z) are vectors. The parameter u is raised to the highest power 3 (called the degree of the curve), so we call the curve a cubic curve.

Due to the flexibility that the spline curve offers, the designer has the freedom to decide on the shape of the curve, i.e., the shape of the curve is fully controlled by the designers. The designer has the task of choosing or placing points in some sequence in 3D space, such that the points when connected or approximated by curves, gives the desired shape. It also similar to fitting a polynomial curve section on a given set of points placed strategically. These strategically positioned sequence of points that are meant to control the shape of the curve are called control points.

In real world there are many analogies to spline curves, for ex: while drawing kolams/ Rangolis during festive occasions, a set of dots are initially placed and they are approximated by curves of choice. Another example being, a road side welding shop where doors, windows, gates, grills of iron are made, it starts by placing long strips of iron on a table that has sequence of strategically arranged firm protrusions or posts on it and using a hand bender they bend the iron strip along the protrusions, to give it a nice curvy shape of choice. Curves that exactly touch these control points are called interpolating curves and curves that approximate the control points are called approximating curves.

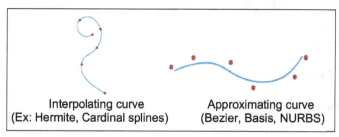

Interpolating curve
(Ex: Hermite, Cardinal splines)

Approximating curve
(Bezier, Basis, NURBS)

As spline is a piece-wise polynomial curve, the many smaller curve sections that make up the curve, must join smoothly at the boundary. To determine how smoothly curve sections join at the boundary, we need to check for boundary conditions / continuity conditions. There are two types of continuity checked for, parametric continuity and geometric continuity.

Parametric Continuity

Two curves, joining at a boundary are said to exhibit levels of continuity as below:

- C_0 (Zero-order) – curves meet

- C_1 (First-order) – tangents equal

- C_2 (Second-order) – curvatures equal

Two curves satisfying C^0 or Zeroeth – Order parametric continuity, just meet at the boundary. The two curves appear as if they have one common boundary position, but do not appear to join smoothly.

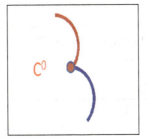

Two curves satisfying C^1 or first – Order parametric continuity, not only meet at the boundary, but their tangents are also equal. The two curves appear as if one curve is smoothly joining with the second curve.

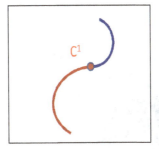

Two curves satisfying C^2 or second – Order parametric continuity, not only meet at the boundary, but their tangents are also equal, and their curvatures are also equal. The two sections appear as if they are pieces of one single smooth curve joined together.

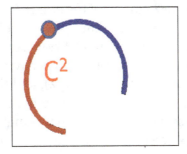

The higher the degree of the curve sections, the smoother they will be joining at the boundary. Some more examples of splines are shown below.

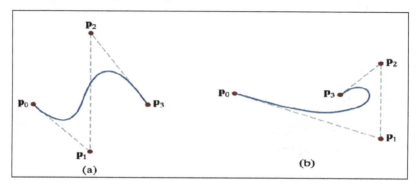

In the above figures, the spline curve is formed by 4 control points, P_0, P_1, P_2, and P_3. The curve touches P_0 and P_3 and approximates P_1, and P_2.

Wire Frame Models

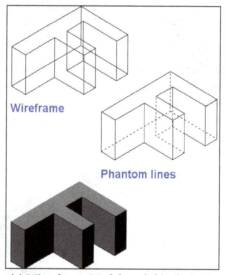

(a) Wire-frame Model; and (b) of a Part.

A wire-frame model of an object is the simplest, but more verbose, geometric model that can be used to represent it mathematically in the computer. It is sometimes referred to as a stick figure or an edge representation of the object. The word "wire-frame" is related to the fact that one may image a wire that is bent to follow the object edges to generate the model. Typically, a wire-frame model consists entirely of points, lines, arcs and circles, conics, and curves. For example, a user may, with three dimensional (3-D) wire-frame models, enter 3-D vertices, say (x, y, z), and then join the vertices to form a 3-D object. An example of 3-D object and its wire-frame model are shown in Figure. Wire-frame modeling is the most commonly used technique and is available in all commercial CAD/CAM systems. Wire-frame modeling is considered a natural extension of traditional methods of drafting. Consequently, it does not require extensive training of users; nor does it demand the use of unusual terminology as surfaces and solids.

Early wire-frame modeling techniques, developed in the 1960s, were strictly two dimensional and were designed to automate drafting and simple NC program verification. In those days, users had to construct the geometry of an object in the desired views independently due to the lack of centralized database systems. Later, in the early 1970s, the centralized database concept enabled modeling of three-dimensional objects as wireframe models that can be subject to three-dimensional transformations. Creating geometry in one view is automatically projected and displayed in other views. This enhances user utilization by saving time and flexibility over manual design and drafting. The major advantage of wire-frame modeling is its simplicity in construction of a model. Therefore, it does not require as much computer time and memory as does surface or solid modeling. However, the user time needed to prepare and/or input data is substantial and increases rapidly with the complexity of the object being modeled. Wire-frame models form the basis for surface models. Most existing surface algorithms require wire-frame entities to generate surfaces. Lastly, the CPU time required to retrieve, edit, or update a wire-frame model is usually small compared to surface or solid models.

Limitations of Wire-frame Modeling

Although wire-frame modeling is simple and straightforward in concept, it has a number of limitations as given below:

- From the point of view of engineering applications, it is not possible to calculate volume and mass properties of a design. Other applications, such as NC path generation, cross-sectioning, and interference detection also encounter problems when wire-frame modeling is used. Because the wire-frame model database contains only low-level information such as points and lines, the wire-frame methods are limited in scope when high-level information is required by particular applications such as process planning.

- In the wire-frame representation, the virtual edges (profile or silhouette) are not usually provided. For example, a cylinder is represented by three edges, that is, two circles and one straight line. But the straight line is not enough to represent the profile or silhouette of a cylinder.

- There are many wire-frame representation schemes. However, ambiguous representations of real objects may be created. For example, the wire-frame model, shown in figure, may be recognized as either a block or an inward corner. Figure may be considered as either a boss or a hole. Figure is just a nonsense object.

- The creation of wire-frame models usually involves more user effort to input necessary information than that of solid models, especially for large and complex parts. For example, consider the creation of a 3-D model of a simple cube. In the wire-frame model, we need to draw 12 lines, whereas with solid modeling methods a cube may be created by providing the positions of three corner points. Furthermore, the latter model provides more information, such as the inside or outside of the part.

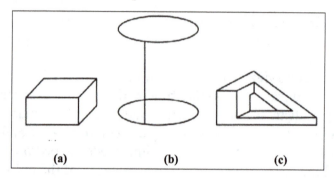

(a) (b) (c)

Wire-frame Entities

All the existing CAD/CAM systems provide users with basic wire-frame entities. Most of the wire-frame models consists of points, lines and arcs, which are the basic entities of model. The entities can be divided into analytical entities and synthetic entities. Analytical entities include points, lines, arcs and circles, fillets and chamfers and conics such as ellipse, parabola and hyperbola. Various types of splines such as cubic spline, β-spline, β and γ-splines and Bezier curves are synthetic entities. Entities are building blocks of geometric models hence mathematical treatment of entities would provide insight into CAD/CAM. Mathematical representation of these entities are given in table.

Absolute coordinate system point by its coordinates P (x, y, z).	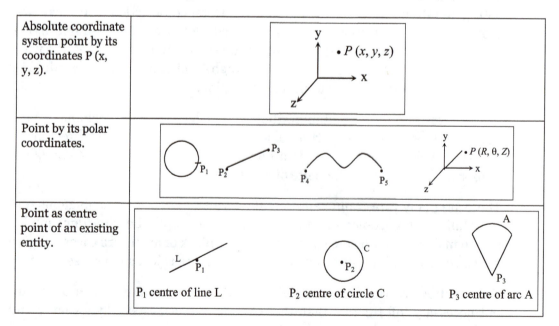
Point by its polar coordinates.	
Point as centre point of an existing entity.	

P₁ centre of line L   P₂ centre of circle C   P₃ centre of arc A

Defining Lines	
Line by two points	
Parallel to or Perpendicular to an existing line	
Tangent to a given circle and passing through a point	
Tangent to two given circles	
Defining Arcs and Circles	
Circle by radius and centre point	
Circle by three points	
Centre and a point on the circle	
Circle by centre and tangent line	
Define Synthetic Entities	
Ellipse by centre and axes length	

Ellipse by four points	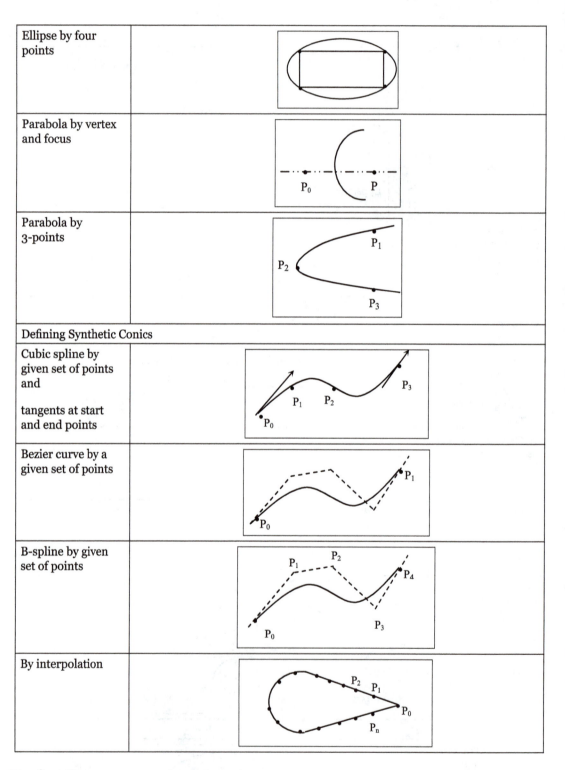
Parabola by vertex and focus	
Parabola by 3-points	
Defining Synthetic Conics	
Cubic spline by given set of points and tangents at start and end points	
Bezier curve by a given set of points	
B-spline by given set of points	
By interpolation	

Bezier Curves

Bezier curves are used in computer graphics to produce curves which appear reasonably smooth at all scales. This spline approximation method was developed by French engineer Pierre Bezier for automobile body design. Bezier spline was designed in such a manner that they are very useful and convenient for curve and surface design, and are easy to implement Curves are trajectories of moving points. We will specify them as functions assigning a location of that moving point (in 2D or 3D) to a parameter t, i.e., parametric curves.

Curves are useful in geometric modeling and they should have a shape which has a clear and intuitive relation to the path of the sequence of control points. One family of curves satisfying this requirement is Bezier curve.

The Bezier curve requires only two end points and other points that control the endpoint tangent vector. Bezier curve is defined by a sequence of N + 1 control points, P_0, $P_1, \ldots, P_n$. We defined the Bezier curve using the algorithm (invented by DeCasteljeau), based on recursive splitting of the intervals joining the consecutive control points.

A purely geometric construction for Bezier splines which does not rely on any polynomial formulation, and is extremely easy to understand. The DeCasteljeau method is an algorithm which performs repeated bi-linear interpolation to compute splines of any order.

De Casteljeau algorithm and Surfaces : The control points P0, P1, P2 and P3are joined with line segments called 'control polygon', even though they are not really a polygon but rather a polygonal curve.

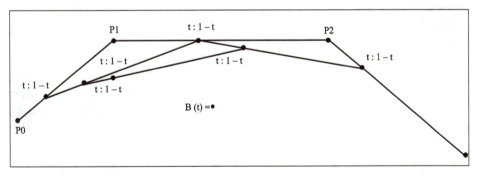

Each of them is then divided in the same ratio t: 1- t, giving rise to the another points. Again, each consecutive two are joined with line segments, which are subdivided and so on, until only one point is left. This is the location of our moving point at time t. The trajectory of that point for times between 0 and 1 is the Bezier curve.

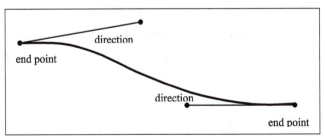

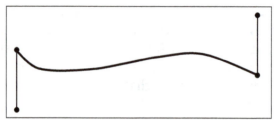

(a): Beizer curve defined by its endpoint vector. (b): All sorts of curves can be specified with different direction vectors at the end points.

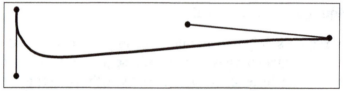

(c): Reflex curves appear when you set the vectors in different directions.

A simple method for constructing a smooth curve that followed a control polygon p with m-1 vertices for small value of m, the Bezier techniques work well. However, as m grows large (m>20) Bezier curves exhibit some undesirable properties.

In general, a Bezier curve section can be fitted to any number of control points. The number of control points to be approximated and their relative positions determine the degree of the Bezier polynomial. As with the interpolation splines, a Bezier curve can be specified with boundary conditions, with a characterizing matrix, or with blending function. For general Bezier curves, the blending-function specification is the most convenient.

Suppose we are given $n + 1$ control-point positions: $p_k = (x_k, y_k, z_k)$ with k varying from o to n. These coordinate points can be blended to produce the following position vector P (u), which describes the path of an approximating Bezier polynomial function between and p_o p_n .

$$p(u) = \sum_{k=0}^{n} p_k b_{k,n}(u), \ 0 \le u \le 1$$

The Bezier blending functions $B_{k,n}(u)$ are the Bernstein polynomials.

$$B_{k,n}(u) = C(n,k) u^k (1-u)^{n-k}$$

Where the C(n, k) are the binomial coefficients:

$$C(n,k) = nC_k = \frac{n!}{k!(n-k)!}$$

Equivalently, we can define Bezier blending functions with the recursive calculation.

$$B_{k,n}(u) = (1-u)B_{k,n-1}(u) + uB_{k-1,n-1}(u), \; n > k \geq 1$$

With $BEZ_{k,k} = u^k$, and $B_{0,k} = (1-u)^k$. Vector equation $p(u) = \sum_{k=0}^{n} p_k b_{k,n}(u), \; 0 \leq u \leq 1$ represents a set of three parametric equations for the individual curve coordinates:

$$x(u) \sum_{k=0}^{n} x_k B_{k,n}(u)$$

$$y(u) \sum_{k=0}^{n} y_k B_{k,n}(u)$$

$$z(u) \sum_{k=0}^{n} z_k B_{k,n}(u)$$

As a rule, a Bezier curve is a polynomial of degree one less than the number of control points used: Three points generate a parabola, four points a cubic curve, and so forth. Figure below demonstrates the appearance of some Bezier curves for various selections of control points in the xy plane (z = 0). With certain control-point placements, however, we obtain degenerate Bezier polynomials. For example, a Bezier curve generated with three collinear control points is a straight-line segment. And a set of control points that are all at the same coordinate position produces a Bezier "curve" that is a single point.

Bezier curves are commonly found in painting and drawing packages, as well as CAD system, since they are easy to implement and they are reasonably powerful in curve design. Efficient methods for determining coordinate position along a Bezier curve can be set up using recursive calculations. For example, successive binomial coefficients can be calculated as shown below through examples of two-dimensional Bezier curves generated from three, four, and five control points. Dashed lines connect the control-point positions.

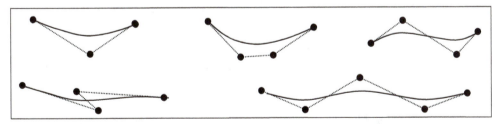

Properties of Bezier Curves

A very useful property of a Bezier curve is that it always passes through the first and last control points. That is, the boundary conditions at the two ends of the curve are:

$$P(0) = p_0$$
$$P(1) = p_n$$

Values of the parametric first derivatives of a Bezier curve at the end points can be calculated from control-point coordinates as,

$$P'(0) = -np_0 + np_1$$
$$P'(1) = np_{n-1} + np_n$$

Thus, the slope at the beginning of the curve is along the line joining the first two control points, and the slope at the end of the curve is along the line joining the last two endpoint. Similarly, the parametric second derivatives of a Bezier curve at the endpoints are calculated as,

$$p''(0) = n)n-1)\left[(p_2 - p_1) - (p_1 - p_0)\right]$$
$$p''(1) = n)n-1)\left[(p_{n-2} - p_{n-1}) - (p_{n-1} - p_n)\right]$$

Another important property of any Bezier curve is that it lies within the convex hull (convex polygon boundary) of the control points. This follows from the properties of Bezier blending functions: They are all positive and their sum is always 1,

$$\sum_{k=0}^{n} B_{k,n}(u) = 1$$

so that any curve position is simply the weighted sum of the control-point positions. The convex-hull property for a Bezier curve ensures that the polynomial will not have erratic oscillations.

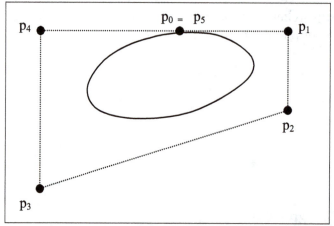

(a): Shows closed Bezier curve generated by specifying
the first and last control points at the same location.

To ensure the smooth transition from one section of a piecewise parametric curve or any Bezier curve to the next we can impose various continuity conditions at the connection point for parametric continuity we match parametric derivatives of adjoining curve section at their common boundary.

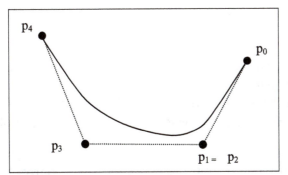

(b): Shows that a Bezier curve can be made to pass closer to a given coordinate position by assigning multiple control points to that position.

Zero order parametric continuity described by C^0 continuity means curves are only meeting as shown in figure while first order parametric continuity referred as C^1 continuity, means that tangent of successive curve sections are equal at their joining point. Second order parametric continuity or C^2 continuity, means that the parametric derivatives of the two curve sections are equal at the intersection. As shown in figure below first order continuity have equal tangent vector but magnitude may not be the same.

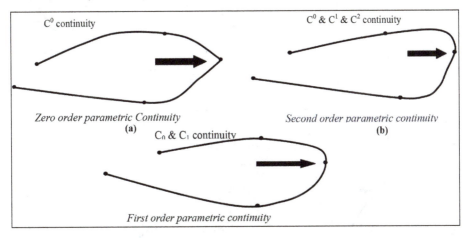

With the second order continuity, the rate of change of tangent vectors for successive section is equal at intersection thus results in smooth tangent transition from one section to another. First order continuity is often used in digitized drawing while second order continuity is used in CAD drawings.

Geometric continuity is another method to join two successive curve sections. G^0 continuity is the same as parametric continuity (i.e., two curves sections to be joined must have same coordinate position at the boundary point) i.e., curve section are joined together such that they have same coordinates position at the boundary point. First order geometric continuity $G^{(1)}$ means that the tangent vectors are the same at join point of two successive curves i.e., the parametric first derivative are proportional at the intersection of two successive sections while second order geometric continuity is G^2 means that both first and second order parametric derivates of the two curve sections are proportional at their boundary. In G^2 curvature of the two successive curve sections will match at the joining position.

Curves such as Spline curve, cubic spline curve are curve fitting method used to produce a smooth curve given a set of points throughout out the path weight are distributed. Spline is used in graphics to specify animation paths, to digitize drawings for computer storage mainly CAD application, use them for automobile bodies design in aircraft design, etc.

Spline curve is constructed using Control points which control the shape of the curve Spline curve is a composite curve formed with sections which are polynomial in nature. These pieces are joined together in such a manner that continuity condition at boundary is maintained. A piecewise parametric polynomial section when passes through each control point curve is known to Interpolate the set of control points refer figure. On the other hand when polynomial is not fitted to the set to very control point it is known to approximate the set of control points.

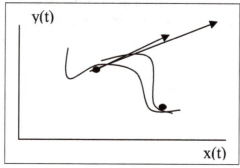

(a): Interpolating curve.

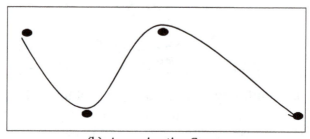

(b): Approximating Curve.

Bezier Surfaces

Two sets of Bezier curve can be used to design an object surface by specifying by an input mesh of control points. The Bézier surface is formed as the cartesian product of the blending functions of two Bézier curves.

$$P(u,v) = \sum_{j=0}^{m} \sum_{k=0}^{n} P_{j,k} B_{j,m}(v) B_{k,n}(u)$$

With $p_{j,k}$ specifying the location of the (m + 1) by (n + 1) control points.

The corresponding properties of the Bézier curve apply to the Bézier surface. The surface does not in general pass through the control points except for the corners of the control point grid. The surface is contained within the convex hull of the control points.

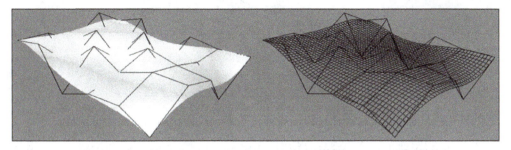

The control points are connected via a dashed line, and solid lenes shows curves of constant u and constant v. Each curve is ploted by varying v over the interval from 0 to 1, with u fixed at one of the values in this unit interval curves of constant v are plotted.

Figures (a), (b), (c) illustrate Bezier surface plots. The control points are connected by dashed lines, and the solid lines show curves of constant u and constant v. Each curve of constant u is plotted by varying v over the interval from 0 to 1, with u fixed at one of the values in this unit interval. Curves of constant v are plotted similarly.

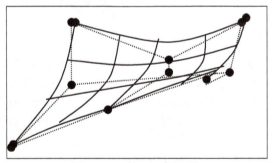

(a): Bezier surfaces constructed for m=3, n=3, Dashed lines connect the control points.

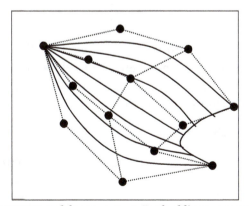

(b): Bezier surfaces constructed for m=4, n=4. Dashed lines connect the control points.

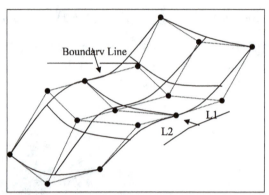

(c): Composite Bezier surface constructed with two Bezier sections, joined at
the indicated boundary line. The dashed lines connect specified control points.

In Figure (c) first-order continuity is established by making the ratio of length L1 to
length L2 constant for each collinear line of control points across the boundary between the surface sections. Figure (c) also illustrates a surface formed with two Bezier
sections. As with curves, a smooth transition from one section to the other is assured by
establishing both zero-order and first-order continuity at the boundary line. Zero-order
continuity is obtained by matching control points at the boundary. First order continuity is obtained by choosing control points along a straight line across the boundary
and by maintaining a constant ration of collinear line segments for each set of specified
control points across section boundaries.

Hermite Splines

Hermite curves are very easy to calculate but also very powerful. They are used to smoothly
interpolate between key-points (like object movement in keyframe animation or camera
control). Understanding the mathematical background of hermite curves will help you to
understand the entire family of splines. Maybe you have some experience with 3D programming and have already used them without knowing that (the so called kb-splines, curves
with control over tension, continuity and bias are just a special form of the hermite curves).

The Math

To keep it simple we first start with some simple stuff. We also only talk about 2-di-
mensional curves here. If you need a 3D curve just do with the z-coordinate what you
do with y or x. Hermite curves work in in any number of dimensions. To calculate a
hermite curve you need the following vectors:

- $P1$: The startpoint of the curve.

- $T1$: The tangent (e.g. direction and speed) to how the curve leaves the startpoint.

- $P2$: The endpoint of the curve.

- $T2$: The tangent (e.g. direction and speed) to how the curves meets the endpoint.

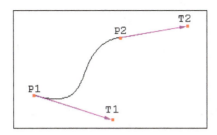

These 4 vectors are simply multiplied with 4 hermite basis functions and added together.

$$h1(s) = 2s^3 - 3s^2 + 1$$

$$h2(s) = -2s^3 + 3s^2$$

$$h3(s) = s^3 - 2s^2 + s$$

$$h4(s) = s^3 - s^2$$

Below are the 4 graphs of the 4 functions (from left to right: h1, h2, h3, h4).

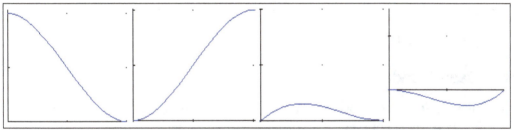

All graphs except the 4th have been plotted from 0,0 to 1,1.

Take a closer look at functions h1 and h2:

- h1 starts at 1 and goes slowly to 0.

- h2 starts at 0 and goes slowly to 1.

Now multiply the startpoint with h1 and the endpoint with h2. Lets go from 0 to 1 to interpolate between start and endpoint. h3 and h4 are applied to the tangents in the same manner. They make sure that the curve bends in the desired direction at the start and endpoint.

The Math in Matrix Form

All this stuff can be expessed with some vector and matrix algebra.

- Vector S: The interpolation-point and it's powers up to 3:

- Vector C: The parameters of our hermite curve:

- Matrix h: The matrix form of the 4 hermite polynomials:

$$| s^3 | \qquad | P_1 | \qquad | 2 \ {-2} \ 1 \ 1 |$$

$$S = \begin{vmatrix} s^2 \\ s^1 \\ 1 \end{vmatrix} \quad C = \begin{vmatrix} P2 \\ T1 \\ T2 \end{vmatrix} \quad h = \begin{vmatrix} -3 & 3 & -2 & -1 \\ 0 & 0 & 1 & 0 \\ 1 & 0 & 0 & 0 \end{vmatrix}$$

To calculate a point on the curve you build the Vector S, multiply it with the matrix h and then multiply with C.

$P = S * h * C$

This matrix-form is valid for all cubic polynomial curves. The only thing that changes is the polynomial matrix. For example, if you want to draw a Bezier curve instead of hermites you might use this matrix:

$$b = \begin{vmatrix} -1 & 3 & -3 & 1 \\ 3 & -6 & 3 & 0 \\ -3 & 3 & 0 & 0 \\ 1 & 0 & 0 & 0 \end{vmatrix}$$

Some Pseudocode

Sure, this C-style pseudo-code won't compile. C doesn't come with a power function, and unless you wrote yourself a vector-class any compiler would generate hundreds of errors and make you feel like an idiot. It's better to present this code in a more abstract form.

```
moveto (P1);                            // move pen to startpoint

for (int t=0; t < steps; t++)

{

   float s = (float)t / (float)steps;   // scale s to go from 0 to 1

   float h1 =  2s^3 - 3s^2 + 1;         // calculate basis function 1

   float h2 = -2s^3 + 3s^2;             // calculate basis function 2

   float h3 =   s^3 - 2*s^2 + s;        // calculate basis function 3

   float h4 =   s^3 -   s^2;            // calculate basis function 4

   vector p = h1*P1 +                   // multiply and sum all funtions

            h2*P2 +                     // together to build the in-
terpolated

            h3*T1 +                     // point along the curve.
```

```
        h4*T2;

  lineto (p)                              // draw to calculated point on
the curve

}
```

Getting Rid of the Tangents

Controlling the tangents is not easy. It's hard to guess what a curve will look like if you have to define it. Also, to make a sharply bending curve you have to drag the tangent-points far away from the curve. we will see how we can turn hermite curves into cardinal splines.

Cardinal Splines

Cardinal splines are just a subset of the hermite curves. They don't need the tangent points because they will be calculated from the control points. We'll lose some of the flexibility of the hermite curves, but as a tradeoff the curves will be much easier to use. The formula for the tangents for cardinal splines is a constant which affects the tightness of the curve.

$$T_i = a * (P_{i+1} - P_{i-1})$$

Catmull-Rom splines

The Catmull-Rom spline is again just a subset of the cardinal splines. You only have to define a as 0.5, and you can draw and interpolate Catmull-Rom splines.

$$T_i = 0.5 * (P_{i+1} - P_{i-1})$$

Catmull-Rom splines are great if you have some data-points and just want to interpolate smoothly between them.

The Kochanek-Bartels Splines

Now we're going down to the guts of curve interpolation. The kb-splines (mostly known from Autodesk's 3d-Studio Max and Newtek's Lightwave) are nothing more than hermite curves and a handfull of formulas to calculate the tangents. These curves have been introduced by D. Kochanek and R. Bartels in 1984 to give animators more control over keyframe animation. They introduced three control-values for each keyframe point:

- Tension: How sharply does the curve bend?

- Continuity: How rapid is the change in speed and direction?

- Bias: What is the direction of the curve as it passes through the keypoint?

The "incoming" Tangent equation:

$$TS_i = \frac{(1-t)*(1-c)*(1+b)}{2}*(P_i - P_{i-1})$$
$$+ \frac{(1-t)*(1+c)*(1-b)}{2}*(P_{i+1} - P_i)$$

The "outgoing" Tangent equation:

$$TD_i = \frac{(1-t)*(1-c)*(1+b)}{2}*(P_i - P_{i-1})$$
$$+ \frac{(1-t)*(1+c)*(1-b)}{2}*(P_{i+1} - P_i)$$

When you want to interpolate the curve you should use this vector:

C =
| P(i) |
| P(i+1) |
| TD(i) |
| TS(i+1) |

You might notice that you always need the previous and next point if you want to calculate the curve. This might be a problem when you try to calculate keyframe data from Lightwave or 3D-Studio.

Speed Control

If you write yourself keyframe-interpolation code and put it into a program you'll notice one problem. Unless you have your keyframes in fixed intervals you will have a sudden change of speed and direction whenever you pass a keyframe-point. This can be avoided if you take the number of key-positions (frames) between two keyframes into account:

N is the number of frames (seconds, whatever) between two keypoints.

$$TD_i = TD_i * \frac{2*N_{i-1}}{N_{i-1}+N_i} \qquad \text{adjustment of outgoing tangent}$$

$$TS_i = TS_i * \frac{2*N_{i-1}}{N_{i-1}+N_i} \qquad \text{adjustment of incoming tangent}$$

B-Splines

The B-Spline Curve – Analytical

A B-spline curve P(t), is defined by:

$$P(t) = \sum_{i=0}^{n} P_i N_{i,k}(t)$$

Where,

- The {Pi : i = 0, 1, ..., n} are the control points.

- k is the order of the polynomial segments of the B-spline curve. Order k means that the curve is made up of piecewise polynomial segments of degree k – 1.

- The Ni,k(t) are the "normalized B-spline blending functions". They are described by the order k and by a non-decreasing sequence of real numbers {ti : i = 0, ..., n + k} .

Normally called the "knot sequence". The Ni,k functions are described as follows:

$$N_{i,1}(t) = \begin{cases} 1 & \text{if } u \in [t_i, t_{i+1}), \\ 0 & \text{otherwise} \end{cases}$$

and if k > 1,

$$N_{i,k}(t) = \frac{t - t_i}{t_{i+k-1} - t_i} N_{i,k-1}(t) + \frac{t_{i+k} - t}{t_{i+k} - t_{i+1}} N_{i+1,k-1}(t)$$

- And $t \in [t_{k-1}, t_{n+1})$.

We note that if, in equation, either of the N terms on the right hand side of the equation are zero, or the subscripts are out of the range of the summation limits, then the associated fraction is not evaluated and the term becomes zero. This is to avoid a zero-over-zero evaluation problem. We also direct the reader's attention to the "closed-open" interval in the equation.

The order k is independent of the number of control points (n + 1). In the B-Spline curve, unlike the Bezier Curve, we have the flexibility of using many control points, and restricting the degree of the polymonial segments.

The B-Spline Curve – Geometric

Given a set of Control Points {P_0, P_1, ..., P_n}, an order k, and a set of knots {t_0, t_1, ..., t_{n+k}}, the B-Spline curve of order k is defined to be,

$$P(t) = P_l^{(k-1)}(t) \text{ if } u \in [t_l, t_{l+1})$$

Where,

$$P_i^{(j)} = \begin{cases} \left(1-\tau_i^j\right)P_{i-1}^{(j-1)}(t) + \tau_i^j P_i^{(j-1)}(t) & \text{if } j > 0, \\ P_i & \text{if } j = 0. \end{cases}$$

and,

$$\tau_i^j = \frac{t - t_i}{t_{i+k-j} - t_i}$$

It is useful to view the geometric construction as the following pyramid:

$$\vdots$$

$$\mathbf{P}_{l-k+1}$$
$$\qquad \mathbf{P}_{l-k+2}^{(1)}$$
$$\mathbf{P}_{l-k+2} \qquad\qquad \mathbf{P}_{l-k+3}^{(2)}$$
$$\qquad \mathbf{P}_{l-k+3}^{(1)} \qquad .$$
$$\mathbf{P}_{l-k+3}$$
$$\qquad\qquad .$$
$$\mathbf{P}_{l-k+4}$$
$$\qquad . \qquad\qquad\qquad\qquad \mathbf{P}_{l-1}^{(k-2)}$$
$$\qquad . \qquad\qquad\qquad\qquad\qquad\qquad \mathbf{P}_l^{(k-1)}$$
$$\qquad . \qquad\qquad\qquad\qquad \mathbf{P}_l^{(k-2)}$$
$$\qquad .$$
$$\mathbf{P}_{l-2} \qquad\qquad \mathbf{P}_{l-1}^{(2)}$$
$$\qquad \mathbf{P}_{l-1}^{(1)} \qquad .$$
$$\mathbf{P}_{l-1} \qquad\qquad \mathbf{P}_l^{(2)}$$
$$\qquad \mathbf{P}_l^{(1)}$$
$$\mathbf{P}_l$$
$$\vdots$$

Any P in this pyramid is calculated as a convex combination of the two P functions immediately to its left.

5

Diverse Aspects of Computer Graphics

There are many applications of computer graphics. Some of them are special effects, web design, computer generated imagery, scientific visualization, morphing, etc. These diverse applications of computer graphics have been thoroughly discussed in this chapter.

Special Effects

Special effects (often abbreviated as SFX, SPFX, or simply FX) are illusions or visual tricks used in the film, television, theatre, video game, and simulator industries to simulate the imagined events in a story or virtual world.

Bluescreens are commonly used in chroma key special effects.

Special effects are traditionally divided into the categories of optical effects and mechanical effects. With the emergence of digital filmmaking a distinction between special effects and visual effects has grown, with the latter referring to digital post-production while "special effects" referring to mechanical and optical effects.

Mechanical effects (also called practical or physical effects) are usually accomplished during the live-action shooting. This includes the use of mechanized props, scenery, scale models, animatronics, pyrotechnics and atmospheric effects: creating physical wind, rain, fog, snow, clouds, etc. Making a car appear to drive by itself and blowing up a building are examples of mechanical effects. Mechanical effects are often incorporated into set design and makeup. For example, a set may be built with break-away doors or walls to enhance a fight scene, or prosthetic makeup can be used to make an actor look like a non-human creature.

Optical effects (also called photographic effects) are techniques in which images or film frames are created photographically, either "in-camera" using multiple exposure, mattes, or the Schüfftan process, or in post-production using an optical printer. An optical effect might be used to place actors or sets against a different background.

A methane bubble bursting

Since the 1990s, computer generated imagery (CGI) has come to the forefront of special effects technologies. It gives filmmakers greater control, and allows many effects to be accomplished more safely and convincingly and—as technology improves—at lower costs. As a result, many optical and mechanical effects techniques have been superseded by CGI.

Developmental History

Early Development

In 1857, Oscar Rejlander created the world's first "trick photograph" by combining different sections of 30 negatives into a single image. In 1895, Alfred Clark created what is commonly accepted as the first-ever motion picture special effect. While filming a reenactment of the beheading of Mary, Queen of Scots, Clark instructed an actor to step up to the block in Mary's costume. As the executioner brought the axe above his head, Clark stopped the camera, had all of the actors freeze, and had the person playing Mary step off the set. He placed a Mary dummy in the actor's place, restarted filming, and allowed the executioner to bring the axe down, severing the dummy's head. Techniques like these would dominate the production of special effects for a century.

It wasn't only the first use of trickery in cinema, it was also the first type of photographic trickery only possible in a motion picture, i.e. the "stop trick". Georges Méliès accidentally discovered the same "stop trick." According to Méliès, his camera jammed while filming a street scene in Paris. When he screened the film, he found that the "stop trick" had caused a truck to turn into a hearse, pedestrians to change direction, and men to turn into women. Méliès, the stage manager at the Theatre Robert-Houdin, was inspired to develop a series of more than 500 short films, between 1914, in the process developing or inventing such techniques as multiple exposures, time-lapse photography, dissolves, and hand painted colour. Because of his ability to seemingly manipulate and transform reality with the cinematograph, the prolific Méliès is sometimes referred to as the "Cinemagician." His most famous film, *Le Voyage dans la lune* (1902), a whimsical parody of Jules Verne's *From the Earth to the Moon*, featured a combination of live action and animation, and also incorporated extensive miniature and matte painting work.

From 1910 to 1920, the main innovations in special effects were the improvements on the matte shot by Norman Dawn. With the original matte shot, pieces of cardboard were placed to block the exposure of the film, which would be exposed later. Dawn combined this technique with the "glass shot." Rather than using cardboard to block certain areas of the film exposure, Dawn simply painted certain areas black to prevent any light from exposing the film. From the partially exposed film, a single frame is then projected onto an easel, where the matte is then drawn. By creating the matte from an image directly from the film, it became incredibly easy to paint an image with proper respect to scale and perspective (the main flaw of the glass shot). Dawn's technique became the textbook for matte shots due to the natural images it created.

During the 1920s and 30s, special effects techniques were improved and refined by the motion picture industry. Many techniques—such as the Schüfftan process—were modifications of illusions from the theater (such as pepper's ghost) and still photography (such as double exposure and matte compositing). Rear projection was a refinement of the use of painted backgrounds in the theater, substituting moving pictures to create moving backgrounds. Lifecasting of faces was imported from traditional maskmaking. Along with makeup advances, fantastic masks could be created which fit the actor perfectly. As material science advanced, horror film maskmaking followed closely.

Several techniques soon developed, such as the "stop trick", wholly original to motion pictures. Animation, creating the illusion of motion, was accomplished with drawings (most notably by Winsor McCay in *Gertie the Dinosaur*) and with three-dimensional models (most notably by Willis O'Brien in *The Lost World* and *King Kong*). Many studios established in-house "special effects" departments, which were responsible for nearly all optical and mechanical aspects of motion-picture trickery.

Also, the challenge of simulating spectacle in motion encouraged the development of the use of miniatures. Naval battles could be depicted with models in studio. Tanks and airplanes could be flown (and crashed) without risk of life and limb. Most impressively, miniatures and matte paintings could be used to depict worlds that never existed. Fritz Lang's film *Metropolis* was an early special effects spectacular, with innovative use of miniatures, matte paintings, the Schüfftan process, and complex compositing.

An important innovation in special-effects photography was the development of the optical printer. Essentially, an optical printer is a projector aiming into a camera lens, and it was developed to make copies of films for distribution. Until Linwood G. Dunn refined the design and use of the optical printer, effects shots were accomplished as in-camera effects. Dunn demonstrating that it could be used to combine images in novel ways and create new illusions. One early showcase for Dunn was Orson Welles' *Citizen Kane*, where such locations as Xanadu (and some of Gregg Toland's famous 'deep focus' shots) were essentially created by Dunn's optical printer.

Color Era

The development of color photography required greater refinement of effects techniques. Color enabled the development of such *travelling matte* techniques as bluescreen and the sodium vapour process. Many films became landmarks in special-effects accomplishments: *Forbidden Planet* used matte paintings, animation, and miniature work to create spectacular alien environments. In *The Ten Commandments*, Paramount's John P. Fulton, A.S.C., multiplied the crowds of extras in the Exodus scenes with careful compositing, depicted the massive constructions of Rameses with models, and split the Red Sea in a still-impressive combination of travelling mattes and water tanks. Ray Harryhausen extended the art of stop-motion animation with his special techniques of compositing to create spectacular fantasy adventures such as Jason and the Argonauts (whose climax, a sword battle with seven animated skeletons, is considered a landmark in special effects).

The Science Fiction Boom

Through the 1950s and 60s numerous new special effects were developed which would dramatically increase the level of realism achievable in science fiction films.

If one film could be said to have established a new high-bench mark for special effects, it would be 1968's *2001: A Space Odyssey*, directed by Stanley Kubrick, who assembled his own effects team (Douglas Trumbull, Tom Howard, Con Pedersen and Wally Veevers) rather than use an in-house effects unit. In this film, the spaceship miniatures were highly detailed and carefully photographed for a realistic depth of field. The shots of spaceships were combined through hand-drawn rotoscoping and careful motion-control work, ensuring that the elements were precisely combined in the camera – a surprising throwback to the silent era, but with spectacular results. Backgrounds of the African vistas in the "Dawn of Man" sequence were combined with soundstage photography via the then-new front projection technique. Scenes set in zero-gravity environments were staged with hidden wires, mirror shots, and large-scale rotating sets. The finale, a voyage through hallucinogenic scenery, was created by Douglas Trumbull using a new technique termed slit-scan.

The 1970s provided two profound changes in the special effects trade. The first was economic: during the industry's recession in the late 1960s and early 1970s, many studios closed down their in-house effects houses. Many technicians became freelancers or founded their own effects companies, sometimes specializing on particular techniques (opticals, animation, etc.).

The second was precipitated by the blockbuster success of two science fiction and fantasy films in 1977. George Lucas's *Star Wars* ushered in an era of science-fiction films with expensive and impressive special-effects. Effects supervisor John Dykstra, A.S.C. and crew developed many improvements in existing effects technology. They developed a computer-controlled camera rig called the "Dykstraflex" that allowed precise repeatability of camera motion, greatly facilitating travelling-matte compositing. Degradation of film images during compositing was minimized by other innovations: the Dykstraflex used VistaVision cameras that photographed widescreen images horizontally along stock, using far more of the film per frame, and thinner-emulsion filmstocks were used in the compositing process. The effects crew assembled by Lucas and Dykstra was dubbed Industrial Light & Magic, and since 1977 has spearheaded most effects innovations.

That same year, Steven Spielberg's film *Close Encounters of the Third Kind* boasted a finale with impressive special effects by *2001* veteran Douglas Trumbull. In addition to developing his own motion-control system, Trumbull also developed techniques for creating intentional "lens flare" (the shapes created by light reflecting in camera lenses) to provide the film's undefinable shapes of flying saucers.

The success of these films, and others since, has prompted massive studio investment in effects-heavy science-fiction films. This has fueled the establishment of many independent effects houses, a tremendous degree of refinement of existing techniques, and the development of new techniques such as CGI. It has also encouraged within the industry a greater distinction between special effects and visual effects; the latter is used to characterize post-production and optical work, while *special effects* refers more often to on-set and mechanical effects.

Introduction of Computer Generated Imagery (CGI)

A recent and profound innovation in special effects has been the development of computer generated imagery, or CGI which has changed nearly every aspect of motion picture special effects. Digital compositing allows far more control and creative freedom than optical compositing, and does not degrade the image like analog (optical) processes. Digital imagery has enabled technicians to create detailed models, matte "paintings," and even fully realized characters with the malleability of computer software.

Arguably the biggest and most "spectacular" use of CGI is in the creation of photo-realistic images of science-fiction and fantasy characters, settings, and objects. Images can be created in a computer using the techniques of animated cartoons and model animation. In 1993, stop-motion animators working on the realistic dinosaurs of Steven Spielberg's *Jurassic Park* were retrained in the use of computer input devices.

By 1995, films such as *Toy Story* underscored that the distinction between live-action films and animated films was no longer clear. Other landmark examples include a character made up of broken pieces of a stained-glass window in *Young Sherlock Holmes*, a shapeshifting character in *Willow*, a tentacle of water in *The Abyss*, the T-1000 Terminator in *Terminator 2: Judgment Day*, hordes of armies of robots and fantastic creatures in the *Star Wars prequel trilogy* and *The Lord of the Rings* trilogy and the planet Pandora in *Avatar*.

Planning and use

Although most special effects work is completed during post-production, it must be carefully planned and choreographed in pre-production and production. A visual effects supervisor is usually involved with the production from an early stage to work closely with the Director and all related personnel to achieve the desired effects.

Live Special Effects

Live special effects are effects that are used in front of a live audience, mostly during sporting events, concerts and corporate shows. Types of effects that are commonly used include: flying effects, laser lighting, Theatrical smoke and fog, CO_2 effects, pyrotechnics, confetti and other atmospheric effects such as bubbles and snow.

Spinning fiery steel wool at night.

Visual Special Effects Techniques

- Bullet time,
- Computer-generated imagery (often using Shaders),
- Digital compositing,
- Dolly zoom,
- In-camera effects,

- Match moving,

- Matte (filmmaking) and Matte painting,

- Miniature effects,

- Morphing,

- Motion control photography,

- Optical effects,

- Optical printing,

- Practical effects,

- Prosthetic makeup effects,

- Rotoscoping,

- Stop motion,

- Go motion,

- Schüfftan process,

- Travelling matte,

- Virtual cinematography,

- Wire removal.

Notable Special Effects Companies

- *Adobe Systems Incorporated* (San Jose, CA),

- *Animal Logic* (Sydney, AU and Venice, CA),

- *Bird Studios* (London UK),

- *BUF Compagnie* (Paris, FR),

- *CA Scanline* (München, DE),

- *Cinesite* (London/Hollywood),

- *Creature Effects, Inc.* (LA, CA, US),

- *Digital Domain* (Venice, LA, CA, US),

- *Double Negative (VFX)* (London, UK),

- *DreamWorks* (LA, CA, US),

- *Flash Film Works* (LA, CA, US),

- *Framestore* (London, UK),
- *Giantsteps* (Venice, CA),
- *Hydraulx* (Santa Monica, LA, US),
- *Image Engine* (Vancouver, BC, CA),
- *Industrial Light & Magic*, founded by George Lucas,
- *Intelligent Creatures* (Toronto, ON, CA),
- *Intrigue FX* (Canada),
- *Legacy Effects*, (Los Angeles, CA),
- *Look Effects*, (Culver City, CA, USA),
- *M5 Industries* (San Francisco i.e. Mythbusters),
- *Mac Guff* (LA, CA, US; Paris, FR),
- *Machine Shop* (London, UK),
- *Makuta VFX* (Universal City, CA) (Hyderabad, India),
- *Matte World Digital* (Novato, CA),
- *The Mill* (London, UK; NY and LA, US),
- *Modus FX* (Montreal, QC, CA),
- *Moving Picture Company* (Soho, London, UK),
- *Pixomondo* (Frankfurt, DE; Munich, DE; Stuttgart, DE; Los Angeles, CA, USA; Beijing, CH; Toronto, ON, CA; Baton Rouge, LA, USA),
- *Rhythm and Hues Studios* (LA, CA, US),
- *Rising Sun Pictures* (Adelaide, AU),
- *Snowmasters* (Lexington, AL, USA),
- *Sony Pictures Imageworks* (Culver City, CA, USA),
- *Strictly FX*, live special effects company,
- *Surreal World* (Melbourne, AU),
- *Super FX*, Special Effects Company, ITALY,
- *Tippett Studio* (Berkeley, CA, US),
- *Tsuburaya Productions* (Hachimanyama, Setagaya, Tokyo, Jap),
- *Vision Crew Unlimited*,

- *Weta Digital,*
- *Zoic Studios* (Culver City, CA, USA),
- *ZFX Inc* a flying effects company,
- *Method Studios.*

Ambient Occlusion

In computer graphics, ambient occlusion is a shading and rendering technique used to calculate how exposed each point in a scene is to ambient lighting. The interior of a tube is typically more occluded (and hence darker) than the exposed outer surfaces, and the deeper you go inside the tube, the more occluded (and darker) the lighting becomes. Ambient occlusion can be seen as an accessibility value that is calculated for each surface point. In scenes with open sky this is done by estimating the amount of visible sky for each point, while in indoor environments only objects within a certain radius are taken into account and the walls are assumed to be the origin of the ambient light. The result is a diffuse, non-directional shading effect that casts no clear shadows but that darkens enclosed and sheltered areas and can affect the rendered image's overall tone. It is often used as a post-processing effect.

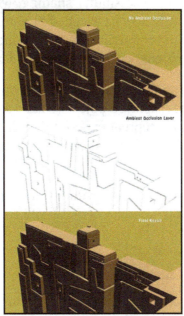

The ambient occlusion map (middle image) for this scene darkens only the innermost angles of corners.

Unlike local methods such as Phong shading, ambient occlusion is a global method, meaning that the illumination at each point is a function of other geometry in the scene.

However, it is a very crude approximation to full global illumination. The appearance achieved by ambient occlusion alone is similar to the way an object might appear on an overcast day.

Implementation

In real-time applications, such as computer games, Screen space ambient occlusion can be used as a faster approximation of true ambient occlusion, using pixel depth rather than scene geometry to form an ambient occlusion map. However, newer technologies are making true ambient occlusion feasible even in real-time.

3D animation of ambient occlusion

Ambient occlusion is related to accessibility shading, which determines appearance based on how easy it is for a surface to be touched by various elements (e.g., dirt, light, etc.). It has been popularized in production animation due to its relative simplicity and efficiency. In the industry, ambient occlusion is often referred to as "sky light".

The ambient occlusion shading model has the nice property of offering a better perception of the 3D shape of the displayed objects. This was shown in a paper where the authors report the results of perceptual experiments showing that depth discrimination under diffuse uniform sky lighting is superior to that predicted by a direct lighting model.

The occlusion $A_{\bar{p}}$ at a point $\bar{p}$ on a surface with normal $\hat{}$ can be computed by integrating the visibility function over the hemisphere Ω with respect to projected solid angle:

$$A_{\bar{p}} = \frac{1}{\pi} \int_{\Omega} V_{\bar{p},\hat{\omega}} (\hat{n} \cdot \hat{\omega}) \mathrm{d}\omega$$

where $V_{\bar{p},\hat{\omega}}$ is the visibility function at $\bar{p}$, defined to be zero if $\bar{p}$ is occluded in the direction $\hat{\omega}$ and one otherwise, and $\mathrm{d}\omega$ is the infinitesimal solid angle step of the integration variable $\hat{\omega}$. A variety of techniques are used to approximate this integral in practice: perhaps the most straightforward way is to use the Monte Carlo method by casting rays from the point $\bar{p}$ and testing for intersection with other scene geometry (i.e., ray casting). Another approach (more suited to hardware acceleration) is to render the view from $\bar{p}$ by rasterizing black geometry against a white background and taking the (cosine-weighted) average of rasterized fragments. This approach is an example of a "gathering" or "inside-out" approach, whereas other algorithms (such as depth-map ambient occlusion) employ "scattering" or "outside-in" techniques.

In addition to the ambient occlusion value, a "bent normal" vector $\hat{n}_b$ is often generated, which points in the average direction of unoccluded samples. The bent normal can be used to look up incident radiance from an environment map to approximate image-based lighting. However, there are some situations in which the direction of the bent normal is a misrepresentation of the dominant direction of illumination, e.g.,

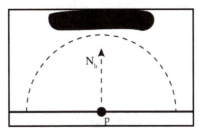

In this example the bent normal N_b has an unfortunate direction, since it is pointing at an occluded surface.

In this example, light may reach the point p only from the left or right sides, but the bent normal points to the average of those two sources, which is, unfortunately, directly toward the obstruction.

Variants

- SSAO-Screen space ambient occlusion,
- SSDO-Screen space directional occlusion,
- HDAO-High Definition Ambient Occlusion,
- HBAO+-Horizon Based Ambient Occlusion+,
- AAO-Alchemy Ambient Occlusion,
- ABAO-Angle Based Ambient Occlusion,
- PBAO,
- VXAO-Voxel Accelerated Ambient Occlusion.

Recognition

In 2010, Hayden Landis, Ken McGaugh and Hilmar Koch were awarded a Scientific and Technical Academy Award for their work on ambient occlusion rendering.

Web Design

Web design encompasses many different skills and disciplines in the production and maintenance of websites. The different areas of web design include web graphic design; interface design; authoring, including standardised code and proprietary software; user experience design; and search engine optimization. Often many individuals will work in teams covering different aspects of the design process, although some designers will cover them all. The term web design is normally used to describe the design process relating to the front-end (client side) design of a website including writing mark up. Web design partially overlaps web engineering in the broader scope of web development. Web designers are expected to have an awareness of usability and if their role involves creating mark up then they are also expected to be up to date with web accessibility guidelines.

History

Web design books in a store.

1988—2001

Although web design has a fairly recent history, it can be linked to other areas such as graphic design. However web design can also be seen from a technological standpoint. It has become a large part of people's everyday lives. It is hard to imagine the Internet without animated graphics, different styles of typography, background and music.

The Start of the Web and Web Design

In 1989, whilst working at CERN Tim Berners-Lee proposed to create a global hypertext project, which later became known as the World Wide Web. During 1991 to 1993 the World Wide Web was born. Text-only pages could be viewed using a simple line-mode browser. In 1993 Marc Andreessen and Eric Bina, created the Mosaic browser. At the time there were multiple browsers, however the majority of them were Unix-based and naturally text heavy. There had been no integrated approach to graphic design elements such as images or sounds. The Mosaic browser broke this mould. The W3C was created in October 1994 to "lead the World Wide Web to its full potential by developing common protocols that promote its evolution and ensure its interoperability." This discouraged any one company from monopolizing a propriety browser and programming language, which could have altered the effect of the World Wide Web as a whole. The W3C continues to set standards, which can today be seen with JavaScript. In 1994 Andreessen formed Communications Corp. that later became known as Netscape Communications, the Netscape 0.9 browser. Netscape created its own HTML tags without regard to the traditional standards process. For example, Netscape 1.1 included tags for changing background colours and formatting text with tables on web pages. Throughout 1996 to 1999 the browser wars began, as Microsoft and Netscape fought for ultimate browser dominance. During this time there were many new technologies in the field, notably Cascading Style Sheets, JavaScript, and Dynamic HTML. On the whole, the browser competition did lead to many positive creations and helped web design evolve at a rapid pace.

Evolution of Web Design

In 1996, Microsoft released its first competitive browser, which was complete with its own features and tags. It was also the first browser to support style sheets, which at the time was seen as an obscure authoring technique. The HTML markup for tables was originally intended for displaying tabular data. However designers quickly realized the potential of using HTML tables for creating the complex, multi-column layouts that were otherwise not possible. At this time, as design and good aesthetics seemed to take precedence over good mark-up structure, and little attention was paid to semantics and web accessibility. HTML sites were limited in their design options, even more so with earlier versions of HTML. To create complex designs, many web designers had to use complicated table structures or even use blank spacer .GIF images to stop empty table cells from collapsing. CSS was introduced in December 1996 by the W3C to support presentation and layout. This allowed HTML code to be semantic rather than both semantic and presentational, and improved web accessibility, see tableless web design.

In 1996, Flash (originally known as FutureSplash) was developed. At the time, the Flash content development tool was relatively simple compared to now, using basic layout and drawing tools, a limited precursor to ActionScript, and a timeline, but it enabled web designers to go beyond the point of HTML, animated GIFs and JavaScript. However, because Flash required a plug-in, many web developers avoided using it for fear of limiting their market share due to lack of compatibility. Instead, designers reverted to gif animations (if they didn't forego using motion graphics altogether) and JavaScript for widgets. But the benefits of Flash made it popular enough among specific target markets to eventually work its way to the vast majority of browsers, and powerful enough to be used to develop entire sites.

End of the First Browser Wars

During 1998 Netscape released Netscape Communicator code under an open source licence, enabling thousands of developers to participate in improving the software. However, they decided to start from the beginning, which guided the development of the open source browser and soon expanded to a complete application platform. The Web Standards Project was formed and promoted browser compliance with HTML and CSS standards by creating Acid1, Acid2, and Acid3 tests. 2000 was a big year for Microsoft. Internet Explorer was released for Mac; this was significant as it was the first browser that fully supported HTML 4.01 and CSS 1, raising the bar in terms of standards compliance. It was also the first browser to fully support the PNG image format. During this time Netscape was sold to AOL and this was seen as Netscape's official loss to Microsoft in the browser wars.

2001—2012

Since the start of the 21st century the web has become more and more integrated into peoples lives. As this has happened the technology of the web has also moved on. There have also been significant changes in the way people use and access the web, and this has changed how sites are designed.

Since the end of the browsers wars new browsers have been released. Many of these are open source meaning that they tend to have faster development and are more supportive of new standards. The new options are considered by many to be better than Microsoft's Internet Explorer.

The W3C has released new standards for HTML (HTML5) and CSS (CSS3), as well as new JavaScript API's, each as a new but individual standard. While the term HTML5 is only used to refer to the new version of HTML and *some* of the JavaScript API's, it has become common to use it to refer to the entire suite of new standards (HTML5, CSS3 and JavaScript).

In 2016, the term "web brutalism" was applied to web design that emphasized simple presentation and fast page loading.

Tools and Technologies

Web designers use a variety of different tools depending on what part of the production process they are involved in. These tools are updated over time by newer standards and software but the principles behind them remain the same. Web designers use both vector and raster graphics editors to create web-formatted imagery or design prototypes. Technologies used to create websites include W3C standards like HTML and CSS, which can be hand-coded or generated by WYSIWYG editing software. Other tools web designers might use include mark up validators and other testing tools for usability and accessibility to ensure their web sites meet web accessibility guidelines.

Skills and Techniques

Marketing and Communication Design

Marketing and communication design on a website may identify what works for its target market. This can be an age group or particular strand of culture; thus the designer may understand the trends of its audience. Designers may also understand the type of website they are designing, meaning, for example, that (B2B) business-to-business website design considerations might differ greatly from a consumer targeted website such as a retail or entertainment website. Careful consideration might be made to ensure that the aesthetics or overall design of a site do not clash with the clarity and accuracy of the content or the ease of web navigation, especially on a B2B website. Designers may also consider the reputation of the owner or business the site is representing to make sure they are portrayed favourably.

User Experience Design and Interactive Design

User understanding of the content of a website often depends on user understanding of how the website works. This is part of the user experience design. User experience is related to layout, clear instructions and labeling on a website. How well a user understands how they can interact on a site may also depend on the interactive design of the site. If a user perceives the usefulness of the website, they are more likely to continue using it. Users who are skilled and well versed with website use may find a more distinctive, yet less intuitive or less user-friendly website interface useful nonetheless. However, users with less experience are less likely to see the advantages or usefulness of a less intuitive website interface. This drives the trend for a more universal user experience and ease of access to accommodate as many users as possible regardless of user skill. Much of the user experience design and interactive design are considered in the user interface design.

Advanced interactive functions may require plug-ins if not advanced coding language skills. Choosing whether or not to use interactivity that requires plug-ins is a critical decision in user experience design. If the plug-in doesn't come pre-installed with most browsers, there's a risk that the user will have neither the know how or the patience to install a plug-in just to access the content. If the function requires advanced coding language skills, it may be too costly in either time or money to code compared to the amount of enhancement the function will add to the user experience. There's also a risk that advanced interactivity may be incompatible with older browsers or hardware configurations. Publishing a function that doesn't work reliably is potentially worse for the user experience than making no attempt. It depends on the target audience if it's likely to be needed or worth any risks.

Page Layout

Part of the user interface design is affected by the quality of the page layout. For example, a designer may consider whether the site's page layout should remain consistent on different pages when designing the layout. Page pixel width may also be considered vital for aligning objects in the layout design. The most popular fixed-width websites generally have the same set width to match the current most popular browser window, at the current most popular screen resolution, on the current most popular monitor size. Most pages are also center-aligned for concerns of aesthetics on larger screens.

Fluid layouts increased in popularity around 2000 as an alternative to HTML-table-based layouts and grid-based design in both page layout design principle and in coding technique, but were very slow to be adopted. This was due to considerations of screen reading devices and varying windows sizes which designers have no control over. Accordingly, a design may be broken down into units (sidebars, content blocks, embedded advertising areas, navigation areas) that are sent to the browser and which will be fitted into the display window by the browser, as best it can. As the browser does recognize the details of the reader's screen (window size, font size relative to window etc.) the browser can make user-specific layout adjustments to fluid layouts, but not fixed-width layouts. Although such a display may often change the relative position of major content units, sidebars may be displaced below body text rather than to the side of it. This is a more flexible display than a hard-coded grid-based layout that doesn't fit the device window. In particular, the relative position of content blocks may change while leaving the content within the block unaffected. This also minimizes the user's need to horizontally scroll the page.

Responsive Web Design is a newer approach, based on CSS3, and a deeper level of per-device specification within the page's stylesheet through an enhanced use of the CSS @media rule.

Typography

Web designers may choose to limit the variety of website typefaces to only a few which are of a similar style, instead of using a wide range of typefaces or type styles. Most browsers recognize a specific number of safe fonts, which designers mainly use in order to avoid complications.

Font downloading was later included in the CSS3 fonts module and has since been implemented in Safari 3.1, Opera 10 and Mozilla Firefox 3.5. This has subsequently increased interest in web typography, as well as the usage of font downloading.

Most site layouts incorporate negative space to break the text up into paragraphs and also avoid center-aligned text.

Motion Graphics

The page layout and user interface may also be affected by the use of motion graphics. The choice of whether or not to use motion graphics may depend on the target market for the website. Motion graphics may be expected or at least better received with an entertainment-oriented website. However, a website target audience with a more serious or formal interest (such as business, community, or government) might find animations unnecessary and distracting if only for entertainment or decoration purposes. This doesn't mean that more serious content couldn't be enhanced with animated or video presentations that is relevant to the content. In either case, motion graphic design may make the difference between more effective visuals or distracting visuals.

Motion graphics that are not initiated by the site visitor can produce accessibility issues. The World Wide Web consortium accessibility standards require that site visitors be able to disable the animations.

Quality of Code

Website designers may consider it to be good practice to conform to standards. This is usually done via a description specifying what the element is doing. Failure to conform to standards may not make a website unusable or error prone, but standards can relate to the correct layout of pages for readability as well making sure coded elements are closed appropriately. This includes errors in code, more organized layout for code, and making sure IDs and classes are identified properly. Poorly-coded pages are sometimes colloquially called tag soup. Validating via W3C can only be done when a correct DOCTYPE declaration is made, which is used to highlight errors in code. The system identifies the errors and areas that do not conform to web design standards. This information can then be corrected by the user.

Homepage Design

Usability experts, including Jakob Nielsen and Kyle Soucy, have often emphasised homepage design for website success and asserted that the homepage is the most important page on a website. However practitioners into the 2000s were starting to find that a growing number of website traffic was bypassing the homepage, going directly to internal content pages through search engines, e-newsletters and RSS feeds. Leading many practitioners to argue that homepages are less important than most people think. Jared Spool argued in 2007 that a site's homepage was actually the least important page on a website.

In 2012 and 2013, carousels (also called 'sliders' and 'rotating banners') have become an extremely popular design element on homepages, often used to showcase featured or recent content in a confined space. Many practitioners argue that carousels are an ineffective design element and hurt a website's search engine optimisation and usability.

Occupations

There are two primary jobs involved in creating a website: the web designer and web developer, who often work closely together on a website. The web designers are responsible for the visual aspect, which includes the layout, coloring and typography of a web page. Web designers will also have a working knowledge of markup languages such as HTML and CSS, although the extent of their knowledge will differ from one web designer to another. Particularly in smaller organizations one person will need the necessary skills for designing and programming the full web page, while larger organizations may have a web designer responsible for the visual aspect alone.

Further jobs which may become involved in the creation of a website include:

- Graphic designers to create visuals for the site such as logos, layouts and buttons.

- Internet marketing specialists to help maintain web presence through strategic solutions on targeting viewers to the site, by using marketing and promotional techniques on the internet.

- SEO writers to research and recommend the correct words to be incorporated into a particular website and make the website more accessible and found on numerous search engines.

- Internet copywriter to create the written content of the page to appeal to the targeted viewers of the site.

- User experience (UX) designer incorporates aspects of user focused design considerations which include information architecture, user centered design, user testing, interaction design, and occasionally visual design.

Computer-generated Imagery

Computer-generated imagery (CGI) is the application of computer graphics to create or contribute to images in art, printed media, video games, films, television programs, shorts, commercials, videos, and simulators. The visual scenes may be dynamic or static, and may be two-dimensional (2D), though the term "CGI" is most commonly used to refer to 3D computer graphics used for creating scenes or special effects in films and television. Additionally, the use of 2D CGI is often mistakenly referred to as "traditional animation", most often in the case when dedicated animation software such as Adobe Flash or Toon Boom is not used or the CGI is hand drawn using a tablet and mouse.

The term 'CGI animation' refers to dynamic CGI rendered as a movie. The term virtual world refers to agent-based, interactive environments. Computer graphics software is used to make computer-generated imagery for films, etc. Availability of CGI software and increased computer speeds have allowed individual artists and small companies to produce professional-grade films, games, and fine art from their home computers. This has brought about an Internet subculture with its own set of global celebrities, clichés, and technical vocabulary. The evolution of CGI led to the emergence of virtual cinematography in the 1990s where runs of the simulated camera are not constrained by the laws of physics.

Static Images and Landscapes

Not only do animated images form part of computer-generated imagery, natural looking landscapes (such as fractal landscapes) are also generated via computer algorithms. A simple way to generate fractal surfaces is to use an extension of the triangular mesh method, relying on the construction of some special case of a de Rham curve, e.g. midpoint displacement. For instance, the algorithm may start with a large triangle, then recursively zoom in by dividing it into four smaller Sierpinski triangles, then interpolate the height of each point from its nearest neighbors. The creation of a Brownian surface may be achieved not only by adding noise as new nodes are created, but by adding additional noise at multiple levels of the mesh. Thus a topographical map with varying levels of height can be created using relatively straightforward fractal algorithms. Some typical, easy-to-program fractals used in CGI are the *plasma fractal* and the more dramatic *fault fractal*.

Fractal landscape

The large number of specific techniques have been researched and developed to produce highly focused computer-generated effects — e.g. the use of specific models to represent the chemical weathering of stones to model erosion and produce an "aged appearance" for a given stone-based surface.

Architectural Scenes

Modern architects use services from computer graphic firms to create 3-dimensional models for both customers and builders. These computer generated models can be more accurate than traditional drawings. Architectural animation (which provides animated movies of buildings, rather than interactive images) can also be used to see the possible relationship a building will have in relation to the environment and its surrounding buildings. The rendering of architectural spaces without the use of paper and pencil tools is now a widely accepted practice with a number of computer-assisted architectural design systems.

Architectural modelling tools allow an architect to visualize a space and perform "walkthroughs" in an interactive manner, thus providing "interactive environments" both at the urban and building levels. Specific applications in architecture not only include the specification of building structures (such as walls and windows) and walk-throughs, but the effects of light and how sunlight will affect a specific design at different times of the day.

A computer generated image featuring a house, made in Blender.

Architectural modelling tools have now become increasingly internet-based. However, the quality of internet-based systems still lags behind those of sophisticated inhouse modelling systems.

In some applications, computer-generated images are used to "reverse engineer" historical buildings. For instance, a computer-generated reconstruction of the monastery at Georgenthal in Germany was derived from the ruins of the monastery, yet provides the viewer with a "look and feel" of what the building would have looked like in its day.

Anatomical Models

Computer generated models used in skeletal animation are not always anatomically correct. However, organizations such as the Scientific Computing and Imaging Institute have developed anatomically correct computer-based models. Computer generated anatomical models can be used both for instructional and operational purposes. To date, a large body of artist produced medical images continue to be used by medical students, such as images by Frank Netter, e.g. Cardiac images. However, a number of online anatomical models are becoming available.

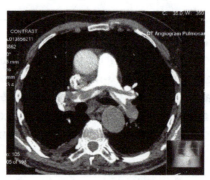

A CT pulmonary angiogram image generated by a computer from a collection of x-rays.

A single patient X-ray is not a computer generated image, even if digitized. However, in applications which involve CT scans a three dimensional model is automatically produced from a large number of single slice x-rays, producing "computer generated image". Applications involving magnetic resonance imaging also bring together a number of "snapshots" (in this case via magnetic pulses) to produce a composite, internal image.

In modern medical applications, patient specific models are constructed in 'computer assisted surgery'. For instance, in total knee replacement, the construction of a detailed patient specific model can be used to carefully plan the surgery. These three dimensional models are usually extracted from multiple CT scans of the appropriate parts of the patient's own anatomy. Such models can also be used for planning aortic valve implantations, one of the common procedures for treating heart disease. Given that the shape, diameter and position of the coronary openings can vary greatly from patient to patient, the extraction (from CT scans) of a model that closely resembles a patient's valve anatomy can be highly beneficial in planning the procedure.

Generating Cloth and Skin Images

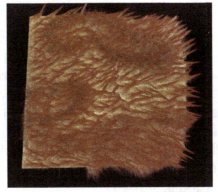

Computer-generated wet fur.

Models of cloth generally fall into three groups:

- The geometric-mechanical structure at yarn crossing.

- The mechanics of continuous elastic sheets.

- The geometric macroscopic features of cloth.

To date, making the clothing of a digital character automatically fold in a natural way remains a challenge for many animators.

In addition to their use in film, advertising and other modes of public display, computer generated images of clothing are now routinely used by top fashion design firms.

The challenge in rendering human skin images involves three levels of realism:

- Photo realism in resembling real skin at the static level.

- Physical realism in resembling its movements.

- Function realism in resembling its response to actions.

The finest visible features such as fine wrinkles and skin pores are size of about 100 μm or 0.1 millimetres. Skin can be modelled as a 7-dimensional bidirectional texture function (BTF) or a collection of bidirectional scattering distribution function (BSDF) over the target's surfaces.

Interactive Simulation and Visualization

Interactive visualization is a general term that applies to the rendering of data that may vary dynamically and allowing a user to view the data from multiple perspectives. The applications areas may vary significantly, ranging from the visualization of the flow patterns in fluid dynamics to specific computer aided design applications. The data rendered may correspond to specific visual scenes that change as the user interacts with the system — e.g. simulators, such as flight simulators, make extensive use of CGI techniques for representing the world.

At the abstract level an interactive visualization process involves a "data pipeline" in which the raw data is managed and filtered to a form that makes it suitable for rendering. This is often called the "visualization data". The visualization data is then mapped to a "visualization representation" that can be fed to a rendering system. This is usually called a "renderable representation". This representation is then rendered as a display-able image. As the user interacts with the system (e.g. by using joystick controls to change their position within the virtual world) the raw data is fed through the pipeline to create a new rendered image, often making real-time computational efficiency a key consideration in such applications.

Computer Animation

While computer generated images of landscapes may be static, the term computer animation only applies to dynamic images that resemble a movie. However, in general the term computer animation refers to dynamic images that do not allow user interaction, and the term virtual world is used for the interactive animated environments.

Computer animation is essentially a digital successor to the art of stop motion animation of 3D models and frame-by-frame animation of 2D illustrations. Computer generated animations are more controllable than other more physically based processes, such as constructing miniatures for effects shots or hiring extras for crowd scenes, and because it allows the creation of images that would not be feasible using any other technology. It can also allow a single graphic artist to produce such content without the use of actors, expensive set pieces, or props.

To create the illusion of movement, an image is displayed on the computer screen and repeatedly replaced by a new image which is similar to the previous image, but advanced slightly in the time domain (usually at a rate of 24 or 30 frames/second). This technique is identical to how the illusion of movement is achieved with television and motion pictures.

Virtual Worlds

A yellow submarine in Second Life

A virtual world is a simulated environment, which allows user to interact with animated characters, or interact with other users through the use of animated characters known as avatars. Virtual worlds are intended for its users to inhabit and interact, and the term today has become largely synonymous with interactive 3D virtual environments, where the users take the form of avatars visible to others graphically. These avatars are usually depicted as textual, two-dimensional, or three-dimensional graphical representations, although other forms are possible (auditory and touch sensations for example). Some, but not all, virtual worlds allow for multiple users.

Metallic balls

In Courtrooms

Computer-generated imagery has been used in courtrooms, primarily since the early 2000s. However, some experts have argued that it is prejudicial. They are used to help judges or the jury to better visualize the sequence of events, evidence or hypothesis. However, a 1997 study showed that people are poor intuitive physicists and easily influenced by computer generated images. Thus it is important that jurors and other legal decision-makers be made aware that such exhibits are merely a representation of one potential sequence of events.

Texture Mapping

Texture mapping is a method for defining high frequency detail, surface texture, or color information on a computer-generated graphic or 3D model. Its application to 3D graphics was pioneered by Edwin Catmull in 1974.

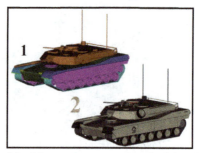

1 = 3D model without textures2 = 3D model with textures

Texture mapping originally referred to a method (now more accurately called diffuse mapping) that simply wrapped and mapped pixels from a texture to a 3D surface. In recent decades the advent of multi-pass rendering and complex mapping such as height mapping, bump mapping, normal mapping, displacement mapping, reflection mapping, specular mapping, mipmaps, occlusion mapping, and many other variations on the technique (controlled by a materials system) have made it possible to simulate near-photorealism in real time by vastly reducing the number of polygons and lighting calculations needed to construct a realistic and functional 3D scene.

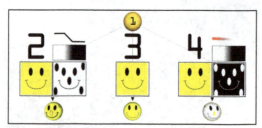

Examples of multitexturing (click for larger image); 1: Untextured sphere, 2: Texture and bump maps, 3: Texture map only, 4: Opacity and texture maps.

Texture Maps

A texture map is an image applied (mapped) to the surface of a shape or polygon. This may be a bitmap image or a procedural texture. They may be stored in common image file formats, referenced by 3d model formats or material definitions, and assembled into resource bundles.

They may have 1-3 dimensions, although 2 dimensions are most common for visible surfaces. For use with modern hardware, texture map data may be stored in swizzled or tiled orderings to improve cache coherency. Rendering APIs typically manage texture map resources (which may be located in device memory) as buffers or surfaces, and may allow 'render to texture' for additional effects such as post processing, environment mapping.

They usually contain RGB color data (either stored as direct color, compressed formats, or indexed color), and sometimes an additional channel for alpha blending (RGBA) especially for billboards and *decal* overlay textures. It is possible to use the alpha channel (which may be convenient to store in formats parsed by hardware) for other uses such as specularity.

Multiple texture maps (or channels) may be combined for control over specularity, normals, displacement, or subsurface scattering for skin rendering.

Multiple texture images may be combined in texture atlases or array textures to reduce state changes for modern hardware. (They may be considered a modern evolution of tile map graphics). Modern hardware often supports cube map textures with multiple faces for environment mapping.

Authoring

They may be acquired by scanning/digital photography, authored in image manipulation software such as Photoshop, or painted onto 3D surfaces directly in a 3D paint tool such as Mudbox or zbrush.

Texture Application

This process is akin to applying patterned paper to a plain white box. Every vertex in a polygon is assigned a texture coordinate (which in the 2d case is also known as a UV coordinates). This may be done through explicit assignment of vertex attributes, manually edited in a 3D modelling package through UV unwrapping tools. It is also possible to associate a procedural transformation from 3d space to texture space with the material. This might be accomplished via planar projection or, alternatively, cylindrical or spherical mapping. More complex mappings may consider the distance along a surface to minimize distortion. These coordinates are interpolated across the faces of polygons to sample the texture map during rendering.

Textures may be repeated or mirrored to extend a finite rectangular bitmap over a larger area, or they may have a one to one unique "injective" mapping from every piece of a surface (which is important for render mapping and light mapping, also known as baking).

Texture Space

Texture mapping maps from the model surface (or screen space during rasterization) into texture space; in this space, the texture map is visible in its undistorted form. UV unwrapping tools typically provide a view in texture space for manual editing of texture coordinates. Some rendering techniques such as subsurface scattering may be performed approximately by texture-space operations.

Multitexturing

Multitexturing is the use of more than one texture at a time on a polygon. For instance, a light map texture may be used to light a surface as an alternative to recalculating that lighting every time the surface is rendered. Microtextures or detail textures are used to add higher frequency details, and dirt maps may add weathering and variation; this can greatly reduce the apparent periodicity of repeating textures. Modern graphics may use in excess of 10 layers for greater fidelity which are combined using shaders. Another multitexture technique is bump mapping, which allows a texture to directly control the facing direction of a surface for the purposes of its lighting calculations; it can give a very good appearance of a complex surface (such as tree bark or rough concrete) that takes on lighting detail in addition to the usual detailed coloring. Bump mapping has become popular in recent video games, as graphics hardware has become powerful enough to accommodate it in real-time.

Texture Filtering

The way that samples (e.g. when viewed as pixels on the screen) are calculated from the texels (texture pixels) is governed by texture filtering. The cheapest method is to use the nearest-neighbour interpolation, but bilinear interpolation or trilinear interpolation between mipmaps are two commonly used alternatives which reduce aliasing or jaggies. In the event of a texture coordinate being outside the texture, it is either clamped or wrapped. Anisotropic filtering better eliminates directional artefacts when viewing textures from oblique viewing angles.

Baking

As an optimization, it is possible to render detail from a high resolution model or expensive process (such as global illumination) into a surface texture (possibly on a low resolution model). This is also known as render mapping. This technique is most commonly used for lightmapping but may also be used to generate normal maps and displacement maps. Some video games (e.g. Messiah) have used this technique. The original Quake software engine used on-the-fly baking to combine light maps and colour texture-maps ("surface caching").

Baking can be used as a form of level of detail generation, where a complex scene with many different elements and materials may be approximated by a single element with a single texture which is then algorithmically reduced for lower rendering cost and fewer drawcalls. It is also used to take high detail models from 3D sculpting software and point cloud scanning and approximate them with meshes more suitable for realtime rendering.

Rasterisation Algorithms

Various techniques have evolved in software and hardware implementations. Each offers different trade-offs in precision, versatility and performance :-

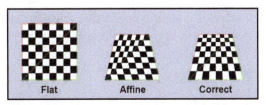

Because affine texture mapping does not take into account the depth information about a polygon's vertices, where the polygon is not perpendicular to the viewer it produces a noticeable defect.

Forward Texture Mapping

Some hardware systems e.g. Sega Saturn and the NV1 traverse texture coordinates directly, interpolating the projected position in screen space through texture space and splatting the texels into a frame buffer. (in the case of the NV1, quadratic interpolation was used allowing curved rendering). Sega provided tools for baking suitable per-quad texture tiles from UV mapped models.

This has the advantage that texture maps are read in a simple linear fashion.

Forward texture mapping may also sometimes produce more natural looking results than affine texture mapping if the primitives are aligned with prominent texture directions (e.g. road markings or layers of bricks). However, perspective distortion is still visible as primitives near the camera. (e.g. the saturn port of Sega Rally exhibited texture-squashing artefacts as nearby polygons were near clipped without UV coordinates.).

This technique is not used in modern hardware because UV coordinates have proved more versatile for modelling and more consistent for clipping.

Inverse Texture Mapping

Most approaches use inverse texture mapping, which traverses the rendering primitives in screen space whilst interpolating texture coordinates for sampling. This interpolation may be affine or perspective correct. One advantage is that each output pixel is guaranteed to only be traversed once; generally the source texture map data is stored in some lower bit-depth or compressed form whilst the frame buffer uses a higher bit-depth. Another is greater versatility for UV mapping. A texture cache becomes important for buffering reads, since the memory access pattern in texture space is more complex.

Affine Texture Mapping

It is cheapest to linearly interpolate texture coordinates across a surface. Some software and hardware systems (such as the original PlayStation), project 3D vertices onto the screen during rendering and linearly interpolate the texture coordinates in screen space between them (inverse-texture mapping). This may be done by incrementing fixed point UV coordinates or by an incremental error algorithm akin to Bresenham's line algorithm.

This leads to noticeable distortion with perspective transformations (see figure – textures (the checker boxes) appear bent), especially as primitives near the camera. Such distortion may be reduced with subdivision.

Perspective Correctness

Perspective correct texturing accounts for the vertices' positions in 3D space rather than simply interpolating coordinates in 2D screen space. This achieves the correct visual effect but it is more expensive to calculate. Instead of interpolating the texture coordinates directly, the coordinates are divided by their depth (relative to the viewer) and the reciprocal of the depth value is also interpolated and used to recover the perspective-correct coordinate. This correction makes it so that in parts of the polygon that are closer to the viewer the difference from pixel to pixel between texture coordinates is smaller (stretching the texture wider) and in parts that are farther away this difference is larger (compressing the texture).

Affine texture mapping directly interpolates a texture coordinate u_a between two endpoints u_0 and u_1 :

$$u_a = (1-\alpha)u_0 + \alpha u_1 \quad 0 \leq \alpha \leq 1$$

Perspective correct mapping interpolates after dividing by depth z , then uses its interpolated reciprocal to recover the correct coordinate:

$$u_a = \frac{(1-\alpha)\dfrac{u_0}{z_0} + \alpha\dfrac{u_1}{z_1}}{(1-\alpha)\dfrac{1}{z_0} + \alpha\dfrac{1}{z_1}}$$

All modern 3D graphics hardware implements perspective correct texturing.

Various techniques have evolved for rendering texture mapped geometry into images with different quality/precision tradeoffs, which can be applied to both software and hardware.

Doom renders vertical spans (walls) with perspective-correct texture mapping.

Classic software texture mappers generally did only simple mapping with at most one lighting effect (typically applied through a lookup table), and the perspective correctness was about 16 times more expensive.

Restricted Camera Rotation

The *Doom engine* restricted the world to vertical walls and horizontal floors/ceilings, with a camera that could only rotate about the vertical axis. This meant the walls would be a constant depth coordinate along a vertical line and the floors/ceilings would have a constant depth along a horizontal line. A fast affine mapping could be used along those lines because it would be correct. Some later renderers of this era simulated a small amount of camera pitch with shearing which allowed the appearance of greater freedom whilst using the same rendering technique.

Some engines with were able to render texture mapped Heightmaps (e.g. Nova Logic's Voxel Space, and the engine for outcast) via Bresenham-like incremental algorithms, producing the appearance of a texture mapped landscape without the use of traditional geometric primitives.

Subdivision for Perspective Correction

Every triangle can be further subdivided into groups of about 16 pixels in order to achieve two goals. First, keeping the arithmetic mill busy at all times. Second, producing faster arithmetic results.

World Space Subdivision

For perspective texture mapping without hardware support, a triangle is broken down into smaller triangles for rendering and affine mapping is used on them. The reason this technique works is that the distortion of affine mapping becomes much less noticeable on smaller polygons. The Sony Playstation made extensive use of this because it only supported affine mapping in hardware but had a relatively high triangle through-put compared to its peers.

Screen Space Subdivision

Software renderers generally preferred screen subdivision because it has less overhead. Additionally, they try to do linear interpolation along a line of pixels to simplify the set-up (compared to 2d affine interpolation) and thus again the overhead (also affine texture-mapping does not fit into the low number of registers of the x86 CPU; the 68000 or any RISC is much more suited).

A different approach was taken for *Quake*, which would calculate perspective correct coordinates only once every 16 pixels of a scanline and linearly interpolate between them, effectively running at the speed of linear interpolation because the perspective correct calculation runs in parallel on the co-processor. The polygons are rendered independently, hence it may be possible to switch between spans and columns or diagonal directions depending on the orientation of the polygon normal to achieve a more constant z but the effort seems not to be worth it.

Screen space sub division techniques. Top left: Quake-like, top right: bilinear, bottom left: const-z.

Other Techniques

Another technique was approximating the perspective with a faster calculation, such as a polynomial. Still another technique uses $1/z$ value of the last two drawn pixels to linearly extrapolate the next value. The division is then done starting from those values so that only a small remainder has to be divided but the amount of bookkeeping makes this method too slow on most systems.

Finally, the Build engine extended the constant distance trick used for Doom by finding the line of constant distance for arbitrary polygons and rendering along it.

Hardware Implementations

Texture mapping hardware was originally developed for simulation (e.g. as implemented in the Evans and Sutherland ESIG image generators), and professional graphics workstations such as Silicon Graphics, broadcast digital video effects machines such as the Ampex ADO and later appeared in arcade machines, consumer video game consoles, and PC graphics cards in the mid 1990s. In flight simulation, texture mapping provided important motion cues.

Modern Graphics processing units provide specialised fixed function units called texture samplers or texture mapping units to perform texture mapping, usually with trilinear filtering or better multi-tap anisotropic filtering and hardware for decoding specific formats such as DXTn. As of 2016, texture mapping hardware is ubiquitous as most SOCs contain a suitable GPU.

Some hardware combines texture mapping with hidden surface determination in tile based deferred rendering or scanline rendering; such systems only fetch the visible texels at the expense of using greater workspace for transformed vertices. Most systems have settled on the Z-buffer approach, which can still reduce the texture mapping workload with front to back sorting.

Applications

Beyond 3d rendering, the availability of texture mapping hardware has inspired its use for accelerating other tasks:

Tomography

It is possible to use texture mapping hardware to accelerate both the reconstruction of voxel data sets from tomographic scans, and to visualise the results.

User Interfaces

Many user interfaces use texture mapping to accelerate animated transitions of screen elements, e.g. Expose in Mac OSX.

Morphing

Morphing is a special effect in motion pictures and animations that changes (or morphs) one image or shape into another through a seamless transition. Most often it is used to depict one person turning into another through technological means or as part of a fantasy or surreal sequence. Traditionally such a depiction would be achieved through cross-fading techniques on film. Since the early 1990s, this has been replaced by computer software to create more realistic transitions.

Three frames form a morph from George W. Bush to Arnold Schwarzenegger showing the midpoint between the two extremes

Early Examples

Though the 1986 movie *The Golden Child* implemented very crude morphing effects from animal to human and back, the first movie to employ detailed morphing was *Willow*, in 1988. A similar process was used a year later in *Indiana Jones and the Last Crusade* to create Walter Donovan's gruesome demise. Both effects were created by Industrial Light & Magic using grid warping techniques developed by Tom Brigham and Doug Smythe (AMPAS).

In 1985, Godley & Creme created a "morph" effect using analogue cross-fades in the video for "Cry". The cover for Queen's 1989 album *The Miracle* featured the technique to morph the four band members' faces into one gestalt image. In 1991, morphing appeared notably in the Michael Jackson music video "Black or White" and in the movies *Terminator 2: Judgment Day* and *Star Trek VI: The Undiscovered Country*. The first application for personal computers to offer morphing was Gryphon Software Morph on the Macintosh. Other early morphing systems included ImageMaster, MorphPlus and CineMorph, all of which premiered for the Commodore Amiga in 1992. Other programs became widely available within a year, and for a time the effect became common to the point of cliché. For high-end use, Elastic Reality (based on MorphPlus) saw its first feature film use in *In The Line of Fire* (1993) and was used in Quantum Leap (work performed by the Post Group). At VisionArt Ted Fay used Elastic Reality to morph Odo for *Star Trek: Deep Space Nine*. Elastic Reality was later purchased by Avid, having already become the de facto system of choice, used in many hundreds of films. The technology behind Elastic Reality earned two Academy Awards in 1996 for Scientific and Technical Achievement going to Garth Dickie and Perry Kivolowitz. The effect is technically called a "spatially warped cross-dissolve". The first social network designed for user-generated morph examples to be posted online was Galleries by Morpheus (morphing software).

In Taiwan, Aderans, a hair loss solutions provider, did a TV commercial featuring a morphing sequence in which people with lush, thick hair morph into one another, reminiscent of the end sequence of the "Black or White" video.

Modern Techniques

An animated example of an ape morphing into a bird.

In the early 1990s computer techniques that often produced more convincing results began to be widely used. These involved distorting one image at the same time that it faded into another through marking corresponding points and vectors on the "before" and "after" images used in the morph. For example, one would morph one face into another by marking key points on the first face, such as the contour of the nose or location of an eye, and mark where these same points existed on the second face. The computer would then distort the first face to have the shape of the second face at the same time that it faded the two faces. To compute the transformation of image coordinates required for the distortion, the algorithm of Beier and Neely can be used.

Later, more sophisticated cross-fading techniques were employed that vignetted different parts of one image to the other gradually instead of transitioning the entire image at once. This style of morphing was perhaps most famously employed in the video that former 10cc members Kevin Godley and Lol Creme (performing as Godley & Creme) produced in 1985 for their song *Cry*. It comprised a series of black and white close-up shots of faces of many different people that gradually faded from one to the next. In a strict sense, this had little to do with modern-day computer generated morphing effects, since it was merely a dissolve using fully analog equipment.

Present Use

Morphing algorithms continue to advance and programs can automatically morph images that correspond closely enough with relatively little instruction from the user. This has led to the use of morphing techniques to create convincing slow-motion effects where none existed in the original film or video footage by morphing between each individual frame using optical flow technology. Morphing has also appeared as a transition technique between one scene and another in television shows, even if the contents of the two images are entirely unrelated. The algorithm in this case attempts to find corresponding points between the images and distort one into the other as they crossfade.

While perhaps less obvious than in the past, morphing is used heavily today. Whereas the effect was initially a novelty, today, morphing effects are most often designed to be seamless and invisible to the eye.

A particular use for morphing effects is modern digital font design. Using morphing technology, called interpolation or multiple master technology, a designer can create an intermediate between two styles, for example generating a semibold font by compromising between a bold and regular style, or extend a trend to create an ultra-light or ultra-bold. The technique is commonly used by font design studios.

Software

- Morpheus
- Nuke

- After Effects

- FantaMorph

- Gryphon Software Morph

- MorphThing

- SilhouetteFX (new algorithms by the above cited Perry Kivolowitz)

- Angelmorph

Molecular Graphics

Molecular graphics (MG) is the discipline and philosophy of studying molecules and their properties through graphical representation. IUPAC limits the definition to representations on a "graphical display device". Ever since Dalton's atoms and Kekulé's benzene, there has been a rich history of hand-drawn atoms and molecules, and these representations have had an important influence on modern molecular graphics. This article concentrates on the use of computers to create molecular graphics. Note, however, that many molecular graphics programs and systems have close coupling between the graphics and editing commands or calculations such as in molecular modelling.

Relation to Molecular Models

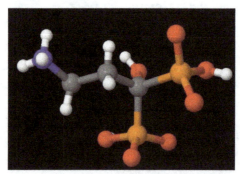

Fig. Key: Hydrogen = white, carbon = grey, nitrogen = blue, oxygen = red,}
and phosphorus = orange.

There has been a long tradition of creating molecular models from physical materials. Perhaps the best known is Crick and Watson's model of DNA built from rods and planar sheets, but the most widely used approach is to represent all atoms and bonds explicitly using the "ball and stick" approach. This can demonstrate a wide range of properties, such as shape, relative size, and flexibility. Many chemistry courses expect that students will have access to ball and stick models. One goal of mainstream molecular graphics has been to represent the "ball and stick" model as realistically as possible and to couple this with calculations of molecular properties.

Figure shows a small molecule (NH3CH2CH2C(OH)(PO3H)(PO3H)-), as drawn by the Jmol program. It is important to realize that the colors and shapes are purely a convention, as individual atoms are not colored, nor do they have hard surfaces. Bonds between atoms are also not rod-shaped.

Comparison of Physical Models with Molecular Graphics

Physical models and computer models have partially complementary strengths and weaknesses. Physical models can be used by those without access to a computer and now can be made cheaply out of plastic materials. Their tactile and visual aspects cannot be easily reproduced by computers (although haptic devices have occasionally been built). On a computer screen, the flexibility of molecules is also difficult to appreciate; illustrating the pseudorotation of cyclohexane is a good example of the value of mechanical models.

However, it is difficult to build large physical molecules, and all-atom physical models of even simple proteins could take weeks or months to build. Moreover, physical models are not robust and they decay over time. Molecular graphics is particularly valuable for representing global and local properties of molecules, such as electrostatic potential. Graphics can also be animated to represent molecular processes and chemical reactions, a feat that is not easy to reproduce physically.

History

Initially the rendering was on early Cathode ray tube screens or through plotters drawing on paper. Molecular structures have always been an attractive choice for developing new computer graphics tools, since the input data are easy to create and the results are usually highly appealing. The first example of MG was a display of a protein molecule (Project MAC, 1966) by Cyrus Levinthal and Robert Langridge. Among the milestones in high-performance MG was the work of Nelson Max in "realistic" rendering of macromolecules using reflecting spheres.

By about 1980 many laboratories both in academia and industry had recognized the power of the computer to analyse and predict the properties of molecules, especially in materials science and the pharmaceutical industry. The discipline was often called "molecular graphics" and in 1982 a group of academics and industrialists in the UK set up the Molecular Graphics Society (MGS). Initially much of the technology concentrated either on high-performance 3D graphics, including interactive rotation or 3D rendering of atoms as spheres (sometimes with radiosity). During the 1980s a number of programs for calculating molecular properties (such as molecular dynamics and quantum mechanics) became available and the term "molecular graphics" often included these. As a result, the MGS has now changed its name to the Molecular Graphics and Modelling Society (MGMS).

The requirements of macromolecular crystallography also drove MG because the traditional techniques of physical model-building could not scale. The first two protein structures solved by molecular graphics without the aid of the Richards' Box were built with Stan Swanson's program FIT on the Vector General graphics display in the laboratory of Edgar Meyer at Texas A&M University: First Marge Legg in Al Cotton's lab at A&M solved the structure of staph. nuclease (1975) and then Jim Hogle solved the structure of monoclinic lysozyme in 1976. A full year passed before other graphics systems were used to replace the Richards' Box for modelling into density in 3-D. Alwyn Jones' FRODO program (and later "O") were developed to overlay the molecular electron density determined from X-ray crystallography and the hypothetical molecular structure.

In 2009 BALLView became the first software to use Raytracing for molecular graphics.

Art, Science and Technology in Molecular Graphics

Both computer technology and graphic arts have contributed to molecular graphics. The development of structural biology in the 1950s led to a requirement to display molecules with thousands of atoms. The existing computer technology was limited in power, and in any case a naive depiction of all atoms left viewers overwhelmed. Most systems therefore used conventions where information was implicit or stylistic. Two vectors meeting at a point implied an atom or (in macromolecules) a complete residue (10-20 atoms).

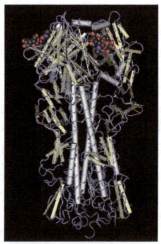

Fig. Image of hemagglutinin with alpha helices depicted as cylinders and the rest of the chain as silver coils. The individual protein molecules (several thousand) have been hidden. All of the non-hydrogen atoms in the two ligands (presumably sialic acid) have been shown near the top of the diagram. Key: Carbon = grey, oxygen = red, nitrogen = blue.

The macromolecular approach was popularized by Dickerson and Geis' presentation of proteins and the graphic work of Jane Richardson through high-quality hand-drawn diagrams such as the "ribbon" representation. In this they strove to capture the intrinsic 'meaning' of the molecule. This search for the "messages in the molecule" has always accompanied the increasing power of computer graphics processing. Typically the depiction would concentrate on specific areas of the molecule (such as the active site) and this might have different colors or more detail in the number of explicit atoms or the type of depiction (e.g., spheres for atoms).

In some cases the limitations of technology have led to serendipitous methods for rendering. Most early graphics devices used vector graphics, which meant that rendering spheres and surfaces was impossible. Michael Connolly's program "MS" calculated points on the surface-accessible surface of a molecule, and the points were rendered as dots with good visibility using the new vector graphics technology, such as the Evans and Sutherland PS300 series. Thin sections ("slabs") through the structural display showed very clearly the complementarity of the surfaces for molecules binding to active sites, and the "Connolly surface" became a universal metaphor.

The relationship between the art and science of molecular graphics is shown in the exhibitions sponsored by the Molecular Graphics Society. Some exhibits are created with molecular graphics programs alone, while others are collages, or involve physical materials. An example from Mike Hann (1994), inspired by Magritte's painting *Ceci n'est pas une pipe*, uses an image of a salmeterol molecule. "*Ceci n'est pas une molecule*," writes Mike Hann, "serves to remind us that all of the graphics images presented here are not molecules, not even pictures of molecules, but pictures of icons which we believe represent some aspects of the molecule's properties."

Colour molecular graphics is often use on chemistry journal covers in an artistic manner.

Space-filling Models

Fig. Space-filling model of formic acid. Key: Hydrogen = white, carbon = black, oxygen = red.

Fig. is a "space-filling" representation of formic acid, where atoms are drawn as solid spheres to suggest the space they occupy. This and all space-filling models are necessarily icons or abstractions: atoms are nuclei with electron "clouds" of varying density surrounding them, and as such have no actual surfaces. For many years the size of atoms has been approximated by physical models (CPK) in which the volumes of plastic balls describe where much of the electron density is to be found (often sized to van der Waals radii). That is, the surface of these models is meant to represent a specific *level of density* of the electron cloud, not any putative physical surface of the atom.

Since the atomic radii (e.g. in Fig.) are only slightly less than the distance between bonded atoms, the iconic spheres intersect, and in the CPK models, this was achieved by planar truncations along the bonding directions, the section being circular. When raster graphics became affordable, one of the common approaches was to replicate CPK models *in silico*. It is relatively straightforward to calculate the circles of intersection, but more complex to represent a model with hidden surface removal. A useful side product is that a conventional value for the molecular volume can be calculated.

The use of spheres is often for convenience, being limited both by graphics libraries and the additional effort required to compute complete electronic density or other space-filling quantities. It is now relatively common to see images of surfaces that have been colored to show quantities such as electrostatic potential. Common surfaces in molecular visualization include solvent-accessible ("Lee-Richards") surfaces, solvent-excluded ("Connolly") surfaces, and isosurfaces. The isosurface in Fig. appears to show the electrostatic potential, with blue colors being negative and red/yellow (near the metal) positive (there is no absolute convention of coloring, and red/positive, blue/negative are often reversed). Opaque isosurfaces do not allow the atoms to be seen and identified and it is not easy to deduce them. Because of this, isosurfaces are often drawn with a degree of transparency.

Technology

Early interactive molecular computer graphics systems were vector graphics machines, which used stroke-writing vector monitors, sometimes even oscilloscopes. The electron beam does not sweep left-and-right as in a raster display. The display hardware followed a sequential list of digital drawing instructions (the display list), directly drawing at an angle one stroke for each molecular bond. When the list was complete, drawing would begin again from the top of the list, so if the list was long (a large number of molecular bonds), the display would flicker heavily. Later vector displays could rotate complex structures with smooth motion, since the orientation of all of the coordinates in the display list could be changed by loading just a few numbers into rotation registers in the display unit, and the display unit would multiply all coordinates in the display list by the contents of these registers as the picture was drawn.

The early black-and white vector displays could somewhat distinguish for example a molecular structure from its surrounding electron density map for crystallographic structure solution work by drawing the molecule brighter than the map. Color display makes them easier to tell apart. During the 1970s two-color stroke-writing Penetron tubes were available, but not used in molecular computer graphics systems. In about 1980 Evans & Sutherland made the first practical full-color vector displays for molecular graphics, typically attached to an E&S PS-300 display. This early color tube was expensive, because it was originally engineered to withstand the shaking of a flight-simulator motion base.

Color raster graphics display of molecular models began around 1978 as seen in this paper by Porter on spherical shading of atomic models. Early raster molecular graphics systems displayed static images that could take around a minute to generate. Dynamically rotating color raster molecular display phased in during 1982-1985 with the introduction of the Ikonas programmable raster display.

Molecular graphics has always pushed the limits of display technology, and has seen a number of cycles of integration and separation of compute-host and display. Early systems like Project MAC were bespoke and unique, but in the 1970s the MMS-X and similar systems used (relatively) low-cost terminals, such as the Tektronix 4014 series, often over dial-up lines to multi-user hosts. The devices could only display static pictures but were able to evangelize MG. In the late 1970s, it was possible for departments (such as crystallography) to afford their own hosts (e.g., PDP-11) and to attach a display (such as Evans & Sutherland's MPS) directly to the bus. The display list was kept on the host, and interactivity was good since updates were rapidly reflected in the display—at the cost of reducing most machines to a single-user system.

In the early 1980s, Evans & Sutherland (E&S) decoupled their PS300 display, which contained its own display information transformable through a dataflow architecture. Complex graphical objects could be downloaded over a serial line (e.g. 9600 baud) and then manipulated without impact on the host. The architecture was excellent for high performance display but very inconvenient for domain-specific calculations, such as electron-density fitting and energy calculations. Many crystallographers and modellers spent arduous months trying to fit such activities into this architecture.

The benefits for MG were considerable, but by the later 1980s, UNIX workstations such as Sun-3 with raster graphics (initially at a resolution of 256 by 256) had started to appear. Computer-assisted drug design in particular required raster graphics for the display of computed properties such as atomic charge and electrostatic potential. Although E&S had a high-end range of raster graphics (primarily aimed at the aerospace industry) they failed to respond to the low-end market challenge where single users, rather than engineering departments, bought workstations. As a result, the market for MG displays passed to Silicon Graphics, coupled with the development of minisupercomputers (e.g., CONVEX and Alliant) which were affordable for well-supported MG laboratories. Silicon Graphics provided a graphics language, IrisGL, which was easier to use and more productive than the PS300 architecture. Commercial companies (e.g., Biosym, Polygen/MSI) ported their code to Silicon Graphics, and by the early 1990s, this was the "industry standard". Dial boxes were often used as control devices.

Stereoscopic displays were developed based on liquid crystal polarized spectacles, and while this had been very expensive on the PS300, it now became a commodity item. A common alternative was to add a polarizable screen to the front of the display and to provide viewers with extremely cheap spectacles with orthogonal polarization for separate eyes. With projectors such as Barco, it was possible to project stereoscopic display onto special silvered screens and supply an audience of hundreds with spectacles. In this way molecular graphics became universally known within large sectors of chemical and biochemical science, especially in the pharmaceutical industry. Because the backgrounds of many displays were black by default, it was common for modelling sessions and lectures to be held with almost all lighting turned off.

In the last decade almost all of this technology has become commoditized. IrisGL evolved to OpenGL so that molecular graphics can be run on any machine. In 1992, Roger Sayle released his RasMol program into the public domain. RasMol contained a very high-performance molecular renderer that ran on Unix/X Window, and Sayle later ported this to the Windows and Macintosh platforms. The Richardsons developed kinemages and the Mage software, which was also multi-platform. By specifying the chemical MIME type, molecular models could be served over the Internet, so that for the first time MG could be distributed at zero cost regardless of platform. In 1995, Birkbeck College's crystallography department used this to run "Principles of Protein Structure", the first multimedia course on the Internet, which reached 100 to 200 scientists.

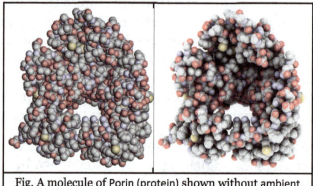

Fig. A molecule of Porin (protein) shown without ambient occlusion (left) and with (right). Advanced rendering effects can improve the comprehension of the 3D shape of a molecule.

MG continues to see innovation that balances technology and art, and currently zero-cost or open source programs such as PyMOL and Jmol have very wide use and acceptance.

Recently the widespread diffusion of advanced graphics hardware has improved the rendering capabilities of the visualization tools. The capabilities of current shading languages allow the inclusion of advanced graphic effects (like ambient occlusion, cast shadows and non-photorealistic rendering techniques) in the interactive visualization of molecules. These graphic effects, beside being eye candy, can improve the comprehension of the three-dimensional shapes of the molecules. An example of the effects that can be achieved exploiting recent graphics hardware can be seen in the simple open source visualization system QuteMol.

Algorithms

Reference Frames

Drawing molecules requires a transformation between molecular coordinates (usually, but not always, in Angstrom units) and the screen. Because many molecules are chiral it is essential that the handedness of the system (almost always right-handed) is preserved. In molecular graphics the origin (0, 0) is usually at the lower left, while in many computer systems the origin is at top left. If the z-coordinate is out of the screen (towards the viewer) the molecule will be referred to right-handed axes, while the screen display will be left-handed.

Molecular transformations normally require:

- Scaling of the display (but not the molecule).

- Translations of the molecule and objects on the screen.

- Rotations about points and lines.

Conformational changes (e.g. rotations about bonds) require rotation of one part of the molecule relative to another. The programmer must decide whether a transformation on the screen reflects a change of view or a change in the molecule or its reference frame.

Simple

In early displays only vectors could be drawn e.g. (Fig.) which are easy to draw because no rendering or hidden surface removal is required.

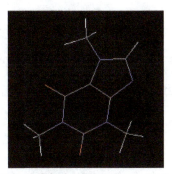

Fig. Stick model of caffeine drawn in Jmol.

On vector machines the lines would be smooth but on raster devices Bresenham's algorithm is used (note the "jaggies" on some of the bonds, which can be largely removed with antialiasing software).

Atoms can be drawn as circles, but these should be sorted so that those with the largest z-coordinates (nearest the screen) are drawn last. Although imperfect, this often gives a reasonably attractive display. Other simple tricks which do not include hidden surface algorithms are:

- coloring each end of a bond with the same color as the atom to which it is at-tached (Fig.).

- drawing less than the whole length of the bond (e.g. 10%-90%) to simulate the bond sticking out of a circle.

- adding a small offset white circle within the circle for an atom to simulate re-flection.

Typical pseudocode for creating Fig. (to fit the molecule exactly to the screen): //

assume:

// atoms with x, y, z coordinates (Angstrom) and elementSymbol

// bonds with pointers/references to atoms at ends

// table of colors for elementTypes

// find limits of molecule in molecule coordinates as xMin, yMin, xMax, yMax

scale = min(xScreenMax/(xMax-xMin), yScreenMax/(yMax-yMin))

xOffset = -xMin * scale; yOffset = -yMin * scale

for (bond in $bonds) {

  atom0 = bond.getAtom(0)

  atom1 = bond.getAtom(1)

  x0 = xOffset+atom0.getX()*scale; y0 = yOffset+atom0.getY()*scale // (1)

  x1 = xOffset+atom1.getX()*scale; y1 = yOffset+atom1.getY()*scale // (2)

  x1 = atom1.getX(); y1 = atom1.getY()

  xMid = (x0 + x1) /2; yMid = (y0 + y1) /2;

  color0 = ColorTable.getColor(atom0.getSymbol())

  drawLine (color0, x0, y0, xMid, yMid)

  color1 = ColorTable.getColor(atom1.getSymbol())

  drawLine (color1, x1, y1, xMid, yMid)

Note that this assumes the origin is in the bottom left corner of the screen, with Y up the screen. Many graphics systems have the origin at the top left, with Y down the screen. In this case the lines (1) and (2) should have the y coordinate generation as:

y0 = yScreenMax -(yOffset+atom0.getY()*scale) // (1)

y1 = yScreenMax -(yOffset+atom1.getY()*scale) // (2)

Changes of this sort change the handedness of the axes so it is easy to reverse the chirality of the displayed molecule unless care is taken.

Advanced

For greater realism and better comprehension of the 3D structure of a molecule many computer graphics algorithms can be used. For many years molecular graphics has stressed the capabilities of graphics hardware and has required hardware-specific approaches. With the increasing power of machines on the desktop, portability is more important and programs such as Jmol have advanced algorithms that do not rely on hardware. On the other hand, recent graphics hardware is able to interactively render very complex molecule shapes with a quality that would not be possible with standard software techniques.

Chronology

Developer(s)	Approximate date	Technology	Comments
Crystallographers < 1960		Hand-drawn	Crystal structures, with hidden atom and bond removal. Often clinographic projections.
Johnson, Motherwell	ca 1970	Pen plotter	ORTEP, PLUTO. Very widely deployed for publishing crystal structures.
Cyrus Levinthal, Bob Langridge, Ward, Stots	1966	Project MAC display system, two-degree of freedom, spring-return velocity joystick for rotating the image.	First protein display on screen. System for interactively building protein structures.
Barry	1969	LINC 300 computer with a dual trace oscilloscope display.	Interactive molecular structure viewing system. Early examples of dynamic rotation, intensity depth-cueing, and side-by-side stereo. Early use of the small angle approximations (a = sin a, 1 = cos a) to speed up graphical rotation calculations.

Developer(s)	Approximate date	Technology	Comments
Ortony	1971	Designed a stereo viewer (British patent appl. 13844/70) for molecular computer graphics.	Horizontal two-way (half-silvered) mirror combines images drawn on the upper and lower halves of a CRT. Crossed polarizers isolate the images to each eye.
Ortony	1971	Light pen, knob.	Interactive molecular structure viewing system. Select bond by turning another knob until desired bond lights up in sequence, a technique later used on the MMS-4 system below, or by picking with the light pen. Points in space are specified with a 3-D "bug" under dynamic control.
Barry, Graesser, Marshall	1971	CHEMAST: LINC 300 computer driving an oscilloscope. Two-axis joystick, similar to one used later by GRIP-75 (below).	Interactive molecular structure viewing system. Structures dynamically rotated using the joystick.
Tountas and Katz	1971	Adage AGT/50 display	Interactive molecular structure viewing system. Mathematics of nested rotation and for laboratory-space rotation.
Perkins, Piper, Tattam, White	1971	Honeywell DDP 516 computer, EAL TR48 analog computer, Lanelec oscilloscope, 7 linear potentiometers. Stereo.	Interactive molecular structure viewing system.
Wright	1972	GRIP-71 at UNC-CH: IBM System/360 Model 40 time-shared computer, IBM 2250 display, buttons, light pen, keyboard.	Discrete manipulation and energy relaxation of protein structures. Program code became the foundation of the GRIP-75 system below.
Barry and North	1972	Oxford Univ.: Ferranti Argus 500 computer, Ferranti model 30 display, keyboard, track ball, one knob. Stereo.	Prototype large-molecule crystallographic structure solution system. Track ball rotates a bond, knob brightens the molecule vs. electron density map.
North, Ford, Watson	Early 1970s	Leeds Univ.: DEC PDP-11/40 computer, Hewlett-Packard display. 16 knobs, keyboard, spring-return joystick. Stereo.	Prototype large-molecule crystallographic structure solution system. Six knobs rotate and translate a small molecule.

Developer(s)	Approximate date	Technology	Comments
Barry, Bosshard, Ellis, Marshall, Fritch, Jacobi	1974	MMS-4: Washington Univ. at St. Louis, LINC 300 computer and an LDS-1 / LINC 300 display, custom display modules. Rotation joystick, knobs. Stereo.	Prototype large-molecule crystallographic structure solution system. Select bond to rotate by turning another knob until desired bond lights up in sequence.
Cohen and Feldmann	1974	DEC PDP-10 computer, Adage display, push buttons, keyboard, knobs	Prototype large-molecule crystallographic structure solution system.
Stellman	1975	Princeton: PDP-10 computer, LDS-1 display, knobs	Prototype large-molecule crystallographic structure solution system. Electron density map not shown; instead an "H Factor" figure of merit is updated as the molecular structure is manipulated.
Collins, Cotton, Hazen, Meyer, Morimoto	1975	CRYSNET, Texas A&M Univ. DEC PDP-11/40 computer, Vector General Series 3 display, knobs, keyboard. Stereo.	Prototype large-molecule crystallographic structure solution system. Variety of viewing modes: rocking, spinning, and several stereo display modes.
Cornelius and Kraut	1976 (approx.)	Univ, of Calif. at San Diego: DEC PDP-11/40 emulator (CalData 135), Evans and Sutherland Picture System display, keyboard, 6 knobs. Stereo.	Prototype large-molecule crystallographic structure solution system.
(Yale Univ.)	1976 (approx.)	PIGS: DEC PDP-11/70 computer, Evans and Sutherland Picture System 2 display, data tablet, knobs.	Prototype large-molecule crystallographic structure solution system. The tablet was used for most interactions.
Feldmann and Porter	1976	NIH: DEC PDP—11/70 computer. Evans and Sutherland Picture System 2 display, knobs. Stereo.	Interactive molecular structure viewing system. Intended to display interactively molecular data from the AMSOM – Atlas of Macromolecular Structure on Microfiche.
Rosenberger et al.	1976	MMS-X: Washington Univ. at St. Louis, TI 980B computer, Hewlett-Packard 1321A display, Beehive video terminal, custom display modules, pair of 3-D spring-return joysticks, knobs.	Prototype (and later successful) large-molecule crystallographic structure solution system. Successor to the MMS-4 system above. The 3-D spring-return joysticks either translate and rotate the molecular structure for viewing or a molecular substructure for fitting, mode controlled by a toggle switch.

Developer(s)	Approximate date	Technology	Comments
Britton, Lipscomb, Pique, Wright, Brooks	1977	GRIP-75 at UNC-CH: Time-shared IBM System/360 Model 75 computer, DEC PDP 11/45 computer, Vector General Series 3 display, 3-D movement box from A.M. Noll and 3-D spring return joystick for substructure manipulation, Measurement Systems nested joystick, knobs, sliders, buttons, keyboard, light pen.	First large-molecule crystallographic structure solution.
Jones	1978	FRODO and RING Max Planck Inst., Germany, RING: DEC PDP-11/40 and Siemens 4004 computers, Vector General 3404 display, 6 knobs.	Large-molecule crystallographic structure solution. FRODO may have run on a DEC VAX-780 as a follow-on to RING.
Diamond	1978	Bilder Cambridge, England, DEC PDP-11/50 computer, Evans and Sutherland Picture System display, tablet.	Large-molecule crystallographic structure solution. All input is by data tablet. Molecular structures built on-line with ideal geometry. Later passes stretch bonds with idealization.
Langridge, White, Marshall	Late 1970s	Departmental systems (PDP-11, Tektronix displays or DEC-VT11, e.g. MMS-X)	Mixture of commodity computing with early displays.
Davies, Hubbard	Mid-1980s	CHEM-X, HYDRA	Laboratory systems with multi-color, raster and vector devices (Sigmex, PS300).
Biosym, Tripos, Polygen	Mid-1980s	PS300 and lower cost dumb terminals (VT200, SIGMEX)	Commercial integrated modelling and display packages.
Silicon Graphics, Sun	Late 1980s	IRIS GL (UNIX) workstations	Commodity-priced single-user workstations with stereoscopic display.
EMBL - WHAT IF	1989, 2000	Machine independent	Nearly free, multifunctional, still fully supported, many free servers based on it
Sayle, Richardson	1992, 1993	RasMol, Kinemage	Platform-independent MG.
MDL (van Vliet, Maffett, Adler, Holt)	1995–1998	Chime	proprietary C++ ; free browser plugin for Mac (OS9) and PCs

Developer(s)	Approximate date	Technology	Comments
MolSoft	1997-	ICM-Browser	proprietary; free download for Windows, Mac, and Linux.
1998-	Marvin-Sketch & MarvinView. MarvinSpace (2005)	proprietary Java applet or stand-alone application.	
Community efforts	2000-	DINO, Jmol, PyMol, Avogadro, PDB, OpenStructure	Open-source Java applet or stand-alone application.
NOCH	2002-	NOC	Open source code molecular structure explorer
LION Bioscience / EMBL	2004-	SRS 3D	Free, open-source system based on Java3D. Integrates 3D structures with sequence and feature data (domains, SNPs, etc.).
San Diego Supercomputer Center	2006-	Sirius	Free for academic/non-profit institutions
Community efforts	2011-	HTML5/JavaScript viewers (GLMol, jolecule, pv, Molmil, iCn3D, 3DMol, NGL, Speck, xtal.js, UglyMol, LiteMol, JSmol)	All Open-source. Require WebGL support in the browser (except for JSmol).

Electronic Richards Box Systems

Before computer graphics could be employed, mechanical methods were used to fit large molecules to their electron density maps. Using techniques of X-ray crystallography crystal of a substance were bombarded with X-rays, and the diffracted beams that came off were assembled by computer using a Fourier transform into a usually blurry 3-D image of the molecule, made visible by drawing contour circles around high electron density to produce a contoured electron density map.

In the earliest days, contoured electron density maps were hand drawn on large plastic sheets. Sometimes, bingo chips were placed on the plastic sheets where atoms were interpreted to be.

This was superseded by the Richards Box in which an adjustable brass Kendrew molecular model was placed front of a 2-way mirror, behind which were plastic sheets of the electron density map. This optically superimposed the molecular model and the electron density map. The model was moved to within the contour lines of the superimposed map. Then, atomic coordinates were recorded using a plumb bob and a meter stick. Computer graphics held out the hope of vastly speeding up this process, as well as giving a clearer view in many ways.

A noteworthy attempt to overcome the low speed of graphics displays of the time took place at Washington University in St. Louis, USA. Dave Barry's group attempted to leapfrog the state of the art in graphics displays by making custom display hardware to display images complex enough for large-molecule crystallographic structure solution, fitting molecules to their electron-density maps. The MMS-4 (table above) display modules were slow and expensive, so a second generation of modules was produced for the MMS-X (table above) system.

The first large molecule whose atomic structure was *partly* determined on a molecular computer graphics system was Transfer RNA by Sung-Hou Kim's team in 1976. after initial fitting on a mechanical Richards Box. The first large molecule whose atomic structure was *entirely* determined on a molecular computer graphics system is said to be neurotoxin A from venom of the Philippines sea snake, by Tsernoglou, Petsko, and Tu, with a statement of being first in 1977. The Richardson group published partial atomic structure results of the protein superoxide dismutase the same year, in 1977. All of these were done using the GRIP-75 system.

Other structure fitting systems, FRODO, RING, Builder, MMS-X, etc. (table above) succeeded as well within three years and became dominant.

The reason that most of these systems succeeded in just those years, not earlier or later, and within a short timespan had to do with the arrival of commercial hardware that was powerful enough. Two things were needed and arrived at about the same time. First, electron density maps are large and require either a computer with at least a 24-bit address space or a combination of a computer with a lesser 16-bit address space plus several years to overcome the difficulties of an address space that is smaller than the data. The second arrival was that of interactive computer graphics displays that were fast enough to display electron-density maps, whose contour circles require the display of numerous short vectors. The first such displays were the Vector General Series 3 and the Evans and Sutherland Picture System 2, MultiPicture System, and PS-300.

Nowadays, fitting of the molecular structure to the electron density map is largely automated by algorithms with computer graphics a guide to the process. An example is the XtalView XFit program.

Scientific Visualization

Scientific visualization (also spelled scientific visualisation) is an interdisciplinary branch of science. According to Friendly (2008), it is "primarily concerned with the visualization of three-dimensional phenomena (architectural, meteorological, medical, biological, etc.), where the emphasis is on realistic renderings of volumes, surfaces, illumination sources, and so forth, perhaps with a dynamic (time) component". It is also considered a subset of computer graphics, a branch of computer science. The purpose of scientific visualization is to graphically illustrate scientific data to enable scientists to understand, illustrate, and glean insight from their data.

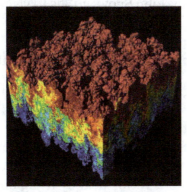

A scientific visualization of a simulation of a Rayleigh–Taylor instability caused by two mixing fluids.

Surface rendering of *Arabidopsis thaliana* pollen grains with confocal microscope.

History

One of the earliest examples of three-dimensional scientific visualisation was Maxwell's thermodynamic surface, sculpted in clay in 1874 by James Clerk Maxwell. This prefigured modern scientific visualization techniques that use computer graphics.

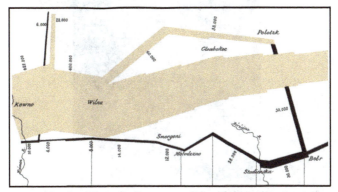

Charles Minard's flow map of Napoleon's March.

Notable early two-dimensional examples include the flow map of Napoleon's March on Moscow produced by Charles Joseph Minard in 1869; the "coxcombs" used by Florence Nightingale in 1857 as part of a campaign to improve sanitary conditions in the British army; and the dot map used by John Snow in 1855 to visualise the Broad Street cholera outbreak.

Methods for Visualizing Two-dimensional Data Sets

Scientific visualization using computer graphics gained in popularity as graphics matured. Primary applications were scalar fields and vector fields from computer simulations and also measured data. The primary methods for visualizing two-dimensional (2D) scalar fields are color mapping and drawing contour lines. 2D vector fields are visualized using glyphs and streamlines or line integral convolution methods. 2D tensor fields are often resolved to a vector field by using one of the two eigenvectors to represent the tensor each point in the field and then visualized using vector field visualization methods.

Methods for Visualizing Three-dimensional Data Sets

For 3D scalar fields the primary methods are volume rendering and isosurfaces. Methods for visualizing vector fields include glyphs (graphical icons) such as arrows, streamlines and streaklines, particle tracing, line integral convolution (LIC) and topological methods. Later, visualization techniques such as hyperstreamlines were developed to visualize 2D and 3D tensor fields.

Scientific Visualization Topics

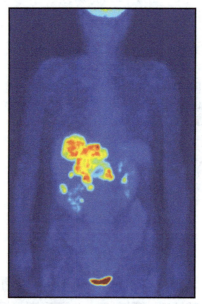

Maximum intensity projection (MIP) of a whole body PET scan.

Scientific visualization of Fluid Flow: Surface
waves in water.

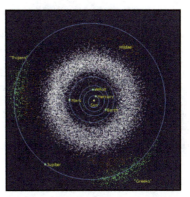

Solar system image of the main asteroid belt
and the Trojan asteroids.

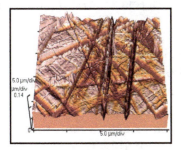

Topographic scan of a glass surface by an
Atomic force microscope.

Chemical imaging of a simultaneous release of
SF_6 and NH_3.

Computer Animation

Computer animation is the art, technique, and science of creating moving images via the use of computers. It is becoming more common to be created by means of 3D computer graphics, though 2D computer graphics are still widely used for stylistic, low bandwidth, and faster real-time rendering needs. Sometimes the target of the animation is the computer itself, but sometimes the target is another medium, such as film. It is also referred to as CGI (Computer-generated imagery or computer-generated imaging), especially when used in films.

Computer Simulation

Computer simulation is a computer program, or network of computers, that attempts to simulate an abstract model of a particular system. Computer simulations have become a useful part of mathematical modelling of many natural systems in physics, and computational physics, chemistry and biology; human systems in economics, psychology, and social science; and in the process of engineering and new technology, to gain insight into the operation of those systems, or to observe their behavior. The simultaneous visualization and simulation of a system is called visulation.

Computer simulations vary from computer programs that run a few minutes, to network-based groups of computers running for hours, to ongoing simulations that run for months. The scale of events being simulated by computer simulations has far exceeded anything possible (or perhaps even imaginable) using the traditional paper-and-pencil mathematical modeling: over 10 years ago, a desert-battle simulation, of one force invading another, involved the modeling of 66,239 tanks, trucks and other vehicles on simulated terrain around Kuwait, using multiple supercomputers in the DoD High Performance Computer Modernization Program.

Information Visualization

Information visualization is the study of "the visual representation of large-scale collections of non-numerical information, such as files and lines of code in software systems, library and bibliographic databases, networks of relations on the internet, and so forth".

Information visualization focused on the creation of approaches for conveying abstract information in intuitive ways. Visual representations and interaction techniques take advantage of the human eye's broad bandwidth pathway into the mind to allow users to see, explore, and understand large amounts of information at once. The key difference between scientific visualization and information visualization is that information visualization is often applied to data that is not generated by scientific inquiry. Some examples are graphical representations of data for business, government, news and social media.

Interface Technology and Perception

Interface technology and perception shows how new interfaces and a better understanding of underlying perceptual issues create new opportunities for the scientific visualization community.

Surface Rendering

Rendering is the process of generating an image from a model, by means of computer programs. The model is a description of three-dimensional objects in a strictly defined language or data structure. It would contain geometry, viewpoint, texture, lighting, and shading information. The image is a digital image or raster graphics image. The term may be by analogy with an "artist's rendering" of a scene. 'Rendering' is also used to describe the process of calculating effects in a video editing file to produce final video output. Important rendering techniques are:

Scanline rendering and rasterisation:

> A high-level representation of an image necessarily contains elements in a different domain from pixels. These elements are referred to as primitives.

In a schematic drawing, for instance, line segments and curves might be primitives. In a graphical user interface, windows and buttons might be the primitives. In 3D rendering, triangles and polygons in space might be primitives.

Ray casting:

Ray casting is primarily used for realtime simulations, such as those used in 3D computer games and cartoon animations, where detail is not important, or where it is more efficient to manually fake the details in order to obtain better performance in the computational stage. This is usually the case when a large number of frames need to be animated. The resulting surfaces have a characteristic 'flat' appearance when no additional tricks are used, as if objects in the scene were all painted with matte finish.

Radiosity:

Radiosity, also known as Global Illumination, is a method that attempts to simulate the way in which directly illuminated surfaces act as indirect light sources that illuminate other surfaces. This produces more realistic shading and seems to better capture the 'ambience' of an indoor scene. A classic example is the way that shadows 'hug' the corners of rooms.

Ray tracing:

Ray tracing is an extension of the same technique developed in scanline rendering and ray casting. Like those, it handles complicated objects well, and the objects may be described mathematically. Unlike scanline and casting, ray tracing is almost always a Monte Carlo technique, that is one based on averaging a number of randomly generated samples from a model.

Volume Rendering

Volume rendering is a technique used to display a 2D projection of a 3D discretely sampled data set. A typical 3D data set is a group of 2D slice images acquired by a CT or MRI scanner. Usually these are acquired in a regular pattern (e.g., one slice every millimeter) and usually have a regular number of image pixels in a regular pattern. This is an example of a regular volumetric grid, with each volume element, or voxel represented by a single value that is obtained by sampling the immediate area surrounding the voxel.

Volume Visualization

According to Rosenblum (1994) "volume visualization examines a set of techniques that allows viewing an object without mathematically representing the other surface. Initially used in medical imaging, volume visualization has become an essential technique for many sciences, portraying phenomena become an essential technique such as clouds, water flows, and molecular and biological structure. Many volume visualization algorithms are computationally expensive and demand large data storage. Advances in hardware and software are generalizing volume visualization as well as real time performances".

Scientific Visualization Applications

This section will give a series of examples how scientific visualization can be applied today.

In The Natural Sciences

Star formation: The featured plot is a Volume plot of the logarithm of gas/dust density in an Enzo star and galaxy simulation. Regions of high density are white while less dense regions are more blue and also more transparent.

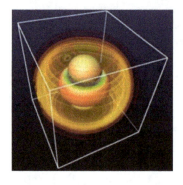

Gravitational waves.

Star formation.

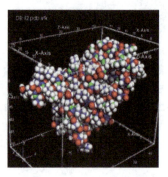

Molecular rendering.

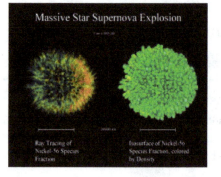

Massive Star Supernovae Explosions.

Gravitational waves: Researchers used the Globus Toolkit to harness the power of multiple supercomputers to simulate the gravitational effects of black-hole collisions.

Massive Star Supernovae Explosions: In the image, three-Dimensional Radiation Hydrodynamics Calculations of Massive Star Supernovae Explosions The DJEHUTY stellar evolution code was used to calculate the explosion of SN 1987A model in three dimensions.

Molecular rendering: VisIt's general plotting capabilities were used to create the molecular rendering shown in the featured visualization. The original data was taken from the Protein Data Bank and turned into a VTK file before rendering.

In Geography and Ecology

Terrain visualization: VisIt can read several file formats common in the field of Geographic Information Systems (GIS), allowing one to plot raster data such as terrain data in visualizations. The featured image shows a plot of a DEM dataset containing mountainous areas near Dunsmuir, CA. Elevation lines are added to the plot to help delineate changes in elevation.

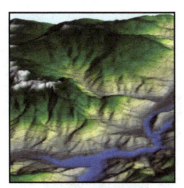

Terrain rendering.

Tornado Simulation: This image was created from data generated by a tornado simulation calculated on NCSA's IBM p690 computing cluster. High-definition television animations of the storm produced at NCSA were included in an episode of the PBS television series NOVA called "Hunt for the Supertwister." The tornado is shown by spheres that are colored according to pressure; orange and blue tubes represent the rising and falling airflow around the tornado.

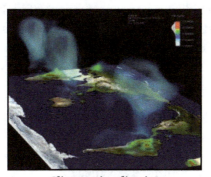

Climate visualization.

Climate visualization: This visualization depicts the carbon dioxide from various sources that are advected individually as tracers in the atmosphere model. Carbon dioxide from the ocean is shown as plumes during February 1900.

Atmospheric Anomaly in Times Square.

Atmospheric Anomaly in Times Square In the image the results from the SAMRAI simulation framework of an atmospheric anomaly in and around Times Square are visualized.

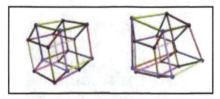

View of a 4D cube projected into 3D: orthogonal projection (left) and perspective projection (right).

In Mathematics

Scientific visualization of mathematical structures has been undertaken for purposes of building intuition and for aiding the forming of mental models.

Higher-dimensional objects can be visualized in form of projections (views) in lower dimensions. In particular, 4-dimensional objects are visualized by means of projection in three dimensions. The lower-dimensional projections of higher-dimensional objects can be used for purposes of virtual object manipulation, allowing 3D objects to be manipulated by operations performed in 2D, and 4D objects by interactions performed in 3D.

In the Formal Sciences

Computer mapping of topographical surfaces: Through computer mapping of topographical surfaces, mathematicians can test theories of how materials will change when stressed. The imaging is part of the work on the NSF-funded Electronic Visualization Laboratory at the University of Illinois at Chicago.

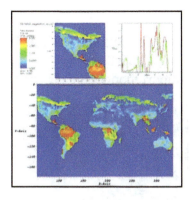

Image annotations.

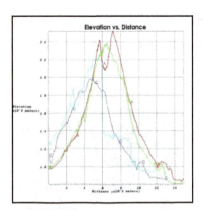

Curve plots.

Curve plots: VisIt can plot curves from data read from files and it can be used to extract and plot curve data from higher-dimensional datasets using lineout operators or queries. The curves in the featured image correspond to elevation data along lines drawn on DEM data and were created with the feature lineout capability. Lineout allows you to interactively draw a line, which specifies a path for data extraction. The resulting data was then plotted as curves.

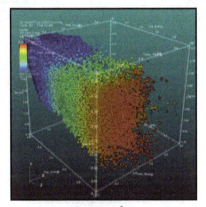

Scatter plot.

Image annotations: The featured plot shows Leaf Area Index (LAI), a measure of global vegetative matter, from a NetCDF dataset. The primary plot is the large plot at the bottom, which shows the LAI for the whole world. The plots on top are actually annotations that contain images generated earlier. Image annotations can be used to include material that enhances a visualization such as auxiliary plots, images of experimental data, project logos, etc.

Scatter plot: VisIt's Scatter plot allows to visualize multivariate data of up to four dimensions. The Scatter plot takes multiple scalar variables and uses them for different axes in phase space. The different variables are combined to form coordinates in the phase space and they are displayed using glyphs and colored using another scalar variable.

In The Applied Sciences

Porsche 911 model (NASTRAN model): The featured plot contains a Mesh plot of a Porsche 911 model imported from a NASTRAN bulk data file. VisIt can read a limited subset of NASTRAN bulk data files, in general enough to import model geometry for visualization.

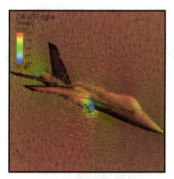

YF-17 aircraft Plot.   Porsche 911 model.

YF-17 aircraft Plot: The featured image displays plots of a CGNS dataset representing a YF-17 jet aircraft. The dataset consists of an unstructured grid with solution. The image was created by using a pseudocolor plot of the dataset's Mach variable, a Mesh plot of the grid, and Vector plot of a slice through the Velocity field.

City rendering.

City rendering: An ESRI shapefile containing a polygonal description of the building footprints was read in and then the polygons were resampled onto a rectilinear grid, which was extruded into the featured cityscape.

Inbound traffic measured: This image is a visualization study of inbound traffic measured in billions of bytes on the NSFNET T1 backbone for the month of September 1991. The traffic volume range is depicted from purple (zero bytes) to white (100 billion bytes). It represents data collected by Merit Network, Inc.

Scientific Visualization Organizations

Important laboratory in the field are:

- Electronic Visualization Laboratory.

- NASA Goddard Scientific Visualization Studio.

Conferences in this field, ranked by significance in scientific visualization research, are:

- IEEE Visualization.

- EuroVis.

- SIGGRAPH.

- Eurographics.

- Graphicon.

Drug Design

Drug design, often referred to as rational drug design or simply rational design, is the inventive process of finding new medications based on the knowledge of a biological target. The drug is most commonly an organic small molecule that activates or inhibits the function of a biomolecule such as a protein, which in turn results in a therapeutic benefit to the patient. In the most basic sense, drug design involves the design of molecules that are complementary in shape and charge to the biomolecular target with which they interact and therefore will bind to it. Drug design frequently but not necessarily relies on computer modeling techniques. This type of modeling is sometimes referred to as computer-aided drug design. Finally, drug design that relies on the knowledge of the three-dimensional structure of the biomolecular target is known as structure-based drug design. In addition to small molecules, biopharmaceuticals and especially therapeutic antibodies are an increasingly important class of drugs and computational methods for improving the affinity, selectivity, and stability of these protein-based therapeutics have also been developed.

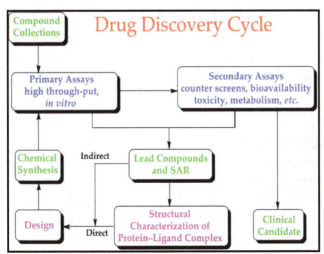

The phrase "drug design" is to some extent a misnomer. A more accurate term is ligand design (i.e., design of a molecule that will bind tightly to its target). Although design techniques for prediction of binding affinity are reasonably successful, there are many other properties, such as bioavailability, metabolic half-life, side effects, etc., that first must be optimized before a ligand can become a safe and efficacious drug. These other characteristics are often difficult to predict with rational design techniques. Nevertheless, due to high attrition rates, especially during clinical phases of drug development, more attention is being focused early in the drug design process on selecting candidate drugs whose physicochemical properties are predicted to result in fewer complications during development and hence more likely to lead to an approved, marketed drug. Furthermore, in vitro experiments complemented with computation methods are increasingly used in early drug discovery to select compounds with more favorable ADME (absorption, distribution, metabolism, and excretion) and toxicological profiles.

Drug Targets

A biomolecular target (most commonly a protein or nucleic acid) is a key molecule involved in a particular metabolic or signaling pathway that is associated with a specific disease condition or pathology or to the infectivity or survival of a microbial pathogen. Potential drug targets are not necessarily disease causing but must by definition be disease modifying. In some cases, small molecules will be designed to enhance or inhibit the target function in the specific disease modifying pathway. Small molecules (for example receptor agonists, antagonists, inverse agonists, or modulators; enzyme activators or inhibitors; or ion channel openers or blockers) will be designed that are complementary to the binding site of target. Small molecules (drugs) can be designed so as not to affect any other important "off-target" molecules (often referred to as anti-targets) since drug interactions with off-target molecules may lead to undesirable side effects. Due to similarities in binding sites, closely related targets identified through sequence homology have the highest chance of cross reactivity and hence highest side effect potential.

Most commonly, drugs are organic small molecules produced through chemical synthesis, but biopolymer-based drugs (also known as biopharmaceuticals) produced through biological processes are becoming increasingly more common. In addition, mRNA-based gene silencing technologies may have therapeutic applications.

Rational Drug Discovery

In contrast to traditional methods of drug discovery (known as forward pharmacology), which rely on trial-and-error testing of chemical substances on cultured cells or animals, and matching the apparent effects to treatments, rational drug design (also called reverse pharmacology) begins with a hypothesis that modulation of a specific biological target may have therapeutic value. In order for a biomolecule to be selected as a drug target, two essential pieces of information are required. The first is evidence that modulation of the target will be disease modifying. This knowledge may come from, for example, disease linkage studies that show an association between mutations in the biological target and certain disease states. The second is that the target is "druggable". This means that it is capable of binding to a small molecule and that its activity can be modulated by the small molecule.

Once a suitable target has been identified, the target is normally cloned and produced and purified. The purified protein is then used to establish a screening assay. In addition, the three-dimensional structure of the target may be determined.

The search for small molecules that bind to the target is begun by screening libraries of potential drug compounds. This may be done by using the screening assay (a "wet screen"). In addition, if the structure of the target is available, a virtual screen may be performed of candidate drugs. Ideally the candidate drug compounds should be "drug-like", that is they should possess properties that are predicted to lead to oral bioavailability, adequate chemical and metabolic stability, and minimal toxic effects. Several methods are available to estimate druglikeness such as Lipinski's Rule of Five and a range of scoring methods such as lipophilic efficiency. Several methods for predicting drug metabolism have also been proposed in the scientific literature.

Due to the large number of drug properties that must be simultaneously optimized during the design process, multi-objective optimization techniques are sometimes employed. Finally because of the limitations in the current methods for prediction of activity, drug design is still very much reliant on serendipity and bounded rationality.

Computer-aided Drug Design

The most fundamental goal in drug design is to predict whether a given molecule will bind to a target and if so how strongly. Molecular mechanics or molecular dynamics is most often used to estimate the strength of the intermolecular interaction between the small molecule and its biological target. These methods are also used to predict the conformation of the small molecule and to model conformational changes in the target that may occur when the small molecule binds to it. Semi-empirical, ab initio quantum chemistry methods, or density functional theory are often used to provide optimized parameters for the molecular mechanics calculations and also provide an estimate of the electronic properties (electrostatic potential, polarizability, etc.) of the drug candidate that will influence binding affinity.

Molecular mechanics methods may also be used to provide semi-quantitative prediction of the binding affinity. Also, knowledge-based scoring function may be used to provide binding affinity estimates. These methods use linear regression, machine learning, neural nets or other statistical techniques to derive predictive binding affinity equations by fitting experimental affinities to computationally derived interaction energies between the small molecule and the target.

Ideally, the computational method will be able to predict affinity before a compound is synthesized and hence in theory only one compound needs to be synthesized, saving enormous time and cost. The reality is that present computational methods are imperfect and provide, at best, only qualitatively accurate estimates of affinity. In practice it still takes several iterations of design, synthesis, and testing before an optimal drug is discovered. Computational methods have accelerated discovery by reducing the number of iterations required and have often provided novel structures.

Drug design with the help of computers may be used at any of the following stages of drug discovery:

1. Hit identification using virtual screening (structure- or ligand-based design).

2. Hit-to-lead optimization of affinity and selectivity (structure-based design, QSAR, etc.).

3. Lead optimization of other pharmaceutical properties while maintaining affinity.

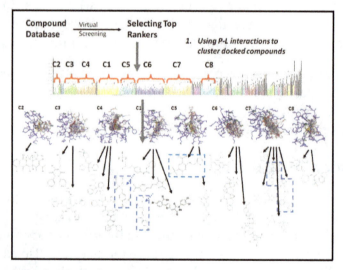

Flowchart of a Usual Clustering Analysis for Structure-Based Drug Design.

In order to overcome the insufficient prediction of binding affinity calculated by recent scoring functions, the protein-ligand interaction and compound 3D structure information are used for analysis. For structure-based drug design, several post-screening analyses focusing on protein-ligand interaction have been developed for improving enrichment and effectively mining potential candidates:

- Consensus scoring:

  o Selecting candidates by voting of multiple scoring functions.

  o May lose the relationship between protein-ligand structural information and scoring criterion.

- Cluster analysis:
    - Represent and cluster candidates according to protein-ligand 3D information.
    - Needs meaningful representation of protein-ligand interactions.

Types

There are two major types of drug design. The first is referred to as ligand-based drug design and the second, structure-based drug design.

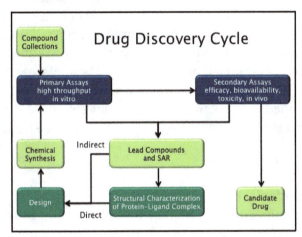

Drug discovery cycle highlighting both ligand-based (indirect) and structure-based (direct) drug design strategies.

Ligand-based

Ligand-based drug design (or indirect drug design) relies on knowledge of other molecules that bind to the biological target of interest. These other molecules may be used to derive a pharmacophore model that defines the minimum necessary structural characteristics a molecule must possess in order to bind to the target. In other words, a model of the biological target may be built based on the knowledge of what binds to it, and this model in turn may be used to design new molecular entities that interact with the target. Alternatively, a quantitative structure-activity relationship (QSAR), in which a correlation between calculated properties of molecules and their experimentally determined biological activity, may be derived. These QSAR relationships in turn may be used to predict the activity of new analogs.

Structure-based

Structure-based drug design (or direct drug design) relies on knowledge of the three dimensional structure of the biological target obtained through methods such as x-ray crystallography or NMR spectroscopy. If an experimental structure of a target is not available, it may be possible to create a homology model of the target based on the experimental structure of a related protein. Using the structure of the biological target, candidate drugs that are predicted to bind with high affinity and selectivity to the target may be designed using interactive graphics and the intuition of a medicinal chemist. Alternatively various automated computational procedures may be used to suggest new drug candidates.

Current methods for structure-based drug design can be divided roughly into three main categories. The first method is identification of new ligands for a given receptor by searching large databases of 3D structures of small molecules to find those fitting the binding pocket of the receptor using fast approximate docking programs. This method is known as virtual screening. A second category is de novo design of new ligands. In this method, ligand molecules are built up within the constraints of the binding pocket by assembling small pieces in a stepwise manner. These pieces can be either individual atoms or molecular fragments. The key advantage of such a method is that novel structures, not contained in any database, can be suggested. A third method is the optimization of known ligands by evaluating proposed analogs within the binding cavity.

Binding Site Identification

Binding site identification is the first step in structure based design. If the structure of the target or a sufficiently similar homolog is determined in the presence of a bound ligand, then the ligand should be observable in the structure in which case location of the binding site is trivial. However, there may be unoccupied allosteric binding sites that may be of interest. Furthermore, it may be that only apoprotein (protein without ligand) structures are available and the reliable identification of unoccupied sites that have the potential to bind ligands with high affinity is non-trivial. In brief, binding site identification usually relies on identification of concave surfaces on the protein that can accommodate drug sized molecules that also possess appropriate "hot spots" (hydrophobic surfaces, hydrogen bonding sites, etc.) that drive ligand binding.

Scoring Functions

Structure-based drug design attempts to use the structure of proteins as a basis for designing new ligands by applying the principles of molecular recognition. Selective high affinity binding to the target is generally desirable since it leads to more efficacious drugs with fewer side effects. Thus, one of the most important principles for designing or obtaining potential new ligands is to predict the binding affinity of a certain ligand to its target (and known antitargets) and use the predicted affinity as a criterion for selection.

One early general-purposed empirical scoring function to describe the binding energy of ligands to receptors was developed by Böhm. This empirical scoring function took the form:

$$\Delta G_{\text{bind}} = \Delta G_0 + \Delta G_{\text{hb}}\Sigma_{h-bonds} + \Delta G_{\text{ionic}}\Sigma_{ionic-int} + \Delta G_{\text{lipophilic}}\left|A\right| + \Delta G_{\text{rot}}NROT$$

where:

- ΔG_o – empirically derived offset that in part corresponds to the overall loss of translational and rotational entropy of the ligand upon binding.

- ΔG_{hb} – contribution from hydrogen bonding.

- ΔG_{ionic} – contribution from ionic interactions.

- ΔG_{lip} – contribution from lipophilic interactions where $|A_{lipo}|$ is surface area of lipophilic contact between the ligand and receptor.

- ΔG_{rot} – entropy penalty due to freezing a rotatable in the ligand bond upon binding.

A more general thermodynamic "master" equation is as follows:

$$\Delta G_{bind} = -RT \ln K_d$$
$$K_d = \frac{[\text{Ligand}][\text{Receptor}]}{[\text{Complex}]}$$

$$\Delta G_{bind} = \Delta G_{desolvation} + \Delta G_{motion} + \Delta G_{configuration} + \Delta G_{interaction}$$

where:

- Desolvation – enthalpic penalty for removing the ligand from solvent.

- Motion – entropic penalty for reducing the degrees of freedom when a ligand binds to its receptor.

- Configuration – conformational strain energy required to put the ligand in its "active" conformation.

- Interaction – enthalpic gain for "resolvating" the ligand with its receptor.

The basic idea is that the overall binding free energy can be decomposed into independent components that are known to be important for the binding process. Each component reflects a certain kind of free energy alteration during the binding process between a ligand and its target receptor. The Master Equation is the linear combination of these components. According to Gibbs free energy equation, the relation between dissociation equilibrium constant, K_d, and the components of free energy was built.

Various computational methods are used to estimate each of the components of the master equation. For example, the change in polar surface area upon ligand binding can be used to estimate the desolvation energy. The number of rotatable bonds frozen upon ligand binding is proportional to the motion term. The configurational or strain energy can be estimated using molecular mechanics calculations. Finally the interaction energy can be estimated using methods such as the change in non polar surface, statistically derived potentials of mean force, the number of hydrogen bonds formed, etc. In practice, the components of the master equation are fit to experimental data using multiple linear regression. This can be done with a diverse training set including many types of ligands and receptors to produce a less accurate but more general "global" model or a more restricted set of ligands and receptors to produce a more accurate but less general "local" model.

Examples

A particular example of rational drug design involves the use of three-dimensional information about biomolecules obtained from such techniques as X-ray crystallography and NMR spectroscopy. Computer-aided drug design in particular becomes much more tractable when there is a high-resolution structure of a target protein bound to a potent ligand. This approach to drug discovery is sometimes referred to as structure-based drug design. The first unequivocal example of the application of structure-based drug design leading to an approved drug is the carbonic anhydrase inhibitor dorzolamide, which was approved in 1995.

Another important case study in rational drug design is imatinib, a tyrosine kinase inhibitor designed specifically for the *bcr-abl* fusion protein that is characteristic for Philadelphia chromosome-positive leukemias (chronic myelogenous leukemia and occasionally acute lymphocytic leukemia). Imatinib is substantially different from previous drugs for cancer, as most agents of chemotherapy simply target rapidly dividing cells, not differentiating between cancer cells and other tissues.

Additional examples include:

- Many of the atypical antipsychotics.
- Cimetidine, the prototypical H_2-receptor antagonist from which the later members of the class were developed.
- Selective COX-2 inhibitor NSAIDs.
- Enfuvirtide, a peptide HIV entry inhibitor.
- Nonbenzodiazepines like zolpidem and zopiclone.
- Raltegravir, an HIV integrase inhibitor.
- SSRIs (selective serotonin reuptake inhibitors), a class of antidepressants.
- Zanamivir, an antiviral drug.

Case Studies

- 5-HT3 antagonists.

- Acetylcholine receptor agonists.

- Angiotensin receptor antagonists.

- Bcr-Abl tyrosine-kinase inhibitors.

- Cannabinoid receptor antagonists.

- CCR5 receptor antagonists.

- Cyclooxygenase 2 inhibitors.

- Dipeptidyl peptidase-4 inhibitors.

- HIV protease inhibitors.

- NK1 receptor antagonists.

- Non-nucleoside reverse transcriptase inhibitors.

- Nucleoside and nucleotide reverse transcriptase inhibitors.

- PDE5 inhibitors.

- Proton pump inibitors.

- Renin inhibitors.

- Triptans.

- TRPV1 antagonists.

- c-Met inhibitors.

Criticism

It has been argued that the highly rigid and focused nature of rational drug design suppresses serendipity in drug discovery. Because many of the most significant medical discoveries have been inadvertent, the recent focus on rational drug design may limit the progress of drug discovery. Furthermore, the rational design of a drug may be limited by a crude or incomplete understanding of the underlying molecular processes of the disease it is intended to treat.

References

- Reynolds CH, Merz KM, Ringe D, eds. (2010). Drug Design: Structure- and Ligand-Based Approaches (1 ed.). Cambridge, UK: Cambridge University Press. ISBN 978-0521887236.

- Wu-Pong S, Rojanasakul Y (2008). Biopharmaceutical drug design and development (2nd ed.). Totowa, NJ Humana Press: Humana Press. ISBN 978-1-59745-532-9.

- Hopkins AL (2011). "Chapter 25: Pharmacological space". In Wermuth CG. The Practice of Medicinal Chemistry (3 ed.). Academic Press. pp. 521–527. ISBN 978-0-12-374194-3.

- Kirchmair J (2014). Drug Metabolism Prediction. Wiley's Methods and Principles in Medicinal Chemistry. 63. Wiley-VCH. ISBN 978-3-527-67301-8.

- Guner OF (2000). Pharmacophore Perception, Development, and use in Drug Design. La Jolla, Calif: International University Line. ISBN 0-9636817-6-1.

- Interactive environments with open-source software: 3D walkthroughs by Wolfgang Höhl, Wolfgang Höhl 2008 ISBN 3-211-79169-8.

- Trends in interactive visualization by Elena van Zudilova-Seinstra, Tony Adriaansen, Robert Liere 2008 ISBN 1-84800-268-8.

- Chaos and fractals: new frontiers of science by Heinz-Otto Peitgen, Hartmut Jürgens, Dietmar Saupe 2004 ISBN 0-387-20229-3.

- Digital modeling of material appearance by Julie Dorsey, Holly E. Rushmeier, François X. Sillion 2007 ISBN 0-12-221181-2.

- Madsen U, Krogsgaard-Larsen P, Liljefors T (2002). Textbook of Drug Design and Discovery. Washington, DC: Taylor & Francis. ISBN 0-415-28288-8.

- Zwicky, E.D, Cooper, S and Chapman, D,B. (2000). Building Internet Firewalls. United States: O'Reily & Associates. p. 804. ISBN 1-56592-871-7.

- Niederst, Jennifer (2006). Web Design In a Nutshell. United States of America: O'Reilly Media. pp. 12–14. ISBN 0-596-00987-9.

- Oleksy, Walter (2001). Careers in Web Design. New York: The Rosen Publishing Group,Inc. pp. 9–11. ISBN 9780823931910.

Permissions

All chapters in this book are published with permission under the Creative Commons Attribution Share Alike License or equivalent. Every chapter published in this book has been scrutinized by our experts. Their significance has been extensively debated. The topics covered herein carry significant information for a comprehensive understanding. They may even be implemented as practical applications or may be referred to as a beginning point for further studies.

We would like to thank the editorial team for lending their expertise to make the book truly unique. They have played a crucial role in the development of this book. Without their invaluable contributions this book wouldn't have been possible. They have made vital efforts to compile up to date information on the varied aspects of this subject to make this book a valuable addition to the collection of many professionals and students.

This book was conceptualized with the vision of imparting up-to-date and integrated information in this field. To ensure the same, a matchless editorial board was set up. Every individual on the board went through rigorous rounds of assessment to prove their worth. After which they invested a large part of their time researching and compiling the most relevant data for our readers.

The editorial board has been involved in producing this book since its inception. They have spent rigorous hours researching and exploring the diverse topics which have resulted in the successful publishing of this book. They have passed on their knowledge of decades through this book. To expedite this challenging task, the publisher supported the team at every step. A small team of assistant editors was also appointed to further simplify the editing procedure and attain best results for the readers.

Apart from the editorial board, the designing team has also invested a significant amount of their time in understanding the subject and creating the most relevant covers. They scrutinized every image to scout for the most suitable representation of the subject and create an appropriate cover for the book.

The publishing team has been an ardent support to the editorial, designing and production team. Their endless efforts to recruit the best for this project, has resulted in the accomplishment of this book. They are a veteran in the field of academics and their pool of knowledge is as vast as their experience in printing. Their expertise and guidance has proved useful at every step. Their uncompromising quality standards have made this book an exceptional effort. Their encouragement from time to time has been an inspiration for everyone.

The publisher and the editorial board hope that this book will prove to be a valuable piece of knowledge for students, practitioners and scholars across the globe.

Index

Printed in the USA
CPSIA information can be obtained
at www.ICGtesting.com
JSHW051905200524
63488JS00005B/168

9 781639 892952